Terror

Also by Leonard A. Cole

The Anthrax Letters: A Medical Detective Story

The Eleventh Plague: The Politics of Biological and Chemical Warfare

Element of Risk: The Politics of Radon

Clouds of Secrecy: The Army's Germ Warfare Tests Over Populated Areas

Politics and the Restraint of Science

Blacks in Power: A Comparative Study of Black and White Elected Officials

Terror

HOW ISRAEL HAS COPED
AND WHAT
AMERICA CAN LEARN

Leonard A. Cole

Indiana University Press
BLOOMINGTON AND INDIANAPOLIS

This book is a publication of
Indiana University Press
601 North Morton Street
Bloomington, IN 47404–3797 USA
http://iupress.indiana.edu

Telephone orders 800-842-6796
Fax orders 812-855-7931
Orders by e-mail iuporder@indiana.edu

The paper used in this publication meets the minimum requirements of American National Standard for Information Sciences—Permanence of Paper for Printed Library Materials, ANSI Z39.48–1984.

MANUFACTURED IN THE UNITED STATES OF AMERICA

Library of Congress Cataloging-in-Publication Data

Cole, Leonard A., date
Terror : how Israel has coped and what America can learn / Leonard A. Cole.
p. cm.
Includes bibliographical references and index.
ISBN-13: 978-0-253-34918-7 (cloth : alk. paper) 1. Terrorism—Israel.
2. Terrorism—Prevention—Israel. 3. Terrorism—United States. I. Title.
HV6433.I75C65 2007
363.325′16095694—dc22

2006037056

1 2 3 4 5 12 11 10 09 08 07

Contents

Prologue

Darryl Moody's eyes widened as he entered the security control tower at Tel Aviv's Ben-Gurion Airport. The half-dozen young women and men working there hardly noticed the small group of American visitors who had stepped into their workspace. Clad in T-shirts and jeans, the Israelis were bantering softly while checking video monitors and making notes. Cartoons hung from the bulletin board. "This is not what I anticipated seeing," Moody thought to himself. He was in Israel for the first time, for a conference on homeland security and behind-the-scenes tours of sensitive sites. Israel's reputation for exacting security measures led him to expect something else. "I had in my mind, you know, high tech, people in military uniforms, disciplined demeanor," he told me. "What I saw was so much more casual." Still, he concluded, their approach evidently worked for them.

It was mid-2005, and for nearly four years, Moody had been working on security issues in the United States. He was a vice president of BearingPoint, a management firm hired by the federal government after the September 11, 2001, attacks to work on enhancing border protection, immigration control, and other security-related issues. His responsibilities included helping to organize the newly established Transportation Security Administration and to improve airport security.

Moody knew that Israeli practices at Ben-Gurion were considered "the gold standard for aviation security," as he put it. While touring the facility, he created a mental checklist of what he witnessed: the long serpentine road from the front gate to the terminal, massive space in the terminal, thick floor-to-ceiling windows of bombproof glass, camera surveillance of cars being unloaded. Helpful as these features might be, recreating them in American airports would not be accepted, he believed. Too difficult, too expensive.

True, some American airports were being renovated to enhance security. Moody thought of Baltimore Airport, which was increasing the distance between entry and passenger check-in. Los Angeles International was restructuring so that parking would be a mile away from the terminal. But in general, he believed, U.S. air travelers were adequately protected by existing methods of passenger screening, x-ray and explosive-detection machines, and armed marshals in planes. Still, on the evidence, Israelis were not satisfied with U.S. procedures. El Al, Israel's national airline, screens its own bags at four of the five American airports out of which it operates—Kennedy in New York, O'Hare in Chicago, Los Angeles International, and Miami International. At Newark International, El Al screeners may recheck luggage that has gone through U.S. detection machines. Isaac Yeffet, El Al's retired head of security, said that El Al screening included the use of more sensitive machines and more rigorous questioning of passengers.[1]

I asked Moody what he found to be different about Israeli procedures at Ben-Gurion. At first he said simply that the Israelis do more screenings. Then with a laugh he added, "The main difference is that in Israel they profile with a capital P. And they don't hide that fact." Darryl Moody is articulate. His smile spreads easily across his round face. As an African American, Moody admitted to keen sensitivity to the issue of profiling. He knows well that at airports and elsewhere in the United States, singling out individuals for scrutiny based on racial, ethnic, or religious background is forbidden. All air passengers, regardless of age or other characteristics, must empty their pockets and remove their shoes and belts for inspection. Individuals undergo additional scrutiny only for cause or through random designation.

What did he personally think about profiling? I asked. "In America we just couldn't do it," Moody replied. He sighed. The Israelis obviously think it is necessary, and it's their country, he said.

"So if you don't like it, don't come to this country." In fact, Israeli screening centers on an interview by a carefully trained inspector. Each individual is asked about the purpose of his visit, length of time in Israel, country of origin. One question builds on another. If the passenger's answers raise concerns, he will be further scrutinized. Otherwise, he quickly moves through the screening process. No removal of shoes or belts. No routine confiscation of nail files and scissors.

Moody thought back to the weeks after 9/11, when some of his colleagues said the United States should just copy the Israeli methods of airport security. Others objected that, besides the issue of profiling, time-consuming interviews of passengers would be unworkable because of the greater volume of U.S. air traffic. Moody believes that national pride also played a part. He recalled that Australia rebuffed his company's offer to go there and produce a biometric identification card for their transportation workers. Rather, the Australians asked him to explain the process so that an Australian firm could implement it. "I found the same attitude in every country where we've tried to provide our expertise," Moody said.

In considering what Americans can learn from Israel's experience, Moody's reactions underscore three truths. First, while Israeli preparedness is commonly acknowledged as advanced, even "the gold standard," preconceived notions about Israeli practices may be inaccurate. The best understanding comes not from hearsay but from personal observation. Second, not every worthwhile measure is easily transferable from one society to another. For example, for cultural, political, or financial reasons, Americans might be unreceptive to certain practices. But third, refusal to learn from others, whether because of national pride or wrong assumptions, can leave a society more vulnerable. By understanding Israelis' experience with terrorism, from adjustments in their daily routines to the country's emergency response procedures, Americans can better discern how to cope and to save lives.

* * *

Although terrorism has been variously defined, it commonly includes deliberate violence against innocent individuals with the aim of influencing political outcomes. For thousands of years murderous assaults against innocent people have occurred in the name of religion or ideology.[2] But terrorist attacks, especially by suicide bombers, increased dramatically toward the end of the twentieth century and into the twenty-first. Their targets were in countries with diverse populations and political systems, including in India, Indonesia, Iraq, Israel, Kenya, Pakistan, Russia, Saudi Arabia, Spain, Sri Lanka, Tanzania, Turkey, the United Kingdom, and the United States. These assaults were carried out largely by Islamic extremists or by secular nationalist militants. The principal example of the latter was in Sri Lanka, where the Tamil Tigers, a Marxist and ethnically based organization, was behind more than eighty suicide bombings.[3]

The 9/11 attacks shocked Americans into recognizing their own vulnerability. Since then, authorities have thwarted plans by terrorists to attack other U.S. targets, including the Brooklyn Bridge, the New York City garment district, and the Los Angeles Airport. Overseas, however, terrorists have been more successful, having set off bombs in Madrid, Istanbul, London—and, with increasing frequency, in Iraq. But no country has endured more systematic terrorism over an extended period than Israel. Elsewhere, intervals between assaults might be measured in months or years. Not in Israel. Beginning in September 2000, a year before the jetliner attacks on America, and throughout the six years following, Palestinians attempted thousands of attacks against Israelis. Most were prevented by Israeli forces, but around four hundred succeeded, including nearly one hundred and fifty suicide bombings.[4] Palestinian bombers blew themselves up in buses, restaurants, shopping malls, dance halls, ice cream parlors, and schools—killing around 1,100 adults and children, and maiming 7,500 more.

The frequency and the random locations of the targets placed the Israelis on edge. Beyond the victims and families who were directly affected, much of the population felt stressed. During the first years of the "intifada," as the Arabs called their uprising, many Israelis stopped dining out or traveling by bus. (The rush of terrorist attacks after 2000 is sometimes called the second intifada, the first and less violent one having extended from 1987 to 1993.) Fewer shoppers went to open markets and department stores. Attendance at movie theaters fell—at least for a while. By 2004, the public's behavior had largely reverted to earlier patterns. Israeli security efforts had succeeded in sharply reducing the number of terror incidents. But even a year earlier, Israelis were drifting back to old form. In 2003, despite three or four suicide bombings per month, markets, stores, movies, and restaurants had again begun to bustle with patrons. Still, the threat of terrorism had influenced the mindset of some people in unexpected ways.

* * *

In the spring of 2003, Lawrence "Levi" Lauer was strolling with his 14-year-old daughter Anya near their Jerusalem home. The Lauers live in a neighborhood known as Old Katamon, a charming residential area where balconies brim with red and yellow begonias. Street crime in Israel is rare, and people have long walked with relative abandon. While the spate of Palestinian attacks that began in 2000 had caused some to hesitate, many Israelis, like the Lauers, maintained their routines.

Interrupting their amiable chat, Anya suddenly suggested that she and her father change their relative positions on the sidewalk. "Dad, I think you should be walking on the outside and I should be on the inside," she said. At first, Levi Lauer thought she was merely observing a quaint tenet of Western etiquette: A gentleman should shield a lady from the splash of passing vehicles. At least that was what Lauer had been taught during his growing-up years in America.

But etiquette was not on Anya's mind. "What if a terrorist bomb should explode from the street?" she asked. "If you died, I think that somehow I would eventually get over it. But if I were killed, I know you could never get over it."

Lauer had left Cleveland in 1976 to live in the Jewish state. Then 31, he was a rabbi in the reform, or progressive tradition of Judaism, with its emphasis on promoting social justice. After settling in Israel, Lauer continued to labor on behalf of the underdog—foreign workers, victims of human trafficking, the poor and needy. He was especially determined that Israel's Arab population be treated justly. After the wave of Palestinian attacks began, Lauer's list of people in distress expanded. At times the number of terror victims and their families seemed to rise by the day. An organization he founded, Atzum (the Hebrew word for powerful), began to raise funds to help these new victims just as it was helping others in need.

Anya's comment stunned her father. "Sure," was all he could say. He changed places with her, anguishing in silence over how his child had been impelled to such calculation. Was this what terrorism had driven Israeli children to worry about? He barely noticed the sun's golden reflection on the Jerusalem-stone homes along their way. Lauer felt sadness more than fear about the effects of the intifada. He and Anya kept on walking.

Terror

1

Terror

Two years before Levi Lauer and his daughter took their stroll in Jerusalem, Yuli Nelimov, 16, stood outside a seaside building in Tel Aviv, 40 miles west. The structure, once a dolphin aquarium, was now a dance hall called the Dolphi Disco. The wall beside the entrance was decorated with cartoon-like depictions of underwater life. Yellow sunfish cavorted against a background of sea anemones. A lazy octopus hovered above them. The dancehall, sometimes referred to as the Dolphinarium, regularly drew a weekend crowd of teenagers, most of them immigrants from the former Soviet Union.

It was nearing 11:30 PM on June 1, 2001, a crisp Friday night. Like the teens in Tel Aviv, others around the world were celebrating the end of their school or work week. Lines of young people awaited entry to a movie in Tokyo, a theater in London, the dance floor at Webster Hall in downtown New York. In their anticipation of a joyful experience, the groups were interchangeable. They also shared a condition of vulnerability. Largely unprotected and unaware, each group was susceptible to the whim of someone intent to do them harm. Those waiting to dance in New York's Webster Hall were as vulnerable and oblivious as those at the Dolphinarium.

Amid the throng waiting for the doors of the Dolphinarium to open, Yuli and her 18-year-old sister Yelena were especially eager. The Nelimov girls had emigrated from Russia five years earlier with their mother, Ella; brother, Sasha, then 9; and their grandmother. Their divorced father had remained in Russia. Both sisters loved to dance, and going to the Dolphi at the end of a school week had become a joyful routine. In fact, that day their fun had begun at home, when they posed for photographs in their mother's dresses. As they dressed for the evening, both girls decided to wear multicolored beaded anklets that they had strung themselves. When Ella saw Yuli painting her fingernails green, she gently chided her. Green nail polish struck her as a bit tawdry. "Oh Mom, it's for fun," Yuli answered, dismissing her mother's fussiness. "The dancehall lights make the green sparkle." Ella shrugged her shoulders, a signal of reluctant surrender to her teenage daughter's whim.

Outside the dancehall, some of the youngsters were on cell phones. Yuli's light brown hair bobbed about her small earrings as she joked with friends. Nearby stood Ilya Gutman, 19, his dark brows arched in a happy expression. He and his family had left Kazakhstan nine years earlier. While helping to care for his disabled brother, he was enrolled in computer studies. Many in the group were similarly devoted to family and schoolwork. Irena Usdachi, 18, was deemed by her high school principal to be remarkably intelligent. Irena Nafmaniashtsy, 16, was, according to her teachers, vivacious and bright. Some who came to dance had arrived in Israel only months earlier: Roman Gurokhovsky, 20, with a shock of hair that curled toward the corner of his eye, and Aleksei Lupalo, 16, whose ironic smile seemed to portend the delivery of a clever one-liner.

The disco manager, Avi Mizrahi, stepped outside and sensed the enthusiasm of the crowd. Standing in front of the entrance, he glanced down the stone promenade past a kiosk 60 feet away that was selling Coke and ice cream. Across the street a bungee jump amusement ride glittered under neon lights. Mizrahi reentered the disco feeling good about the party atmosphere.

Earlier that day, while Yuli and Yelena were draping themselves in their mother's attire, Sa'id Hutari was preparing to wrap himself in something less seemly. Born in Jordan twenty years earlier, Sa'id was heir to a family grievance. His grandfather was among 750,000 Arabs who were displaced in 1948 during Israel's war of independence. The previous year, the Jewish population of Palestine had accepted the United Nations plan to divide the land into separate Jewish and Arab states. But the neighboring Arab countries rejected the plan and attacked the nascent Jewish state.

In the ensuing conflict, some Arabs fled their homes when their leaders promised a quick return after the Jews were defeated. Some were pressed to leave by Jewish armed forces. Others fled to avoid deadly crossfire as people often do in wars. No matter the reason. And no matter that around the same period 850,000 Jews were forced to leave their homes in Arab countries. These Jews, like millions of other displaced persons from Europe, China, and the newly established states of India and Pakistan, settled in different countries. But more than a half-century later, only the Arabs continued to claim a "right of return."[1] And of all the world's displaced persons of that time, only the Arabs remained in refugee camps.

The neighboring countries that set up the camps—Egypt, Lebanon, Syria, Jordan—largely refused to absorb their inhabitants and encouraged their continuing hostility to Israel. Third and fourth generations were born into the crowded camps, steeped in resentment. These descendants were bred to believe that the only acceptable resolution of their grievances was to regain the homes of their grandparents or great-grandparents. Whether or not the homes still existed was immaterial to their proclaimed "right of return" to what was now the state of Israel. Insisting on this "right" would mean that perhaps 4 million—the estimated number of Palestinian descendants—could take residency in Israel. Since Israel's population consists of about 5.5 million Jews and 1.3 million Arabs, a large influx of Arabs would, of course, mean the end of the Jewish state.

The hatred bequeathed to Sa'id Hutari left him susceptible to virulent manipulation. Organizations like Hamas and Islamic Jihad openly called for killing Jews as a means to end Israeli occupation. But for them, the occupation was on all the land between the Jordan River and the Mediterranean Sea, including the state of Israel.

The 1993 Oslo Accord provided for recognition of Israel by Yasser Arafat's Palestinian Authority, along with steps toward creation of a Palestinian state. The borders were to be negotiated, though by general understanding the new Palestinian state would be created from land that came under Israeli control after the 1967 Israel-Arab war. On the one hand, that meant the Gaza strip, a wedge of land along Israel's border with Egypt. And on the other, the West Bank, an area between Israel and Jordan, west of the Jordan River.

Between 1948 and 1967, the West Bank was under the control of Jordan. Before then, for thirty years, it had been under the authority of Britain as part of the Palestine Mandate. (The mandate, granted by the League of Nations after World War I, initially included what later became Jordan as well as Israel and the area between them.) For centuries before World War I, the Ottoman Turks had ruled the area. In fact, the last time an indigenous population was sovereign in the land of Palestine, including the West Bank, was two thousand years earlier, when it was part of ancient Israel. Jewish sovereignty ceased when the Romans conquered the area and sent much of the population into exile eighty-seven years after the death of Christ.

Under the guidance of Hamas's Qassam Brigades, that June evening in 2001, Sa'id Hutari donned a garment variously described as a harness or belt. It was packed with explosives and inch-long nails, screws, washers, and ball bearings. Hamas and other terrorist groups, including Islamic Jihad and the Al Aqsa Martyrs Brigades, were prompting young people like Sa'id toward actions incompatible with civilized society.

Sa'id's father spoke of his son as a quiet, happy boy who did well in school. After becoming an electrician, Sa'id moved to the West Bank. Some two million Arabs now live there in addition to 240,000 Jews who moved there after 1967. The Jews are commonly referred to as "settlers," and the land as "occupied territory." (Many Israelis insist the term should be "disputed territory," since sovereignty and border issues remain unresolved.)

Sa'id had rehearsed his assignment under the direction of Jamal Mansur, a Hamas leader who worked from an office in Nablus, an Arab town in the West Bank.

Alighting from a Subaru, Sa'id made his way across a parking lot to the Dolphinarium. Scarcely older than the Israeli teenagers gathered near the entrance, he wedged his way among them. His bulky jacket drew no particular attention as he moved within feet of Yuli and Yelena. Nor did the 30-odd pounds of concealed explosives impede his movement. A wire attached to the deadly cargo extended to a triggering device in his pants pocket. A few minutes past 11:30 PM Sa'id Hutari reached into his pocket, placed his finger on the button, and pressed.

A flash of light leaped upward from his chest, accompanied by a deafening blast. In an instant, bodies were thrown into the air. Limbs were sundered, and pieces of arms, legs, and hands flew in every direction. A burgeoning fireball engulfed an area 50 feet across as strips of human membrane were catapulted far beyond the edge of the fire.

The metal pieces that had been packed with the explosives sprayed outward as fast as bullets. In less than a second, a nail could puncture a victim as cleanly as a hypodermic needle. Drilling farther inward, it could slice through an artery and end up lodged in the heart. A screw might take a different trajectory. Turned into a propeller, its rotary force could tear open a wad of skin and grind into the underlying muscle and nerve tissue, converting them into a mushy mass. A second screw might spin through the spinal cord, severing the motor connections between brain and limbs and leaving the victim permanently paralyzed.

For an instant after the detonation everything was silent. Then screams and moans. Young people, some whole, some in pieces, lay scattered on the pavement made soft from the heat of the explosion.

Blood gushed from ripped abdomens and from openings where an arm or leg was torn away. The ground was dotted with pieces of skin and of scalp with hair attached.

Blood was spattered on automobiles parked far from the epicenter and on the walls of the distant kiosk along the promenade. Danny Shamalov, 17, whose foot was punctured by nails, recalled the carnage the next day from a hospital bed: "I saw a young girl sitting without a leg; she was screaming and didn't let anyone get near her. Next to her someone lay dead. I saw a boy running and holding his torn arm, and I saw another girl without an eye."[2]

The outer wall of the Dolphinarium was pockmarked with shards of metal. The overhang above the entryway was charred, though inexplicably, the adjacent mural was undamaged, its still-life fish eerily placid amid the chaos. Within minutes, vehicles poured into the scene, their sirens screaming, blue and red lights flashing. Police cordoned off the area.

Scores of emergency medical workers made their way through the dead and maimed. The workers began to administer first aid as they placed the injured onto stretchers and loaded them into ambulances. Survivors were quickly dispatched to area hospitals, where teams of doctors and other health workers were scrambling in preparation. Priority attention went to the living, while the dead victims were covered with white plastic sheets and left on the ground. As the bodies awaited transportation to the morgue, their motionless arms and legs extended beyond the sheets. Among the twenty who lay dead were Yuli and Yelena Nelimov, Ilya, the two Irenas, and Roman and Aleksei. Another 120 were injured, many of them critically, including one who died days later.

Within an hour the victims had been removed, though remnants of recent life remained pervasive. Into the next day, clean-up crews labored to remove the traces. Caked blood had colored patches of the ground burgundy-black. Segments of skin turned dark from the searing heat remained stuck to the pavement, and bone fragments lay scattered far from the epicenter.

Minutes after the attack, radio and television bulletins announced what had happened. Ella Nelimov was driving with a friend when she heard the radio bulletin. As with other parents trying frantically to reach their children at the Dolphinarium, Ella's calls to her girls' cell phones went unanswered. Her middle-of-the-night trek began at Ichilov, the main hospital in Metropolitan Tel Aviv, the first stop in Ella's search. When she arrived, she encountered a growing crowd of desperate parents who were also seeking word about their children. She reached a hospital aide and described her daughters, Yuli and Yelena. The aide said that identification of the newly arrived patients was not yet complete and that Ella would have to wait. She sat quietly along the lobby wall and eventually was told that her daughters were not at the hospital. Ella's friend then drove her to Tel Aviv University's Wolfsohn Hospital on the southern edge of the city. As at Ichilov, Ella's girls were not among the newly admitted patients. Perhaps, Ella thought, someone might have information at the Dolphinarium, and she went there next. As she approached the perimeter an hour and a half after the bombing, the smell of the carnage was still fresh. She told a police officer of her search at the two hospitals and wondered if anyone at the scene might know where her daughters had been taken. The officer advised her to check at the morgue.

The morgue, part of the National Forensic Institute, was less than a mile from the Dolphinarium, and when Ella arrived she found herself among grieving families. Mothers, upon learning the worst, had collapsed on the building's grounds and were being treated by paramedics. She walked past them and went inside. She was escorted to a room that contained the unidentified remains of two victims. At first she could not recognize the mangled figures, but a soft gasp escaped from her throat as her eyes glided to a hand. The fingernails were painted green. Then she saw the ankles of each figure encircled with the multicolored beads that her girls had strung. Though overwhelmed with sadness, she remained stoic.

A year later Ella Nelimov still seemed uncomprehending. At a graveside memorial service for her daughters, she stared at the two black marble headstones. Like most Jews from the former Soviet

Union, she grew up uninformed about religious practices. Centuries-old Russian anti-Semitism had been reinforced by the Soviet regime's own version as well as its general antipathy to religion. Many Jews had grown distant from the traditions of their parents or grandparents. Still, during the Cold War, a core of Jewish activists pressed for the right to emigrate and openly practice their religion. They were less likely to receive permission to leave than to be sent to prison for their effrontery.

Only in the late 1980s, when the Soviet regime was near collapse, were Jews able to emigrate in large numbers. Reattachment to their historical roots prompted nearly one million Jews from the former Soviet Union to move to Israel in little more than a decade. Ella's daughters, Yuli and Yelena, felt especially drawn to a sense of peoplehood and convinced their mother to make the move. After their deaths, Ella told a rabbi that she knew little about rituals and asked him to guide her through Jewish mourning. "We are here in Israel, we're Jews, and I wanted to do what they do here," she said. Subsequent months were difficult, but she kept her equilibrium. She had attained a better-paying government job and was receiving support from friends and from a volunteer community group.

Now, dressed in a black blouse and pants, she stood before her daughters' graves clasping a bouquet of flowers. "I can see in my mind what they looked like just before they went out that night," she said. "I can see it like it was yesterday."

Months after the attack, Australian television broadcast a documentary that included an interview with Sa'id's father. Mr. Hutari said that he had no forewarning that Sa'id was going to blow himself up but that he was proud of what his son did. "I hope that my other three sons will do the same," he said. "I would like all members of my family, all the relatives, to die for my nation and my homeland."[3]

Unlike most Israeli facilities that have been have been bombed, the Dolphinarium was not quickly repaired and returned to its original condition. Three year after the attack, the building remained closed and barred. On a June evening much like that tragic evening in 2001, flashes of moonbeam bounced from waves along the nearby beachfront. They shone on a simple memorial several feet from the entrance to the former dancehall. A life-size iron silhouette depicts a boy and girl holding hands. Not far away are the names of the victims, and a simple inscription: "We will not stop dancing."

* * *

The attack at the Dolphinarium, though widely reported, seemed distant to many outside Israel. Few patrons of public establishments elsewhere in the world changed their habits or felt threatened as a consequence. But three months later, on September 11, 2001, dancing at Webster Hall and elsewhere in the New York area came to a halt. In the following days the slogan, "We are all Israelis now," became a commonplace for many, at least for a while.[4]

As Americans were jolted into recognizing their own vulnerability, more began to pay attention to how the Israelis were dealing with terrorism. Information exchanges between United States and Israeli officials grew in a variety of areas, from law enforcement to medical preparedness. These concerns led to numerous conferences, including one at New York University Medical School on the eve of the second anniversary of the jetliner attacks. Dr. David Applebaum, chief of emergency medicine at Shaare Zedek Hospital in Jerusalem, was invited to share his experiences in caring for hundreds of victims of terrorist attacks. After making his presentation, on Monday, September 7, 2003, he quickly left the conference to return to Israel.

In anticipation of his daughter Nava's marriage three days later on September 10, Applebaum, 50, seemed to wear a perpetual smile. His dark pepper-and-salt beard contrasted with glistening white teeth. As they posed for a photograph, 20-year-old Nava leaned toward her father's chest. The joyful glint in their eyes matched perfectly. Now, with his return to Israel, he could give full attention to his daughter and the imminent celebration.

Born in Detroit, David attended the Hillel Elementary School, a Jewish school at which his father was the principal. Miriam Seagle, a childhood friend, remembers afternoons at David's home when they were seven, stuffing down hotdogs and watching television. *Howdy Doody* was a favorite program. David's family moved to Chicago when he was a teenager, after which Miriam rarely saw him. But decades later, on a visit to Israel with her husband, they reconnected. She chuckled as she recalled her impression: "He was still sweet and funny, just like he was as a kid."

After David completed college, he became an ordained rabbi, but he also earned a masters degree in biology from Northwestern University. He then attended the Medical College of Ohio in Toledo, graduated in 1978, and worked as an emergency room doctor in Cleveland. After immigrating to Israel in 1982, he divided his time between the United States and Israel, performing emergency medicine at each.

During the next two decades, Dr. Applebaum forged a reputation as a creative clinician and organizer. He developed a life-saving procedure that can dissolve clots in the first moments after a heart attack. And he responded to the often-crowded conditions in hospital emergency departments by creating an alternative service. He established a privately owned system of clinics called Terem, which grew to include eight urgent and primary care facilities in the Jerusalem area. Many patients with sore throats, upset stomachs, and minor injuries now seek care at a Terem clinic, and hospital emergency departments have become less clogged.

Miriam Dombey, David's assistant at a Jerusalem clinic he directed, recalled an incident in which a Jewish woman did not want to be treated by an Arab physician on staff. Dr. Applebaum would have none of it. He intervened, telling the patient that nationality played no part in determining the qualifications of staff members. "Our staff has a right to be here and complies with our professional standards," he said. Staring directly at her, he warned: "You can accept treatment by our doctor or go elsewhere."

With his wife, Debra, who had grown up in Cleveland, David had six children. Nava, their oldest daughter, had just completed two years of national service, working with children suffering from cancer. She was planning to enter college and study genetics. Meanwhile, relatives from America and Canada had arrived to join with hundreds of Israeli friends and family to celebrate Nava's marriage to Hanan Sand, a student at a religious school.

Café Hillel, a lively gathering place in Jerusalem, attracts young and old. Salads and sandwiches are common fare, along with a specialty drink of the house, a mug of cappuccino. The café, on Emek Refaim Street, is easily accessible. Just beyond two security guards, the door opens directly into the dining area. Inside, to the left, patrons place their orders at the counter. Behind the counter a crew of young sandwich-makers labor to keep pace with demand. On the opposite wall, large windowpanes give full view to an outdoor eating section. People linger over drinks, and relaxed conversation is the rule.

Not surprisingly, the café would seem a pleasant place for a father-daughter chat. For David and Nava, their late-evening snack and the take-home desserts they promised the rest of the family carried special significance. Nava's marriage the next day meant that this night was to be the last with her family before beginning her own household.

From their home a few blocks away, David and Nava made their way to Emek Refaim Street. They crossed the alleyway that borders the restaurant and walked under a black awning. The white lettering on the forward flap simply said: "Café Hillel." Nava passed the security guards and entered. David, a few feet behind, had not quite reached the door. Suddenly, from 30 feet down the street, near the adjacent pizza parlor, a man yelled, "Stop him. Stop him." Yitzak Mor was shouting and pointing frantically to a man in a white shirt, halfway between David and himself.

Mor had been working as a guard at Pizza Meter for only one week. Stocky and dark, he was barely older than the Jewish state. He was one year old when his family emigrated from Morocco in 1948, the year that Israel was established. Skilled with his hands, Yitzak previously worked as an electrician and machinist. Israel's economy had soured in recent years, and work was harder to find. But the intifada had also created a new industry. The demand for security guards mushroomed, and Yitzak found employment at a security agency. He was initially assigned to a nursery school, then to an elementary school, and later to the Pizza Meter next to the Café Hillel.

Seven months after his frantic shouts, Yitzak Mor and his wife, Chava, recounted the experience to me. Their modest third-floor apartment is in Gilo, a section on the edge of Jerusalem. Yitzak stretched his arm along the back of a worn green couch. A pack of Time cigarettes lay on the coffee table between us.

"That day, I came to work at 5 PM," he recalled. It was Tuesday, September 9, and he was expected to stay until midnight. "When I arrived, I saw more police and security people than usual, and I asked, 'What's going on?'" He learned that a warning had been issued that a terrorist might be in the vicinity.

Mor had never encountered a terrorist. Like other guards he carried a pistol, but he had fired it only during practice. A government security man nearby said, "If you see the terrorist, just grab him quietly if you can." Mor asked, "Is that a joke?" "No." He wandered up to the corner and heard the same warning from the two private guards in front of the Café Hillel. He felt unsettled. How would he know if he'd seen a terrorist?

He returned to his post outside the Pizza Meter. Customers came and went uneventfully. Toward the end of his shift, around 11:20 PM, a man walked past him toward the café. When Mor saw the man from the rear he became alarmed. "It looked like there was a square suitcase on his back. He had a white shirt, and this thing under it bulked out," he recalled.

Mor called at him to stop, but the man kept moving. Then Mor bellowed the words that have echoed in his mind ever since: "Stop him. Stop him." Fearful that shooting at the man from behind might detonate the bulk, Mor hoped a guard at the café would fire from the front. But to no avail.

A flash of light and a deafening explosion erupted from the man. "I felt like I was flying," Mor said. The blast lifted him and spun him around. He lay in the street riddled with shrapnel, barely conscious. With sirens wailing, police cars, ambulances, and other emergency vehicles quickly arrived.

The scene was littered with bodies and blood. Part of the roof of the café had collapsed, and the awning bearing the name "Café Hillel" dangled precariously. Plastic coffee cups, napkins, and broken glass covered the street along with body parts and torn clothing. Perah Tiab had been walking up the alley next to the café and was showered with debris. Sobbing, the 41-year-old woman said, "It was like the sky was bleeding."

At the hospital it became clear that Mor's injuries were serious but not life-threatening. "It was a miracle," he said wistfully. "I was the same distance away from the bomber as Dr. Applebaum." With a nod of disbelief he added: "But he was killed with his daughter and I wasn't."

Mor expressed grief over their deaths and then turned inward: "To have gone through this and lived is another type of affliction." His wife Chava interjected: "I was in shock. I saw my husband on television in a wheelchair and that's how I learned. I tried calling and calling but couldn't reach him at the hospital. Then they called me."

Mor was discharged from the hospital after a few days to convalesce at home. His wounds were healing, but he continued to spend much of the time in bed. Chava evinces frustration: "He remained unable to walk, but it was clear that the problem was not just with physical injury." When we spoke in 2004, seven months after the attack, Yitzak rose to his feet. He hesitantly navigated around the coffee table before sinking again into the couch. "My psychiatrist says I don't have any physical problem with my legs. But I can hardly walk—my legs don't work."

Yitzak's experience had brought his wife to despair. "Now I can't even look for work. I have to stay with him all the time." She sounded disbelieving. "His personality is different." They were living off of a small government stipend and help from the volunteer group, Atzum.

Yitzak, shoeless and in white socks, stretched backwards. At a glance, he seemed physically fit, garbed as he was in a turtleneck jersey and green running pants. But as he talked, the malaise became evident. He spoke haltingly about his efforts to go out in public. "If I get on a bus, I feel my heart pounding, so I get off after a few blocks. I keep trying, but when I get on the bus I start to shake, and I hold on to people." Chava nodded knowingly. With a half-smile she said that not all the strangers appreciated being grabbed. She shook her head about the toll the event had taken. "You wouldn't recognize him from the way he was before." Yitzak listened impassively. "Now he can't even change a light bulb."

Their grown children and other family members visit and try to help. But Yitzak was psychologically traumatized, a victim of post-traumatic stress disorder.

As I was about to leave, Yitzak looked at me quizzically and asked, "How does a man have the will to blow himself up? Do you have an answer for that?" The question seemed as much philosophical as related to his experience. I shrugged and responded with another question: "How does his mother come to say that she is happy that her son blew himself up?" Without pause, Chava offered a long "Ahhhh," and asked, "How does a woman with children become a suicide terrorist?" It was a reminder that women and even children as young as 11 had been suicide bombers. We looked at each other in silent wonderment.

The night of the bombing, victims were rushed to local hospitals. The most severely injured were taken to Hadassah, where advanced care is available in specialties like neurosurgery and microsurgery. But fourteen victims, including Yitzak Mor, were brought to Shaare Zedek. Ordinarily, Dr. David Applebaum would have tended to him. David was invariably among the first to arrive at the hospital upon notice of an attack, offering comfort to patients and encouragement to staff. But even after the ambulances began to deliver the wounded, he had not shown up. The hospital director, Jonathan Halevy, suspected that his absence might have meant that he was part of the tragedy.

Minutes later, word filtered back to the hospital that Dr. Applebaum and Nava were among the dead. An unusual quiet fell over the staff as they continued to work, many brushing away tears. "I felt as if we'd been orphaned," nurse Simcha Hacohen said. "He was an amazing human being," she added. "As soon as he arrived each day, he would go around wishing everyone 'Good morning,' staff members and patients alike."

The suicide bombing that night, for which Hamas claimed credit, killed seven people and injured fifty-seven. But the loss of David and his daughter seemed especially cruel. Dr. Halevy recalled David's many innovations to emergency care, including his introduction of computer technology to follow each patient's course of treatment. "Thousands of Jerusalemites owe their lives to him," Halevy said. At the funeral the next day, David was extolled as a scholar of the Bible, a humanitarian, a loving family man. He treated Arabs and Jews without distinction and took pride in having an ethnically mixed staff. A former Chief Rabbi of Israel, Yisrael Meir Lau, called him "one of God's emissaries."

At his sister's funeral service the same day, Yitsak Applebaum, 22, said, "Nava was always smiling, always happy, always surrounded by her many friends." He added, "She will be an eternal bride." After Nava's coffin was lowered into the grave, Hanan, her fiancé, made his way to the edge and dropped a small red box into the cavity. It contained the wedding ring he had planned to place on her finger that night.

Miriam Dombey and her husband Moshe had been friends of the Applebaums long before she began working for him in 1996. In June 2004, nine months after David and Nava's death, when I asked how the family was faring, she said they had been "amazing." "Of course we don't know what they feel in private—it must be sad," she posited. "But in public they show great strength."

The family was living out the promise that the oldest son,

Natan, had offered soon after the funerals. "We are not a family that is afraid," said the 24-year-old. "We go to cafés and take buses, and we will continue to do so. We do not live for the moment; we live for the future."[5]

Months later, Natan became the father of a baby boy. As is Jewish custom, the child was named after a deceased and honored family member, in this case, David. He was also given the middle name Avi Chai, which in this context meant "my father lives."

The legacy of David Applebaum continues in other ways as well. His deeds have been celebrated through a variety of medical and religious memorials. Perhaps the most unusual was in August 2004, when fifteen physicians and their families emigrated from North America to Israel as part of an Applebaum Fellowship program. The program was established by Nefesh B'Nefesh, an organization that offers grants and encouragement to people interested in moving to Israel. The doctors' decisions to immigrate arose in part from their religious commitment. But Dr. Applebaum's own behavior had been inspirational. One of the doctors, Michael Chernofsky, who had been a hand surgeon in Pennsylvania, recalled a conversation with David two years earlier about practicing in Israel. David's encouragement, he said, helped influence his family's decision. Jeremy Halberstadt, a pediatrician from Queens spoke of David's example. "The greatest hope of physicians like myself who are arriving here is to be able to contribute to the Jewish people in the way Dr. Applebaum did," he said.[6]

* * *

The stroll that Levi Lauer took with his daughter Anya, the Dolphinarium memorial, the activities of the Applebaum family, and the return of diners, dancers, and commuters all carried the same message. The Israeli public was determined to live. Of course, they lived with a continuing burden of uncertainty. For those most directly affected by the terrorism—the victims and families—the consequences are profound and often long-lasting. Suffering from depression or post-traumatic stress disorder, they may need treatment for years afterward. Indeed, the terrorism has imposed a condition of permanent stress on the entire population. But the stress is part of a strange norm. It is tucked into the collective psyche, often beyond consciousness. Even with the anticipation of further terrorist attacks, anxiety is overshadowed by determined resilience.

The ability to cope with stress is certainly not peculiar to Israeli society. At the same time, some new Israeli institutions, whether born of tradition or necessity, have addressed the waves of terrorist attacks in ways that are unique to the Jewish state. One such example derives from the religious tradition of reverence not only for life but of respect for the dead.

2

ZAKA

The centerfold photograph in the brochure shows thirty men in protective outerwear, including thick rubber gloves and boots, gas masks at the ready. Some are wearing luminous yellow vests with Hebrew lettering that spells ZAKA, an acronym for Identification of Disaster Victims. A few are on sleek motorcycles, seemingly prepared to speed off at a moment's notice. Behind each rider, above the rear wheel, a white box contains emergency medical supplies. A blinking red light atop the box beams out an insistent warning that this vehicle has the right of way.

The men in the picture appear intent, some smiling, some peering straight ahead. To the untutored observer, certain features about them may seem incongruous. Men in their 20s and 30s, a few older, they are wearing kippahs, skullcaps that signify religious piety. Several have full beards and long curly sideburns. Their ultra-Orthodox appearance is reminiscent of Tevya, the pious nineteenth-century patriarch in *Fiddler on the Roof*. The *Fiddler* story itself is a throwback to hundreds of years of Jewish life in Russia and elsewhere in Eastern Europe. Only today's Tevya is covered in twenty-first-century emergency rescue gear.

Connected by beepers and cell phones, ZAKA volunteers are among the first to arrive at a disaster scene, whether of a terror attack or traffic accident. Along with traditional medical responders, they help with emergency care. But unlike the other medics, they also fervently try to locate body parts for burial with the corpse.

In the ZAKA centerfold, Isaac Bernstein stands near one of the motorcycles. His delicate features are visible through a reddish-brown beard. Isaac's lean frame and expressive gestures were also evident in a television documentary shown in 2003 on Israel's Channel 2 about how ZAKA volunteers were coping with stress.

In the spring of 2004, I met with Isaac and other ZAKA members at the organization's headquarters on Jaffa Road in Jerusalem. I arrived with a friend, Dr. Zev Alexander, who during the previous year had spent much time with the members. An American, he was in the midst of a two-year Fulbright grant to study ZAKA. Just before arriving in Israel, Zev had completed medical school at Brown University in Providence, Rhode Island. At the end of his Fulbright project in 2005, he returned to the United States to begin a residency in psychiatry. He'll be carrying on a family tradition—his father and grandfather were psychiatrists.

Zev and I were ushered down a corridor past a half-dozen offices to an unadorned conference room. Light plastic chairs were positioned irregularly around a circular table. A small bookcase against the wall contained some telephone directories and prayer books. One shelf carried two-dozen weighty volumes in Hebrew. Zev, fluent in Hebrew, informed me that they were Kabbalist tracts of mystical teaching.

Hanging on the wall near the table were a half-dozen photographs of eminent bearded rabbis. On the opposite wall were posters of ZAKA volunteers in action—on a motorcycle streaming toward a scene, cradling an injured victim, soaking up blood with paper towels after a terror bombing.

A few minutes passed, and Isaac Bernstein bounded into the room. "Shalom," he said cheerfully, using the multipurpose word for hello, goodbye, and peace. Now 30, he had recently become a full-time employee of ZAKA. Previously, he had worked in the manufacture of textiles. Zev translated for us.

When did he become a ZAKA volunteer? I asked. "About four years ago," Bernstein replied. He was relaxed, not at all ponderous. "I had friends who were in ZAKA, not just helping at terror attacks but also at car accidents. They would tell me about their experiences, and I was moved by how much they were doing from the heart. I felt jealous. I joined."

I mentioned the TV documentary on ZAKA. In the video Bernstein had told a psychologist that in a sense all the ZAKA people were crazy. What did he mean by that? I asked.

He acknowledged with a grin that the statement might seem puzzling. "During the days they were filming the documentary, there was a terrorist attack. I am in the film with the others working at the site. The attack was 7 AM, and three hours earlier my wife had given birth to a son. When I had my son, I was the happiest person." Isaac smiled, kissed the tips of his fingers, and flipped them outward in a gesture of immense pleasure.

"Then I went home to sleep, but after 30 minutes my beeper woke me. There had been an explosion. I went to the scene immediately. It was Bus Number 20 and a lot of people were killed, including children."

He slowly exhaled as he noted the date of the attack, November 21, 2002. "Here I had been the most happy guy in the world, then at the scene I see the backpacks of small children and a father searching for his kids." As he was returning home he remained deeply conflicted. "How can I laugh and play with my children after anything like that?" he thought. "It all seems totally crazy."

Around nine hundred ZAKA volunteers are available for call throughout Israel. Augmented by seventy-five motorcycles and two-dozen ambulances, they are trained both as medics and as body handlers. But their vaunted efficiency came about only recently, as did their coordination with other government agencies, including the police, the Magen David Adom (MDA, Israel's equivalent to the Red Cross), and the army's Home Front Command.

The roots of ZAKA lie in religious tradition. Orthodox communities have long had burial societies whose members handle the deceased with sacred care. A severed finger or scrap of flesh are considered no less holy than the rest of the corpse. Collecting them for burial with the body is considered part of the biblical mandate to bury the dead "on the same day." If any of these men happened to be near a serious accident or other violent scene, they might call friends to come and help fulfill this holy obligation.

Such an incident occurred in August 1995. An explosion on a Jerusalem bus drew a stream of ultra-Orthodox men from homes nearby. They fumbled around and tried to help as they searched for pieces of flesh and bone. As at other earlier rescue operations, they sometimes got in the way of professional emergency responders. Yehuda Meshi-Zahav, the 45-year-old founder of ZAKA recalls that officials were fed up: "The police told us either to get serious and complete a professional training course or never again come to the scene of a crime."[1]

With that incentive, under Meshi-Zahav's leadership, ZAKA evolved into a sophisticated operation. The volunteers now must undergo months of emergency medical and rescue instruction. The work of ZAKA has also softened resentment by Israel's Jewish secular majority about special treatment accorded to the religious community. Perhaps 20 percent of Israel's Jewish population engages in regular religious practices. The ultra-Orthodox are only part of this minority. They are sometimes called "Haredi," Hebrew for trembling, a reference to the fervent physical animation they display during prayer.

Resentment has arisen from the fact that unlike the rest of the Jewish population, Haredi men and women are not required to serve in the military and their religious schools receive special government subsidies. But the dedication of ZAKA volunteers at one terror scene after another drew admiration from all Israelis. An example of this respect was offered early in the TV documentary about the stress experienced by the ZAKA workers.

The video was titled "Shock Treatment." At the outset, a woman in a pale green police uniform sat at the head of a table with a few other police officers. In front of them, in a semi-circle, were some twenty men in ZAKA vests. The woman identified herself as Commander Esther Domininski. "It is an honor for me to be here with you today," she began, softly but with authority. "We know this isn't easy for you—physically, but first and foremost emotionally." All eyes were on her. The sad expression on a clean-shaven young ZAKA man seemed to say, "You have no idea how true that is." They were assembled in a conference room at a Jerusalem hotel.

Domininski continued: "It imposes an emotional burden on each and every one of you. . . . " One man slowly brushed his hand across his beard. Another closed his eyes in contemplation, then fixed his attention again on the commander as she finished her thought, "after recovering body parts, severed body parts."

At the time of filming, in the fall of 2002, Palestinian attacks were occurring as often as two or three a week. Each bombing meant more death and dismemberment. The disturbing effects on the volunteers prompted Meshi-Zahav to seek the help of mental health professionals. Commander Domininski's remarks were a prelude to the main purpose of the day. She introduced Dr. Rony Berger, who was seated to her right. A specialist in the treatment of traumatic stress, Berger, a psychologist, began: "We didn't come here today to tell you that we think you're the victims." A ZAKA man in steel rimmed glasses and beard, about 40, looked quizzical. Berger continued: "We're coming from a place where we have the utmost respect for 'True Benevolence.' Your benevolence is one for which there is no reward."

Berger slowly pulled his arms toward his chest as if to draw the audience in. "We are aware of all this, and we want to reinforce you."

The film jumped ahead to a close-up of a man in an open ZAKA vest. His name appeared on the screen: "Isaac Bernstein, ZAKA volunteer." This was the first time I saw the man I would later meet at the ZAKA headquarters. He spoke in response to a prompt from Berger for the men to share their feelings. "What can I tell him?" Bernstein asked, looking around the room at no one in particular.

"That I arrived at the scene of an attack and lifted up an arm"—Bernstein raised his hand, enacting a lifting motion—"thinking I was taking a person out, but I was left with the arm in my hand?" He turned to a man at his left as if to ask, Now what? Then he continued aloud: "I'm serious, true story. So what am I supposed to tell the psychologist?"

Bernstein offered an ironic smile. Addressing the rest of the room, he seemed to question whether Dr. Berger could help any of them. "First, let's ask him if he's ever seen someone dead in a road accident. We'll go for the simplest thing." Before Bernstein's rhetorical challenge to Berger was answered, the film changed abruptly to a disaster scene in a section of Jerusalem called Kiryat Menachem. The date was November 21, 2002. The incident was the one that Bernstein mentioned to me eighteen months later when we met at the ZAKA headquarters.

The bus had exploded minutes earlier, and responders were at the scene. Isaac was scurrying amid other volunteers from ZAKA and the MDA, Israel's emergency response units. Some were working their way through the gnarled bus, looking for pieces of former life. The windows were blown out, and light was pouring in through their empty frames.

Police in abundance were keeping the area clear of nonessential personnel as medical responders in white coveralls carried away lifeless victims. Those in ZAKA vests and white booties over their shoes were also searching for limbs.

Bernstein called to a nearby worker, "Stop, stop, get me some water." The man handed him a canteen. Bernstein crunched a sheet of paper toweling, moistened it, and bent down. Reaching past a collection of rubble to a low stonewall he dabbed at the red stain. Another worker was already blotting with moist cotton. The paper and cotton, newly crimson, were placed in plastic bags marked for location and contents. Other ZAKA volunteers were scraping pieces of flesh from the road into plastic bags. The contents would be delivered to a forensic examiner for DNA identification, if possible in time for burial with the body.

Later, a TV interviewer turned to a ZAKA man standing off to the side. The man, beardless, was identified as Haim Weingarten. The interviewer asked: "Even though you're used to it, how does it make you feel?"

Weingarten squeezed his eyes shut before responding, "I'm not used to it—it's hard every time all over again."

I met with Haim Weingarten at the ZAKA offices in 2004. Although 34, he looked a decade younger. Weingarten ran a telemarketing firm, but like all ZAKA volunteers, he would drop everything to rush to a disaster scene. In the previous four years he had been to every event in the Jerusalem area. How many? I asked. He was not sure—too many to count.

I asked if any particular experience stood out in his memory. He thought a bit and mentioned Bus Number 2 on the evening of August 19, 2003, when a suicide bomber, dressed as an Orthodox Jew, boarded the bus at Shmuel Hanavi Street in Jerusalem and detonated himself.

Weingarten, who lived in the neighborhood, arrived by motorcycle just after the explosion. He knew some of the injured, including a young man who grabbed his hand. "He looked me in the eyes and said, 'Haim, help me.'" With the help of another worker, Weingarten applied a portable ventilator to his friend's face, trying to squeeze breaths into him. "But I felt his grasp on me was getting weaker and weaker. Then the doctor told me to stop."

Weingarten's friend was among the 23 killed and 130 injured at that scene. As he described the experience, his voice weakened: "I know I did the right thing, but I had this feeling that I didn't do enough." His lower jaw jutted forward, a slight quiver. "After that I couldn't do anything else at that event. I just got into one of the ambulances, brought some of the injured to the hospital, and didn't return."

The film returned to Dr. Berger instructing the men in front of him: "What we're asking you to do is one very simple thing. Sit in your chair in a comfortable position. Lean back and close your eyes." Berger lightly tapped his own eyelids. "And go into your body for a few minutes, okay? No more than five."

One man laughed, "Any longer and I'll fall asleep."

"That's okay too," Berger responded.

The exchange elicited nervous chuckles. The men seem relieved by the diversion.

Berger persisted: "Come on, close your eyes. No one's going to eat you. I'll close my eyes with you."

A voice called out: "Then who will see the clock?"

Laughter. But Berger patiently stayed on course. "It'll be five minutes; we have a sense of time. Close your eyes for a few minutes and try to connect with your body . . . " One by one the men shut their eyes as Berger continued in soothing tones, " . . . and with the way the air goes in and out."

Berger's hands rested on his lap. "Feel the weight of your shoulder and focus only on your breathing."

Unlike the others, Isaac Bernstein had not shut his eyes. He was leaning back, hands clasped behind his head. His extended elbows looked like stiffened wings against a current. But his apparent resistance eventually gave way, and gradually he lowered his lids.

The large circle of yellow-vested men, eyes shut, heads at odd angles, seemed as if they were in a trance. Berger's reading glasses swung from the strap around his neck. Then he urged a volcanic thought: "Try to think or see an attack you were at—and recall what happened at that terrible attack. What broke your heart? What caused you pain?"

Despite the evocative prompts, no one stirred. The horrors remained hidden beneath their placid exteriors. Then Isaac Bernstein's lips tightened, a hint of agitation. He alone revealed a visible sting brought on by a difficult recollection.

As the film cut to the next scene, Isaac and the others were given a novel outlet to express their recollections. Berger asked them to make pictures related to their experiences. Paintbrushes in hand, the men gathered around tables. They dipped their brushes into palettes of paint and applied the colors to white paper.

Bernstein painted a tangle of dots, lines, and circles. Most were encased in a rectangle, though a few extended farther down the page. The walls of the rectangle were blue, the dots and lines mostly red. "It's the attack at the Moment Café," Isaac said.

He was referring to the bombing on Saturday night, March 9, 2002. At 10:30 PM, a Palestinian man entered the café and blew himself up, killing eleven and injuring fifty-four. Afterward, the Palestinian group Hamas claimed responsibility for the attack.

The Moment was a gathering place for artists and professionals, many in their 20s and 30s. Located at Azza and Ben-Maimon Streets, it was near the prime minister's residence. Peace Now activists had been demonstrating outside the residence for much of the day. A dozen of them had stopped in for coffee at the Moment and had left just before 10:30 PM. When they reached home and turned on the television, they were in shock. They had been demonstrating against violence "on both sides," as Arie Arnon put it, and now could scarcely believe they escaped with their own lives.[2]

Bernstein explained that the lines of his rectangle were the walls inside the café. "This is what my eyes saw." He stared at the paper, pointed to brightly colored splotches and lines, and said, "Lots of people lying here on the floor, dead."

The back of his hand rubbed against his lips. "We started taking people out from inside." The dots and lines represented pieces of bodies. "All this blood," he said pointing to some red circles. "Because the people inside hadn't been killed, they were injured."

His finger moved up the page and stopped at a blue horizontal line: "There was a girl here. She wasn't missing anything. Outwardly she looked perfect." Isaac's voice was calm, but his half-closed eyes betrayed consternation. "The doctor had just arrived, and he checked her. I asked him: 'Should I put her in the ambulance?'" Bernstein's eyes widened, seemingly still surprised by the doctor's answer. "He said, 'She's dead.' And I said 'What?' He said, 'Now go tend to the people inside.'"

Another voice: "I've kept this bottled up inside for too long." The speaker was Haim Fuchsman, sunglasses arched atop his head. He pointed to a purple and green configuration that he had drawn. "This is supposed to be a stroller upside down on the sidewalk," he said.

Fuchsman stretched his thumb and pinky apart over the paper as if measuring the length of the image. "I went over to move the stroller away," he continued. "When I turned it over, I saw the most horrifying sight—a few-months-old baby still fastened in the stroller . . . " He looked down at the floor. " . . . but without a head."

After a long pause, he said, "I never thought I'd see a sight like that. People say that sights stay with you for days." He covered his eyes with his fingers and said, "That one stays with me to this day."

Haim Fuchsman continued in an even voice: "When I go at night to check on my kids, if I see one of them sleeping in a certain position, whether it's with an arm like this"—he raised his right arm above his head, palm forward—"or the legs in a position that reminds me of a dead body sprawled out on the street, in a bus, a restaurant, wherever, I always straighten out their arms and legs, make sure they're okay, and then I calm down."

The man next to him asked, "Why didn't you quit ZAKA after this experience?"

Fuchsman answered: "Faith—it's a spiritual thing. But mainly it's because I feel the work I do is so important."

The man responded: "But there are many other Orthodox men in Jerusalem who could do this work."

"I don't think so."

A voice from the group added, "I don't think there's anyone like him in Jerusalem."

Without a hint of superiority, Fuchsman agreed. When he turned over the stroller, he said, ZAKA volunteers were standing by, along with forensics specialists and others from the bomb squad. "And they all walked away." He had to unfasten the safety belt from the baby and put him in a body bag "all by myself, because nobody else could handle such a sight."

The eyes of the men near Fuchsman were pinched shut, their lips taut.

"And after they took that baby away to the victims' tent, when the guy from forensics reached that body, he called for me. I don't want to sound pretentious, but I have more strength to do these things than other people."

Fuchsman rose from his chair and left the circle. The room remained silent. He reached the far wall and sank into a large soft chair. After lighting a cigarette, he rubbed his eyes, slumped down, and fixed his gaze away from the group.

By the time I met with Haim Fuchsman in 2004, he had responded to another fifty or sixty attacks. I mentioned the video and asked if he remembered the date of the event with the stroller. Without a moment's pause, he said March 2, 2002. That was just one week before the event at the Moment Café, though this one was in Beit Yisrael, an ultra-Orthodox neighborhood in Jerusalem. People had been gathered near a yeshiva, a school for religious studies, about to join in a bar mitzvah celebration. It was 9:15 PM when the terrorist exploded himself near a group of women waiting with their baby carriages for their husbands to leave a nearby synagogue. Twelve people were killed and more than fifty injured. Among the dead were Shiraz Nehmad, 7; her sister Liran, 3; Avraham Nehmad, 7; and Ya'akov Avraham, 7 months. Presumably it was Ya'akov and his stroller that Haim Fuchsman attended to. The Al-Aqsa Martyrs Brigades, a group that was part of Yasser Arafat's Fatah movement, claimed credit for the attack.

Fuchsman's wife, Haya, serious and dark-eyed, recalled that day while sitting in their living room. "That was the hardest night out of all the attacks, simply because there were babies and little kids there." As his wife spoke, Fuchsman listened passively from the couch. Their 4-year-old daughter, Avital, squeezed next to him.

Haya continued: "When he saw our kids, those images must have come back to him, and he thought that our kids could have been there—God forbid. And when our son cried that night, he yelled and said, 'You go to him. I can't look. I can't see him.'" Haya waved her hand in despair. "I didn't know when it would end, when he'd get over it. It really scared me."

As she spoke, Eli, 2, climbed up next to his sister Avital. He smiled and twisted restlessly during his mother's somber comments. Fuchsman lightly patted his son's rear and expanded on Haya's observations about the night just after the attack. "When I looked at Eli, all the horrifying images of the baby from the attack came back to me." Fuchsman idly flipped through the pages of a book on the coffee table and then jerked his shoulders back. "I ran out of the room and asked my wife to tend to him."

At first, Haya thought her husband would not continue with ZAKA after a few attacks. She knew him to be sensitive, "not a rough, tough kind of guy," she said. As she spoke, Avital moved to Haya's lap and tugged playfully at her mother's chin. Haya smiled as she confessed surprise to learn that her husband was considered among the most stalwart of the ZAKA volunteers. "How come I didn't know that side of him?" she wondered aloud. Her smile was short-lived. "Then I realized that it's not really him. He works like a robot."

* * *

Dr. Rony Berger asked the ZAKA group if what their wives said was true, "that after attacks you detach yourselves from what happened?"

"No way," Haim Weingarten replied.

He recalled that after returning home from an attack, one of his daughters complained that her sister had taken her doll. "So what?" he responded to her. "You should be grateful to be alive." With an embarrassed grin, he added, "But then I got a grip on myself." Staring at Berger, he said, "There's a direct connection, definitely, at first."

"Of course there's a direct connection," echoed Isaac Bernstein, looking at Weingarten. "You get home and maybe your wife fixed some meat for lunch. And I don't know anyone here who touches meat after an attack."

The scene shifted to Haim Weingarten in light protective outerwear entering his apartment. "Shalom," he intoned musically. His two daughters rushed to him. Standing behind them was his wife, Yehudit. Her attractiveness transcended her full-length sleeves and long dark skirt, traditional attire among Orthodox women. First Michal, 10, and then Shere, 5, responded softly, "Shalom." "How are you?" asked Yehudit, knowing he had come from an attack.

As he bent to embrace his daughters, Yehudit raised her hands and gently reminded him to wait. "Go shower first," she said.

He walked to the dining room table and began to empty the pockets of his outerwear. First the pager, then the cell phone. Michal trailed him closely and said, "Daddy, this morning I saw a dead man on TV." She was holding the back of a dining room chair. "And his arm came off. Did you take care of him?"

Weingarten paused. "He wasn't dead. He was injured." He patted Michal's cheek, overriding his wife's charge not to touch anyone until showering. Michal said nothing more about the arm or her father's explanation.

Yehudit retrieved a large plastic bag from the kitchen and held it open for him. After stuffing his outer garment into the bag, he took it from her, sealed it, then left for the shower.

The Weingartens' kitchen is compact, though comfortably modern. Next to a row of shoulder-level cabinets, Yehudit reached into the refrigerator for a bowl of raw potatoes. Peeler in hand, she began to scrape off the skins. "It's very hard," she said. "He doesn't feel like the same person he was before. He's usually a very happy-spirited person, but after a gruesome attack he's edgy and stressed."

She continued to peel. "He doesn't talk much, he doesn't pour his heart out. You have to squeeze it out of him."

Michal, the older daughter, seemed oblivious to her mother's commentary. In tan coveralls, she was on the floor, drawing pictures with crayons.

After showering, Weingarten reentered the kitchen, buttoning the sleeves of his fresh blue shirt. He lightly tapped Michal's head and asked, "What are you doing?"

"Drawing a picture."

He sat down at the small kitchen table, sipped some cola, and turned to his wife. "How's it going?" he asked.

She ignored the question. "OK. What happened?" she wanted to know.

"There was an explosion, that's what happened." Neither Weingarten nor Yehudit made eye contact.

She wanted to hear more. "Tell me," she said. He gestured with his hand that there was nothing more to tell.

Then Michal climbed on his lap, and he looked at her plaintively. "What did you see?" he asked. "What did you tell me that you saw?"

"I saw a man, and his arm came off. At first Mommy told me it was a knapsack, but I said, 'No it can't be.'" Michal's voice seemed empty of emotion. "It looked like an arm, but Mommy said it was a knapsack."

Yehudit had been stone silent, but now acknowledged to her husband, "I didn't want her to be afraid."

Trying to sound reassuring, Haim said it was probably someone who was injured and who will get better. "Pray at school that he'll get better," he told Michal.

Michal looked at him and then down toward her lap. Her sister Shere, perhaps too young to comprehend the conversation, continued to draw with her crayons.

Without further word, Weingarten rose from his chair and retrieved his prayer shawl and phylacteries, two small boxes containing scripture. He took the thin black straps attached to the boxes and affixed one box to his left arm and the other to his forehead in the manner of religious tradition. He draped the shawl over his head and began to pray with visible energy. Michal pulled herself up into the seat next to her sister. She pushed her hair back, and together they colored pictures as their father expressed his devotion to God.

* * *

Toward the end of one of the day-long sessions with the ZAKA workers, Rony Berger asked them what they had gained from the session's exercises. Haim Weingarten said, with evident surprise, that he learned that he was "normal like every one else here and that the others think the same as I do." Isaac Bernstein, skeptical at the beginning, now realized that "talking is very important." With an elfish grin, he said he also learned "that we're all nutcases. But the good kind." Chuckles echoed around the room.

By the time I met with the ZAKA volunteers, more than a year later, they had been called to many additional attacks. I asked if their sessions with the psychologist had helped them cope. "Yes, yes," Haim Fuchsman responded. "Now, each time I come back from a suicide bombing or something like that, I try to talk to my wife about it. I didn't do that before. Now it doesn't matter when I get home, midnight or 4 o'clock in the morning, my wife says, 'Tell me about it, what you saw, what you did.'" Fuchsman's new-found relief was palpable. "Then I tell her, and I realize when I talk about it, it makes me feel much better."

Haim Weingarten echoed the other Haim: "Psychology is not such an acceptable thing in the ultra-Orthodox community, so personally that was not my thing. Initially, I went to the counseling session with the other ZAKA guys more to be with them, but I thought it would be a waste of time. But the first time we went and spoke, many things came out, and I had never thought about them as my feelings before."

Has it helped? I asked.

"It has been very helpful. I continue to speak with Dr. Berger through his organization (Natal) when there is an event. I haven't a need for personal therapy, but I enjoy the group sessions."

In the United States, no organization exists that is comparable to ZAKA. But the techniques used to treat ZAKA workers are suitable in general for responders at terror events and for others who have suffered trauma. In fact, Berger is among many Israeli psychologists who have addressed American audiences of educators, police, and mental health workers. Built into their presentations is knowledge based on the Israeli experience in helping ZAKA and others to cope.

In seeking to understand further the influence of the attacks on their attitudes, I wondered how the ZAKA men felt about the perpetrators. I asked Isaac Bernstein and the two Haims whether they ever saw the remains of any suicide bombers. All three said yes, many times. What did they think about these people? I asked. Bernstein seemed vexed by my question.

"I take care of them with every concern for doing it the proper way," he answered.

How did he feel inside? I asked. Bernstein took a deep breath, slowly exhaled, and answered with a single word: "Difficult." I pressed further: How did he feel about the Arabs who were responsible for these killings? Did he hate them?

After a long silence, he came up with a measured response. "It is possible to hate them, yes. But not all Arabs. I have Arab friends. The ones who come to explode themselves, yes. But I believe in what I do, and for that reason I also gather their remains."

When I asked Haim Fuchsman what he thought of the perpetrators, he noted that often he would see only the head, because there's nothing left of the rest of his body. Then he became reflective: "It's hard, but what can you do? You have to put the head away." Then he added, "A terrorist is also created in the image of God, and no matter how hard it is, you take care of it."

Haim Weingarten told me he had seen the remains of Palestinian suicide killers dozens of times. When I asked what this meant to him, he, like the other Haim, said that every person is born in the image of God. "But I don't know what kind of people they are—able to kill children and toddlers going to nursery school."

Did he ever hate these people? I asked.

"No, no. It's not a matter of hate. It's just that you see this, and you pray that it will end."

3

Buses

In 2004, the Web site for Israel's largest transportation company, Egged (pronounced "EGG-ed"), displayed a lustrous green bus in motion. The company logo, which appears prominently on the side of the bus, features a large *aleph,* the first letter of the Hebrew alphabet. The image offers the sense of a first-rate, swift, and reliable vehicle. The site also announced the recent acquisition of a fleet of two hundred sleek new buses equipped with low-pollution engines.[1]

There was not a hint in Egged's descriptive material that since the beginning of the intifada in late 2000, Palestinian attackers, mostly suicide bombers, had blown up forty Israeli buses or bus stops—or maybe the hint is implicit. Traffic signs, like most public notices in Israel, are commonly posted in three languages: Hebrew, Arabic, and English. A large influx of immigrants from the former Soviet Union in the 1990s has prompted more notices in Russian as well. But the Egged Web site in 2004 was available only in Hebrew and Russian. The absence of Arabic is unusual. Most Palestinians, unlike Israeli Arabs, are not conversant in either Hebrew or Russian, so their access to schedule information would be more complicated.

Whether intended or not, the Web site seemed at least a symbolic denial to those who would use the information to cause harm.

The bombings deterred some Israelis from riding buses, but not most. Egged's fleet of 3,200 buses continued to service routes throughout the country. In 2003, despite the periodic assaults, more than a million passengers continued to ride buses every day. Probably out of necessity, most people did not alter their travel habits. But even if they were anxious, many recognized that the odds of becoming a victim on any given ride were near zero. According to the Egged company, its buses run around 26,000 trips on service routes every day. Certain routes may have seemed more likely targets than others. Still, the risk was minimal.

For example, Bus 14A was exploded in Jerusalem by a suicide bomber on February 22, 2004, shortly after 8:30 AM. But Bus 14A and the similarly routed Bus 14 run as often as every 15 minutes, from 6 AM to midnight. The route is traversed about fifty times a day, 1,200 times a month, 15,000 times a year. Attacks came more often during the day than the night. But even during rush hours, a preferred time for the terrorists, the frequency of bus runs was high, while the odds of an attack on any particular bus were minuscule.

Levels of anxiety are not governed by statistics alone. The emotional impact of every bombing rippled through the country. However small the risk to any individual, the cumulative effects of the attacks can generate anxiety. But even though an individual attack could be devastating, much of the commuter population maintained their travel habits.

* * *

Erik Schechter made his way unevenly down the corridor of his office building. As he approached me, the rhythm of his limp became clear: a strong thrust forward with the right leg and a dragging catch-up with the left. On January 29, 2004, Erik was on Bus 19 in Jerusalem when it was blown up by a suicide bomber. Now, three months later, his quick smile hid any suggestion that he was in distress. He had returned to his job as a reporter for the *Jerusalem Post* a few weeks before we met.

"Hi, nice to see you," Erik said in the anteroom of his newspaper's building where I had been waiting. He nodded to the security guard stationed at the entrance, confirming that he had been expecting me. I followed Erik to a large conference room for a conversation about his experience. At 31, he had been with the *Post* for one year, and before that with the *Jerusalem Report* magazine. Both are English-language publications. Erik specialized in military affairs, and his assignments at the newspaper had taken him to Egypt, Iraq, Turkey, and Jenin, a West Bank town from which several suicide bombers had come. His beat was exciting, he said, but neither his reporting nor any other activity prepared him for his experience on Bus 19.

"January 29 was a Thursday," he began, "and I got on the bus a little before 9 in the morning." Erik boarded near his home at the stop on Azza and Rav Berlin Streets. "The bus is very crowded, and I'm on it for about five minutes as we get to Azza and Arlozorov Streets." The intersection is in a comfortable residential area, not far from the home of then-Prime Minister Ariel Sharon. The streets are lined with low walls of Jerusalem stone. The houses behind them, surrounded by greenery, are also constructed of this exquisite yellow-tan stone. The bus slowed down to turn the corner where 30-foot fir trees partially obscured the buildings behind them. "I'm standing, facing toward the rear door and the street." Beyond the door, the trees were in full view.

As Erik spoke his eyes narrowed as if recapturing that moment. His narrative had the air of a classroom lecture, an image that was enhanced by the dry-erasure board behind him. He paused and glanced over his shoulder past the board to a framed page of an old edition of the *Palestine Post,* as the paper was called at its inception in 1932. *The Palestine Post* had vigorously supported the Zionist dream of a renascent Jewish homeland in Palestine. In 1950, two years after Israel became an independent state, the word "Palestine" in the paper's title was replaced by "Jerusalem." The page on the wall was from August 1939. The lead story pronounced that Hitler had accused Poland of committing atrocities against Germans. Days later, on September 1, Germany invaded Poland, and World War II was underway.

Erik peered through rimless glasses. Close-cropped hair and a high forehead accentuated the roundness of his face. A hint of whimsy seemed part of his permanent expression, but his story was deadly serious. "So the bus is crowded and I'm standing. All of a sudden there's a brilliant flash." He raised his hands to his ears. "And then a piercing sound. It was like the sound when you'd see a test pattern on TV and hear an announcement that 'this is a test.' Only it was ramped up and continued for 10 seconds." Jarred by the intensity of the sound, he said, he remained standing, unable to move. "All I could see was straight ahead, which was toward the door at the rear of the bus. But there was no door there anymore, and I could see onto the street." At first he thought he was in a dream. But the odor of smoke and the smoldering heat thrust him back to reality. "In a few seconds I go from, 'I can't move, is this a dream?' to 'No, it's a bombing.' And then, 'I'm dying.'" After some moments, he slid down against a crush of fellow victims. From there he noticed rows of singed bodies slumped in their seats. Inches to his right, a young man sat motionless, his neck snapped as if it had been garroted. Severe pain in Erik's legs prompted him to glance down. He was aghast. "Just below my left knee I saw a piece of flesh torn open." The flesh was mangled, pink, dappled with blood. He guessed he would lose the leg. The blast had also damaged Erik's lungs, and he felt as if he were suffocating.

"All of a sudden I see a policeman in front of me, and I just said, 'Help me, I can't breathe.'" The policeman carried him out of the bus and laid him on the ground near other victims. "Next thing I know, the paramedics are tending to me." One of them did something with the mangled flesh that left him incredulous. "He pulls off the piece of meat from my leg. It was someone else's. Phew, it's not mine." He repeated softly, "It was a piece of someone else." The sense of relief was transitory. Fragments of metal had fractured his left knee and shoulder blade. The rush of recollections made him wince, "It was all very painful."

While on the ground waiting for an ambulance, he was seized by an odd impulse. He felt an urge to call in his story to the *Jerusalem Post* offices. He fumbled for his cell phone, but to no avail. His hands were so burned and bloody that he could not retrieve it. He cursed the thought that another reporter might get the by-line. "Finally I just said, 'Screw it, someone else will write the story.'" The next day the paper printed several articles about the attack. The lead story, by Etgar Lefkovits, announced that the bus bombing killed ten and injured fifty.[2] One of the critically injured victims died later, raising the number killed to eleven. Both Hamas and the al-Aqsa Martyrs Brigades claimed credit for the attack.

Another story mentioned that Erik, the paper's military correspondent, had suffered "moderate" wounds that included "a broken left knee and a severed vein in the calf below it; puncture wounds in his right leg and back, from slices of metal packed into the explosives; a broken shoulder," and more. He was also bleeding internally, which required transfusions of five pints of blood.

After arriving at Shaare Zedek Hospital in Jerusalem, Erik overheard the doctors discussing whether his leg could be saved. A flood of scenarios entered his mind. "You hear this and you start negotiating—not with God, but sort of with yourself. I couldn't move my toes, and I thought, well, if I just lose a few toes and keep the foot that would be okay. Or, if I just were able to keep the toes even if they would never be able to move again." In the end, the doctors were able to seal the bleeding vessels, reattach tendons, and reset the bone. His leg would be saved, though with permanent effects from the battering. He continued to have nightmares, usually related to a foot or leg. In one, he was trying to walk home when his foot gave way and he crawled along the street looking for help. In another, he tried to jump over a precipice but couldn't make it. In yet another, more bizarre dream, shoe stores in the United States that were owned by religious Jews were being bombed by a neo-Nazi group. Erik told me he was functioning well at work, but when I asked how he felt psychologically, he hesitated. "I can't say that I'm a hundred percent," he answered. "I don't go on city buses. I'm not up to doing that." How does he travel to work or otherwise get around? "I take a cab or walk."

In the hospital he asked why he had heard the shrill piercing sound but not the bomb blast. The doctors explained that close proximity to a powerful explosion could damage the bones of the inner ear and render a blast inaudible. The screeching that he heard could have resulted from a torn eardrum through which air traveled in and out. That probably explained why people talking "sounded like they were under water," he said.

During the previous year, Erik had reported on a range of issues related to security and the Middle East conflict. One of his articles was about the economic effects of the intifada on Arab shops in the Old City of Jerusalem, a traditional attraction for visitors. Tourists and shoppers had become scarce, and the stores there were nearly empty. Another article examined frustrations with the American-led effort to stabilize Iraq. A third discussed the work of Israeli military censors, who were seen as sometimes overly vigilant in blocking information. But one story that Erik wrote in April 2003, nine months before his terror experience, was portentous. He examined suicide attacks from a historical perspective.[3]

His article recalled the efforts of the 3,500 Japanese kamikaze pilots in World War II who crashed into Allied targets in the Pacific theater. Although they sank more than fifty ships, the suicide attacks were less successful than conventional air raids. He also referred to the study by Robert Pape that examined suicide bombing around the world between 1980 and 2001. Pape concluded that making concessions to terrorists whets their appetite for more—that "almost any concession at all will tend to encourage the terrorist leaders further about their own coercive effectiveness."[4]

Perhaps this knowledge helped steel Erik's resolve. During our conversation he admitted to a "bubbling anger" toward people he considered naïve about suicide terrorists. His anger was not outwardly evident. More with irony than bitterness, he wondered about the people who opposed the security fence being built in the West Bank. He questioned why anyone would be more concerned about inconveniencing Palestinian farmers than about preventing terrorists from entering Israel and killing Jews.

I asked whether his experience on Bus 19 had changed his views about politics or the Israeli-Palestinian conflict. Not really, he answered. "I'm still a secular classical liberal—sort of capitalist, separation of church and state, that sort of thing."

As for the Palestinians: "The only thing I feel, really, is pity for a society that makes heroes of people like suicide bombers. What are they going to say in their history books? That when they get to this period in their history their most popular people, their heroes, were mass murderers?"

* * *

Under the auspices of ZAKA and an organization called Christians for Israel, the bus that Erik had ridden was sent on an unusual trip after the bombing. The wrecked remains were shipped to the Hague in the Netherlands just before February 23, 2004. On that day the International Court of Justice was to begin hearings on the barrier that Israel was building in the West Bank. The demarcation, around 450 miles of fence and 15 miles of solid wall, was intended to prevent terrorists from crossing into Israel.

Several countries viewed the fence as an encroachment on Palestinian land. Pressed by the Arab countries, the UN General Assembly voted to ask the International Court of Justice for an opinion on whether the Israeli action violated international law. Many countries, including members of the European Union, refused to support the effort. Some felt that even if the barrier was inappropriate, the issue was political, not legal. Accordingly, it was not a matter for the ICJ. The General Assembly vote was 90 in support of the request to the ICJ, 8 against, and 74 abstentions.

Israelis fumed at the decision, contending that the United Nations was failing to acknowledge the effectiveness of the barrier against terror attacks. The Jewish state refused to participate in the Court's proceedings, as did the United States.

But Israelis hoped that displaying the wreckage of Bus 19 might help sensitize the ICJ to the terror ordeal that the fence would mitigate. I asked a member of ZAKA, Haim Fuchsman, who was with the bus while it was on display in the Netherlands, how he felt about the experience. When we spoke, in April 2004, the ICJ had not yet rendered its decision. Fuchsman was optimistic: "People from all over the world had come to the Hague. The atmosphere was almost holy, as if the world had been silent, but now they were seeing how the Israelis had been suffering. Many people saw the bus and shed tears. I felt that I was a representative there for everyone who had been killed." The hearings lasted three days, after which the bus was returned to Israel. ZAKA and Christians for Israel felt so encouraged by people's reactions in the Netherlands that in May they brought Bus 19 to the United States. It was to be displayed in Washington, D.C., Indianapolis, Denver, Chicago, and New York City.

On May 28, 2004, I visited the offsite location where Bus 19 was stored when not on public display. It was in an industrial park in Ashburn, Virginia, outside of Washington. The remains seemed so mangled that I wondered if the condition had worsened from the country-to-country shipping. But photographs of the original scene in Jerusalem confirmed that the wreckage looked about the same in May as it had minutes after the attack in January.

As Erik Schechter indicated, the bomber had entered the bus through the rear door, located just past the midsection. The explosion blew out every window of the vehicle. I saw shattered glass piled near the driver's seat, though most shards had been cleared away on day one. The force had twisted the metal frame into waves and bulges. Areas of red-brown metal shaded into burnt black. Struts from the framework leaned in every direction, some dangling precariously. Myriad cables and pipes, ordinarily out of sight, were now visible through holes in the floor and roof.

I boarded the bus opposite the driver's seat through the front door frame—the door itself had been torn away. The front seats remained in place, though pieces of the roof, sides, and floor lay piled between them. Striped beige seat covers in the first three rows were intact. In row 4, sections of the cloth covers were missing, and the sponge cushions, ordinarily covered, were in full view. The missing sections had been cut away by ZAKA volunteers after the attack. The material had been so drenched with blood that it could not be drained off by blotting. The stained cloth was collected for burial with the other human remains. In the sixth row, I tried unsuccessfully to wedge into a seat. The frame was so mangled that whoever had been sitting there must have been crushed. In the rear half, the ceiling had been blasted away entirely. Through the uncovered top, sunlight reflected off jagged metal that once connected the ceiling to the sides. The damage was most severe in the back rows, where the bomber had detonated himself. There the seats had been torn from their bases and lay askew. Their metal backs were twisted like the bent clocks in a Salvatore Dali painting. Above the frame of a blown-out window, a small sign was intact. In three languages—Hebrew, English, and Arabic—its neat red lettering offered an admonition: Don't Put Head or Hands Out of the Window.

* * *

Five months before the bombing of Bus 19, Ora and Shalom Cohen decided to celebrate their ninth wedding anniversary with an unusual outing. On August 19, 2003, they squeezed into a taxi with their five children, ages one month to seven years, and headed to the Western Wall, the holiest of Jewish sites. The 20-minute ride from their apartment in the Ramat Eshkol section of Jerusalem was brief enough to minimize the children's restlessness. The large plaza in front of the Wall would provide ample space for them to run around amid other families, tourists, and pious Jews who came to pray before the ancient stones.

The Western Wall lies within the Old City of Jerusalem, which itself is enclosed by an imposing stone wall. The outer wall was completed in 1541 when Jerusalem and the surrounding regions were part of the Ottoman Empire, then ruled from Constantinople by Suleiman the Magnificent. The Old City's third-of-a-square-mile area is crowded with dwellings, shops, churches, mosques, and synagogues. The space is divided into Jewish, Muslim, Christian, and Armenian Quarters, and, in the southeast corner, the Temple Mount.

The Mount is an elevated area the size of twelve football fields. It is the site on which the sacred Jewish Temple stood until it was destroyed by the Roman army in CE 70. Known as the Second Temple, it had replaced an earlier sanctuary razed by Babylonian invaders in 586 BCE. Only the Western Wall remains of the original Temple Mount structure. Made of huge blocks of limestone, the visible portion of the Western Wall measures 60 feet high and 160 feet long, though its full length extends another 1,400 feet, mostly under the ground. During the centuries, this longer section became covered with earth and can now be accessed only through a tunnel.

It was during the rule of King Herod in the first century BCE that the walls of the Temple Mount were built and the Sanctuary was renovated. The facade was described by a contemporary eyewitness, Flavius Josephus:

> Viewed from without, the Sanctuary had everything that could amaze either mind or eyes. Overlaid all round with stout plates of gold, the first rays of the sun . . . reflected so fierce a blaze of fire that those who endeavored to look at it were forced to turn away as if they had looked straight at the sun. To strangers as they approached it seemed in the distance like a mountain covered with snow; for any part not covered with gold was dazzling white.[5]

When the Roman army destroyed the Temple, it also banished the Jews from their holy city. In subsequent years Jews drifted back, but reclamation of Jewish sovereignty over Jerusalem awaited the birth of the modern state in 1948. Meanwhile, the advent of Mohammed in the seventh century introduced the Islamic religious tradition to the region. Early in the eighth century, two mosques were built on portions of the Temple Mount, an area that Muslims refer to as Haram al-Sharif. Both mosques stand today: one is Al Aqsa, and the other the lustrous gold-colored Dome of the Rock. The mosques and the Western Wall draw the faithful every day. Although Muslim clerics are granted authority over the Islamic holy places, Israel claims all of Jerusalem as its sovereign capital. Palestinians dispute the claim, and Israeli soldiers are positioned to quell any possible disorder. But the area is largely peaceful as Jews pray freely at the Wall and Muslims in the mosques.

Israel's victory in the 1967 war enabled Jews to regain access to the Old City, which had been denied them for the nineteen years that Jordan controlled that area. An expansive plaza was later built near the Wall. Along with nearby archeological displays and shopping locations, the area draws visitors like the Cohens for recreation as well as spiritual fulfillment.

After their evening of snacks and celebration, Ora and Shalom Cohen gathered up their children and waited at the nearby bus station. At 9 PM they boarded Bus 2, whose route included a stop near their home. Ora took a seat in the middle and perched her one-month-old son, Elchanan, on her lap. Two daughters, Meirav, 7, and Orly, 4, squeezed next to her. Across the aisle, her husband Shalom sat with their other two children, Shira, almost 2, and Daniel, 6. The bus was packed with young families like theirs, tired and pleased to be heading home.

Night comes late in August, and the glow of daylight had just begun to fade. As the bus skirted the outer perimeter of the Old City, passengers could see the city lights come on and bathe its golden walls. To the east of the Old City rose the dry terraces of the Mount of Olives. Its ancient slopes, which were visited by Jesus, contain the oldest continuously used Jewish cemetery. As the bus proceeded north on Bar-Lev Street, Ora discreetly covered Elchanan with a blanket and began to nurse him. The street unofficially divides a largely Arab population toward the right from Jewish residents on the left. Ten minutes into the trip, the bus turned left for one block and then right onto a major thoroughfare, Shmuel Hanavi Street. There it stopped to discharge passengers.

At that moment, halfway between the Wall and home, for Ora Cohen everything turned black. A 29-year-old Arab, dressed as an ultra-Orthodox Jew, pushed his way through the back door of the bus and blew himself up.

"I actually didn't hear anything—supposedly you never do," Ora recalled. "There was just this thick silence for a long moment while people tried to grasp what had happened. And then the shrieking began." Ora's eardrums were ruptured, and she was barely conscious. As she was being transported to the hospital, she murmured, "My baby, my baby," but the paramedics were not focused on her words. She was one of 150 victims in the midst of a frantic rescue operation.

Ora was taken to Shaare Zedek Hospital with more than forty other victims. The staff was attending to the injured, and questions about missing family members were secondary to life-saving therapy. Ora persisted, however, and soon learned that her husband and their three older children were also at Shaare Zedek. Her injuries were severe. The roof of the bus had fallen on her, and she lay immobilized with broken bones in her back, chest, and nose. But she was overcome with grief at the thought that she had lost Elchanan and Shira.

After the living victims were carried from the bus, workers returned to remove the dead. Several lay heaped on the floor near the seat that Ora had occupied. As a worker lifted a body from the top of the pile, he heard a whimper below. He pulled away two more bodies and found a tiny baby covered with blood but alive. The baby was rushed to Hadassah's Ein Kerem Hospital.

Nava Braverman, a Hadassah nurse and coordinator of the hospital's women's health center, weighed the baby and guessed he was about one month old. The baby's right ear was leaking fluid, and he had difficulty breathing, a symptom of injury to the lungs. Braverman also knew that another unidentified victim in the hospital, a one- or two-year-old girl, was attached to a respirator and undergoing surgery for shrapnel wounds.

Braverman contacted social workers at Hadassah and other area hospitals to find out if any patients were missing a child. Her initial inquiry went unanswered because most severely injured patients were not in any condition to speak to the social workers. Hours later, Hadassah received a call from a man who said that his neighbors had been hospitalized at Shaare Zedek and they were looking for their baby and young girl.

The man then went to Hadassah but could not positively identify the two children, who were in hospital gowns and connected to life-saving machinery. Braverman gave him photographs of the children and plastic bags containing their clothes. "Show these to the mother," she said. If the mother did not recognize them, he was to "bring everything back because we'll probably need it again."

As the man sped across town to Shaare Zedek, Braverman received a call from a social worker at that hospital. A woman there was wailing hysterically that her baby "flew out of my arms" and that now he must be dead. Soon after, with the arrival of the photos and clothing, Ora Cohen sobbed with relief. For hours after the bombing, she said, she had five children, "but I didn't know how many of them were alive."

Elchanan's injuries were less severe than his sister Shira's. Eight months later, in April 2004, Elchanan had apparently recovered. He played on the floor of the family's apartment amid a sea of toys. But two-year-old Shira bore visible scars. The skin of her cheeks, like that of the rest of her body, was textured with crevices from shrapnel. Her right eye, which had been pierced by a shard of glass, was still covered by a bandage. At first doctors thought she would lose the eye, but they became more hopeful after repeated surgeries.

Ora sat at her kitchen table to recount her family's ordeal. Born in Iran, she had lived in the United States before coming to Israel a decade earlier. With no other relatives in Israel, she and her husband lacked the intimate support network available to many others. She is all the more grateful for the financial and psychological help from Atzum, the volunteer group founded by Levi Lauer. Atzum seeks out victims of terrorism like the Cohens, who have little other support. The organization's representatives visit them, shop for them, and provide counseling.

Still, Ora's penetrating dark eyes revealed a continuing tension. She admitted to unremitting anger at what happened to her family and felt suspicious of Arabs. Did she still ride the bus? I asked. Her voice tightened.

"Not really," she answered. "Sometimes I try and then get off after one or two stops. I never get to the destination. I get off and take a taxi."

* * *

The next afternoon, on August 20, 2003, Zev Alexander and I boarded Bus 14A on Jaffa Street across from Jerusalem's Central Bus Station. Though Zev had lived in Jerusalem for the past year, he rarely used public transportation, preferring instead the convenience of his car. I felt no qualms about riding the bus, nor did Zev admit to any when he agreed to accompany me. Seated toward the rear, we watched the reactions of passengers as they boarded, found seats, sometimes stood, and then debarked. We remained on board for 45 minutes through nineteen stops during the north-to-south ride that ended in the Talpiyot industrial zone at the edge of the city. The passenger load ranged from light to standing room only.

At an early stop, Zev pointed to the right and said, "There's Mahane Yehuda." He didn't have to explain further. The entrance to this well-known outdoor market stood yards from us. The market contained rows of stalls with culinary choices appealing to both eye and palate. Stalls displayed florid tomatoes, oranges, rich red pomegranates. Some specialized in assorted nuts and cheeses. Farther along, behind chilled glass enclosures, lay cuts of beef and chicken, sea bass from the Mediterranean, trout from an Israeli fish farm. The market drew patrons of many backgrounds, including Jews, Christians, and Muslims. On Fridays it is filled with Jews preparing for the Sabbath dinner.

On July 30, 1997, three years before the heightened intensity of the terrorism, two consecutive suicide bombings at the Mahane

Yehuda market killed 16 people and wounded 178. Then, on November 2, 2000, scarcely a month into the intifada, a car bomb near the market killed two and injured ten. On April 12, 2002, a crowded Friday, a 21-year-old Arab woman blew herself up at the bus stop next to the market where we were now taking on passengers. The explosive device, which included three plastic pipes and a battery, were concealed in her purse. In the aftermath, six people lay dead and 104 wounded.

The next year, on Wednesday, June 11, 2003, at 5:30 PM, an Arab man dressed as an Orthodox Jew boarded Bus 14A at this same bus stop. Minutes later, he detonated himself, killing seventeen and wounding more than one hundred. On February 22, 2004, while nearing a park along the route, another Bus 14A exploded. A suicide bomber on board took the lives of eight people and injured sixty, eleven of them schoolchildren.

As Zev and I continued our journey along the 14A route, I beheld each of these tragic locations. Passengers boarded and exited. What were they thinking? The Mahane Yehuda market, the site of so many hits, was bustling with shoppers. Two young women in jeans climbed aboard and never lost the rhythm of their conversation. A middle-aged man with sideburns took a seat and gazed casually out the window. A tall scholarly looking man, standing, clutched the steel pole as the bus accelerated.

These people surely knew of the terror sites, yet they appeared oblivious to them. I saw no darting eyes. No one seemed anxious or suspicious. The most notable movement was the sway of standing passengers when the bus lurched to a stop.

Toward the end of the ride, I asked Zev how he felt. He seemed relaxed throughout, and I was surprised to hear him say he was nervous when we started, though less so as the ride progressed. Why did he go from nervous to calm? I asked. "No reason. I don't know."

Suppose I asked him to ride again tomorrow on this bus. Would today's experience have made a difference? I asked.

"That's a good question. Perhaps," he answered. "You get used to things during a lull, though you get anxious right after a terror event."

Zev became contemplative and confided that a reason he enjoyed living in the Mahane Yehuda area was its proximity to the market. "I enjoy spending time there, the colorful personalities of the shopkeepers, hand-picking my fruit," he said. "So I purposely chose to live near a favorite place even though it might seem dangerous by some standards." But he also admitted to avoiding other places that had been scenes of terror attacks. Acknowledging his inconsistency, Zev smiled, shrugged, and said, "Strange."

* * *

Later, I thought about bus and metro rides I had taken in New York, Paris, and London, and their similarity to the one in Jerusalem. The bland expressions of most passengers seemed interchangeable, whatever the city. Still, on reflection I recognized something different about the Jerusalem experience. On buses and subways in other cities, passengers might be absorbed in a newspaper, a novel, perhaps a textbook. Not on Bus 14A. No eyes were lowered toward a written page. Though seemingly nonchalant and indirect, the passengers' gazes remained at eye-level, taking in the scope of what was around them.

4

Survivors

Beginning on May 24, 1991, in the course of thirty-six hours, round-the-clock Israeli flights brought 14,000 eager black Ethiopian Jews to Israel. The fly-out, known as Operation Solomon, became possible only after Israel agreed to pay the Ethiopian government $40 million. The departing Jews were then believed to be the last of a 3,000-year-old community whose prayers had linked them to Jerusalem. Squeezed into one of the crowded planes, 11-year-old Natan Sendeke, like others on board, had never before experienced indoor electricity or running water. With the encouragement of the community's elders, the Ethiopian Jews had walked hundreds of miles from their remote villages to Addis Ababa, the capital. There, through prearrangement with Israeli and Ethiopian authorities, they boarded huge strange birds. The flights transported them in three hours from a fifteenth-century bucolic existence to a fast-moving modern society.

The lifestyle and language gap between the two societies was daunting—most Ethiopians spoke only Amharic. But youngsters like Natan adapted more easily than their elders. For the first time in his life he went to school, where he learned Hebrew and English and the ways of his new home. Upon graduating from high school in 1998, Natan, like most 18-year-old Israelis, joined the army. Plans for college would be delayed until after his three-year military tour.

Natan was assigned to the border police near the eastern section of Jerusalem with its large Arab population. Along Hanaviim Street, he patrolled past century-old homes and regal stone buildings like the Bikur Cholim Hospital and Hadassah College, venerable institutions that served Arabs and Jews alike. The neighborhood was also home to ultra-Orthodox Jews, who could readily be identified by their manner of dress—the men in black hats and long black coats.

At 7 AM on Thursday, September 4, 2001, a woman ran up to Natan, pointed back down the street, and said a suspicious man was there. "Why suspicious?" Natan asked.

"He's wearing a black coat and kippah (a skullcap worn by observant Jews), and a backpack." As Natan pondered the odd combination of black coat and backpack, the woman added, "I could smell alcohol on his breath."

Natan strode quickly in the direction she pointed and spotted the man. Upon seeing the uniformed officer, the figure in the black coat and backpack began to run. Natan pursued him, yelling, "Stop," but to no avail. Natan drew his gun but hesitated to shoot because he was not sure the man was a terrorist. As Natan closed the distance between them to a few yards, the man turned and smiled. That was the last thing Natan remembered. The suicide bomber had detonated himself. Unconscious, severely burned, and with nails in his lungs, Natan was taken to Hadassah Hospital at Ein Kerem.

Micha Feldmann, a 60-year-old Israeli, had long helped immigrants adjust to their new society. Fluent in Amharic, he had known Natan and his family since their arrival in Israel. In 2005 he sat with Natan and me in the Tel Aviv offices of Selah, the volunteer organization with which he worked. Selah is a Hebrew acronym for Israel Crisis Management Center.

As often happens when a new immigrant is hospitalized, the organization had been asked to send someone over to lend support. Micha described his arrival at the intensive care unit after Natan's admission.

"I saw his parents outside, and they told me which bed he was in. I didn't see anybody there at first, just a bed covered with linen. Then I looked more carefully and saw a nose sticking out with a tube in it." That was all Micha could see of Natan. He wondered how much Natan's parents understood about their son's situation. Their grasp of Hebrew was tenuous, and he spoke to them in Amharic. "Do you know what is going on with Natan?" he asked.

"Well, they talk to us, but we don't understand," Natan's father replied. Micha nodded and said he would be right back. He found one of Natan's doctors and asked him to explain Natan's condition to the parents, which Micha would translate for them. Micha recounted to me what happened next. "The doctor tells the whole story, and I translate. But his last line is, 'Natan has less than a 50 percent chance to survive.' I thought, 'How do you say something like that to parents?'"

He did not feel he should alter the doctor's words, he said. "So I translated everything. But I added a sentence of my own. I said, 'From my experience, many people in this condition have survived.'"

Micha had no such experience, and his translation implied that the sentence came from the doctor. As he related the tale, his furrowed brows registered discomfort. Then his face brightened: "And after two weeks, Natan woke up and saw his mother's face. She was smiling, and that is the first thing he sees and still remembers."

Natan, who had been sitting quietly beside Micha, nodded in agreement. With a grin, he interjected softly: "The doctors said my recovery was a miracle."

When we met in 2005, Natan's tall, lean figure seemed a picture of health. The wisp of frizzy black hair on his chin seemed more a brush than a beard. A white scar across his throat was the only visible sign of his ordeal. Natan noted that no other Israelis were wounded or killed by the blast because of his intervention. "I know that I saved lives," he said unabashedly. Natan's story had been widely reported in the Israeli media, and he was acclaimed a national hero.

Natan related how support groups were vital to his recovery. Selah provided a psychologist for him and assigned volunteers to continue to look after him. The organization purchased household needs for his family, including an air conditioner and furniture. In 2005 Natan was planning to study social work in college but was already in a routine of helping others. He counseled youngsters who dropped out of school and coached a soccer team. Among his best moments, he said, were visits to other victims of terrorism, especially Ethiopians, soldiers, and their families. "When I visit and I help, that helps me get stronger," he said.

Was he bitter or angry because of the terror incident? I wondered. Natan answered comfortably, "I think the experience taught me to be a better person. I have more appreciation now for everything around me." I asked if the event left any other impressions on him. He paused and acknowledged at least one lingering anxiety. He will not ride a bus.

Micha, with a big smile, added, "And of course one of the most important things about Natan is that now he's good friends with Hillary Clinton."

Hillary Clinton?

"Yes, she was in Israel a few months after his attack, and she visited him in the hospital."

Before I could question how a single encounter could make them good friends, Micha said that the following year, he accompanied Natan to New York City's annual Israel Day parade in May. When they reached the reviewing stand, Natan expressed excitement upon learning that Senator Clinton was expected to appear. Micha told him, "Natan, don't fool yourself. She won't recognize you." But when Hillary approached the stand, she began to shout 'Natan, Natan!' After hugs, she sat him down next to her in the front row. Micha chortled as he recalled the afternoon, "Well, at least I got to sit behind them in the second row."

* * *

Elad Wassa arrived in Israel at age eight, in 1985, six years before Natan. He was part of Operation Moses, the first large-scale immigration of Ethiopian Jews to Israel. In that venture, 8,000 Ethiopian Jews were airlifted in Israeli planes out of neighboring Sudan. The passengers had migrated to Sudanese camps months earlier, hoping that their trek would be a step toward reaching Jerusalem. The exodus ended in January 1985, when the Ethiopian government blocked further migration—until Operation Solomon in 1991.

When I talked to him in 2005, Elad recalled how difficult the month-long walk across Ethiopia had been. Threatened during the day by human marauders and at night by wild animals, he and his family lived in constant fear. Like other black Jews who made their way across Ethiopia, they arrived at the Sudanese camps ragged and hungry. There they waited anxiously for months until Israel could arrange for their departures.

For Elad, as for Natan Sendeke and other Ethiopian youngsters, the adjustment to life in Israel was simpler than for their elders. The family settled in Netanya, a northern city along the Mediterranean coast, where Elad attended school and became an avid runner and soccer player. After completing army service, he worked at a vegetable stand in Netanya's main shopping market.

On May 19, 2002, a Palestinian suicide bomber, dressed as an Israeli soldier, entered the market and detonated himself. Three people died and fifty-nine were injured. The explosive was laced with nails that lodged in Elad's head, neck, shoulder, chest, arms, and spine. When Elad awoke at the Hillel Yaffe Hospital in nearby Hadera, he learned that a nail had penetrated his spinal cord. His legs were paralyzed.

Three years later, Elad spoke to me about his early misery. As he struggled through rehabilitation, he said, "I refused to speak to anyone, even my mother." He was disheartened during his brief visits home when friends would see him in a wheelchair and cry. But by the time we met in 2005, Elad, though wheelchair-bound, exhibited not a trace of self-pity. His grin was at once coy and infectious. Attired in a gray athletic suit, Elad's hands and upper body moved expressively as he described his difficult experience—not only the physical pain, but awakening from dreams in which he was walking and running. During the year after the bombing, he began to shed his anger and replace despair with determination. "I said to God, 'You've taken away my legs, but you left me with strong arms and a head. So now I have to use them.'"

Elad put his hands in his pockets and stretched his shoulders upward. "Now I talk with friends and I visit other victims and I encourage them." With a glint in his eye, he added, "And I play wheelchair basketball." Beit Halochem is a center where disabled soldiers and terror victims continue to pursue athletic activities.

That center is just one of the many organizations that provide support. Elad also received help from volunteer groups, including Selah and the OneFamily Fund, an organization established during the intifada. They were instrumental in helping him to become self-sufficient. Now, without assistance he can shop, cook, and drive a car equipped with hand controls.

Is he angry with the Palestinians? I asked. He seemed surprised, as if he had never thought about the matter before. His voice lowered: "You can't be angry. You know, in every group there are good people and bad people."

As with Natan Sendeke, Elad's experience also prompted a brush with an American celebrity. Christopher Reeve, the American film actor, had become paralyzed from the shoulders down after a horse-riding accident in 1995. Convinced that stem cell research would eventually lead to a cure, Reeve wanted to learn about Israeli advances in that field. In 2003, the year before he died, Reeve visited Israel to meet with scientists there. When Elad learned about the impending visit, he wrote to the "Superman" star and mentioned his own condition. The letter left a deep impression on Reeve, who told friends that he was eager to meet him.

Elad had already been inspired by the documentary, *Christopher Reeve: Courageous Steps,* which portrayed the actor's determination to live to the fullest despite his disability. Upon Reeve's arrival, the two men faced each other in wheelchairs, and Elad announced "Welcome to Israel. You are my hero." Reeve emerged from their conversation saying he felt "great" to be with Elad. "This young man is incredible," he said.

Upon learning of Reeve's death in 2004, Elad recalled the sentiments he expressed about Reeve during his trip to Israel. "He brings encouragement to people who feel as if their whole world has been destroyed," he said at the time. "I'm one of them."

* * *

While at the Jewish Museum, Kinneret Chaya Boosany paused in front of the "Portrait of a Young Woman," a painting by Amedeo Modigliani. She was immersed in New York City's art offerings during a visit to the city in the fall of 2004. The day before, at the Whitney Museum, she lingered over Ana Mendieta's sculpted explorations of the female body. Now it was Modigliani.

Kinneret gazed intently at the long-necked subject of the painting. The Young Woman's pursed lips leave a viewer wondering what was on her mind. Kinneret's own expression matched that of the enigmatic figure in the century-old classic. Behind Kinneret's soft smile lay a strange mix of pain and joy that later prompted her to say, "I am 26 with the experience of a 100-year-old—who was born two and a half years ago."

Kinneret's easy stride and thin frame hint at her talent as a dancer. Earlier photographs also reveal an exquisite face. In the aftermath of wounds, scars, and broken bones, her beauty, though transformed, remains no less compelling.

On Saturday evening, March 30, 2002, Kinneret was serving soft drinks and cocktails from behind the bar at "My Coffee Shop" on Tel Aviv's busy Allenby Street. She was working to earn money for studies toward a career in alternative medicine. At 9:30 PM a young Arab man entered, ordered coffee from her, and blew himself up. As the flames leaped toward Kinneret, she was thrown back against the wall. Seconds later she was buried under broken bottles, wall fixtures, and a refrigerator ripped from its moorings. A rescue worker could see only her scorched hand protruding from the rubble. Though he cradled the hand gently, loose skin sloughed off.

Kinneret was rushed to Ichilov Hospital a mile away. With 85 percent of her body burnt, doctors doubted she would live through the night. Unconscious and attached to a ventilator to help her breathe, she was plied with antibiotics and other drugs, and wrapped in lotions and bandages. Kinneret had suffered severe damage to her lungs, eyes, ears, and limbs. Days later her condition had barely improved, but the fact that she was still alive widened the wedge of hope. Kinneret's parents and two sisters were continuously at her bedside. When Sheila Raviv, a family friend, visited the hospital, she noted in a diary that Kinneret's mother, Yaffa, had "found a tiny unburned spot on her head where she can stroke her."

Weeks went by, and Kinneret's prognosis remained uncertain. Hints of emerging consciousness were blurred by heavy sedation to overcome the pain from her wounds, repeated skin grafts, and other surgeries. Sheila Raviv indicated in her diary six weeks after the attack that Kinneret's lung condition had improved but that new infections were impeding her respiration. Sheila also commented about the effects of the ordeal on Kinneret's mother and father and their family. "Yaffa looks terribly tired and very emotional, Moshe too, but he is better at covering his emotions. Kinneret's aunts and sisters were there too, to care for the 'carers' with hugs, cookies, and home-baked bourekas [cheese pastries]."

Kinneret herself has little memory of those first months. In 2004, when I asked her how long she was in a coma, she said four months, though not exactly. Part of the time her coma was drug-induced to spare her the excruciating pain from the burns. "I did have some consciousness during those four months. I remember a lot of inner struggling. I remember people talking. I always looked, in my mind, for the voice and touch of my mom. I heard her, but sometimes I didn't, and I wanted to know, Where is she? Where is she? So it was like crazy."

Kinneret's first clear recollection upon regaining consciousness was of a young woman on crutches, leaning over her with a large smile. Maytal Wax routinely visited new terror victims and their families. She knew their feelings of desperation, their doubts about whether they could return to a productive life. Six years earlier, she had faced the same questions.

In March 1996, during the holiday of Purim, Maytal, then 26, and her brother Assaf, 21, were at a Tel Aviv shopping center when a bomber blew himself up. Assaf was killed. Most of Maytal's body, like Kinneret's, was burned, though her injuries also included the loss of her right leg and the mangling of the left.

The bombing predated the torrent of attacks against Israelis that began in 2000. But it is a reminder that Israelis have been targets of violence even when prospects for peace seemed encouraging. In September 1993, Israeli Prime Minister Yitzak Rabin and Yasser Arafat, head of the Palestine Liberation Organization, signed the Oslo Accord in the presence of President Bill Clinton at the White House. The terms, which were initially explored between Israelis and Palestinians in Oslo, Norway, provided for an interim self-government for the Palestinians and for negotiations toward a final status agreement. In an exchange of letters between the parties, Arafat renounced terrorism.

Months later, in February 1994, an Israeli extremist, Baruch Goldstein, entered a Muslim religious site in the West Bank and sprayed gunfire at the worshippers. Twenty-nine Muslims lay dead before the enraged crowd subdued and killed him. Reflecting the sentiment of most Israelis, Rabin disdained Goldstein's terrorist action: "Sensible Judaism spits you out," he declared. "You placed yourself outside the wall of Jewish law. You are a shame on Zionism and an embarrassment to Judaism."

Goldstein's action was a rare instance of wanton murder of innocent Arabs by an Israeli. Meanwhile, in 1994 through July 1995, Hamas and Islamic Jihad launched at least ten attacks against Israelis, most of them suicide bombings. In those attacks, the bombers killed 91 Israelis and injured hundreds.[1]

Arafat's response was troubling. While condemning suicide

bombings, he referred to the perpetrators as martyrs, and he invariably condemned retaliation by Israeli forces against the terrorist groups. Arafat's failure to act meaningfully to stop the terrorism left many Israelis frustrated. But despite opposition to the Oslo agreement by the Likud Party and others on the right, most of the electorate continued to support Rabin and his Labor-led government. Then, in November 1995, a right-wing Israeli zealot assassinated Rabin.

Shimon Peres, a Labor Party veteran with a strong commitment to the Oslo Accord, succeeded Rabin. Elections were scheduled for May 1996, and Peres at first seemed likely to prevail over the Likud candidate, Benjamin Netanyahu. But by early March the situation had changed. On February 25 a suicide bomber on a bus in Jerusalem and another at a bus stop in Ashkelon killed 28 Israelis. On March 3, a bomber in Jerusalem killed 18. The next day, the bombing at the Tel Aviv shopping center killed Assaf Wax and 19 others, and gravely injured his sister Maytal. The battery of attacks soured Israelis on prospects for peace and eroded their confidence in the Labor Party leadership. The May election resulted in a victory for Likud, and Netanyahu became Prime Minister.

During this period, Maytal's thoughts were distant from politics. While grieving over the loss of her brother, she struggled to come to terms with her own injuries. After a trying year, her upbeat disposition began to surface, and she became determined to help others. Kinneret's first encounter with Maytal's smile is embedded in her memory. "Before I met her, I didn't know you could live a normal life with that body. She showed me that it's possible."

Maytal moves about mostly by wheelchair because using her artificial leg and crutches for more than brief periods causes pain. In the years since her injuries, she has acquired a master's degree in library science, begun swimming, and, within the limits of her disability, taken up folk dancing. When Maytal met Kinneret, she was working as a librarian at Tel Aviv University. Around that time she read about an unusual commemoration planned for the first anniversary of the September 11 attacks in the United States. In honor of the victims, a bicycle ride was to begin at the site of the World Trade Center and end at the Pentagon. Maytal wanted to participate to honor her brother. For four months she trained on a hand-cycle, and then went to New York to join the cluster of 1,250 cyclists who began the trip on September 20, 2002.

The pack of riders traveled 270 miles over three days, sleeping in tents at night. During one stretch, Alan Scharfstein, a cyclist from New Jersey rode alongside Maytal in wonderment. She told him how she lost her leg and spoke of her subsequent determination: "I had to decide whether to remain a victim or to actually live the rest of my life." Before the ride ended, a third of the starters had dropped out, but not Maytal. On the third day, around 4:30 PM, in the midst of the remaining cyclists, Maytal reached the Pentagon's north parking lot. The roar of the waiting crowd overwhelmed Maytal and she became speechless. Later she told a reporter that she felt honored to have completed the trip, "because I think I can give hope to people who need it."

For Kinneret, Maytal shone as an indomitable role model. A year passed before Kinneret could leave the hospital and its rehabilitation center. During that time and after, Kinneret underwent surgery so often that she and her family lost count. Skin grafts were interspersed with repeated operations on her eyes, ears, nose, legs, hands, and lungs.

Once out of the hospital, Kinneret tried to reclaim a normal life. She turned to a new career interest and began to study film-making, but she also continued to visit other victims of terror. When we talked in 2004, Kinneret brought her gloved hands together as she reflected on her current routine. "The suffering that I see every day when I go to the rehab center—the orphans, the cripples, the mothers without kids. It's so painful to me, especially when I see them at the beginning of their process." She paused and quietly uttered the name "Maytal." Picking up her thoughts, she said, "You know, like Maytal came to me, I just want to show them that you can live through this and can live a normal life." Kinneret had become part of Israel's extraordinary support network for terror victims. She continues to pass the baton of hope that Maytal had handed to her.

Kinneret smiled as she spoke of the many people she had encountered in the past few years. "Amazing" was her favorite adjective to describe family and friends, but also doctors, rehabilitation aides, well-wishers, and new friends.

One of the "amazing" people Kinneret met was Gillian Laub, an American photographer three years older than Kinneret whose work has appeared in prominent publications including the *New Yorker, Newsweek,* and the *New York Times.* Gillian visited Israel in October 2002 to explore her own feelings about the country. Declaring herself apolitical, she set about to speak with Jews and Arabs in a variety of settings. While visiting medical centers in Tel Aviv, she met a representative of OneFamily, an organization that helps victims of terrorism, who took her to meet Kinneret. "I was just floored by her, pretty much like everyone else is," Gillian later recalled to me. "Here she was, in a very, very bad physical state. I mean she was hard to look at. She still had open wounds. Her eye was half open. I had never seen somebody that was so badly burned. It was a shock to me."

As we spoke, in 2004, Gillian squeezed her eyes together, and the corners of her mouth turned downward. I interjected that I did not think that Kinneret was hard to look at now.

"Of course not, now, after all her operations," Gillian responded. Her expression lightened: "I find her incredibly beautiful. But even then, after about ten minutes, for me that all changed. When she smiled or spoke, I was blown away by this woman."

How did she explain that? I asked.

Gillian was drawn to her not only because they were about the same age but also because she admired her toughness. "She's a victim, but actually she's so strong that I don't look at her as a victim. I look at her as a survivor. I can't explain it exactly, but I just felt this affection for her. I didn't feel pity for her. I was like, wow. She is a tough woman."

Did Gillian take her picture at that time? I asked.

"No, no," she chuckled. "The way I approach picture taking is—you know, what I do is research. I just wanted to get a feeling, record my feelings. I talk to people and I take notes. You have to know when you're taking a picture what you're trying to say."

After returning to the United States, Gillian continued to think about the impact that Kinneret had on her. The following spring she received a grant from World Press Photo, an organization based in the Netherlands that promotes press photography. The funding would enable her to take pictures on any subject in Israel, with an anticipated showing in Amsterdam in the fall.

Gillian spent the summer of 2003 in Israel and reconnected with Kinneret. Building on her earlier experience there, she shot pictures of people at the seashore, in their homes, idling in the streets. Among her subjects were Israelis and Palestinians who had been wounded by violence. These photographs were so compelling that the *New York Times Magazine* published several, along with comments by the subjects. The collection, titled "The Maimed," led with a single huge photograph across one-and-a-half pages. A young woman was encased in a pressure suit, sitting on her heels, knees pointing forward. The skin-tight suit helped minimize swelling in the aftermath of skin operations. The woman's bare upper legs were brown with scars, as were areas of her face. Head tilted to the side, she gazed wistfully at the camera. Only her half smile saved the image from a projection of gloom. Her expression recalled the enigmatic smile in the painting by Modigliani. The woman in the photograph was Kinneret, saying: "This is my goal, to show the world that life is stronger than everything, and love and the will of living, it's all that matters."[2]

Two years after the picture was taken, in 2005, I sat with Kinneret on a cool September morning in a café on Christopher Street in New York. She was in the United States to consult with an American plastic surgeon about more operations on her face. I asked if she was bitter about what happened to her. There were moments of anger, she conceded, mainly during the first year in the hospital, especially after painful surgeries. But she moved past those emotions with the help of a psychologist. "I think bitterness is a waste of energy. It leads you nowhere. Really, you need your strength to do something else, not bitterness or anger."

Kinneret cut into an omelet. Her fingers, parts of which were lost in the bombing, protruded from skin-tight partial gloves. The long sleeves of her stylish blue denim jacket covered her scarred arms. Whether wielding a fork or a pen, the left-handed Kinneret maneuvered unself-consciously. The confidence of her movements reflected her persona, with not a hint of self-pity. This woman, blind in one eye, deaf in one ear, breathing with one lung, still undergoing reconstructive surgery, told me that she felt lucky. "I really love what I'm doing now, filmmaking, and also talking about my life to help others and help people understand. I've been to places and met people that I wouldn't have met except for that incident."

She refers to these people as angels. "Sometimes I say to myself, oddly, that I am thankful for what happened because it brought these people into my life."

* * *

On April 6, 1994, seven months after Arafat and Rabin signed the Oslo peace agreement, an Arab driver detonated his car, full of explosives, at a bus station in the inland city of Afula. Eight Israelis were killed and dozens injured, including Anna Krakovich. She had been an English teacher in the Ukraine before coming to Israel two years earlier, when she was 37, with her 10-year-old daughter, Irene. They settled in Haifa, and soon after, Anna found a position teaching high school English in Afula, 30 miles away. Anna's daily routine included a late afternoon bus commute home from the Afula station.

After the blast, Anna, suffering from broken bones and severe burns, was transported by helicopter to Haifa's Rambam Hospital. At that point she had few friends in Israel, and when she awoke from a coma days later, the first thing she heard was a stranger saying, "Don't worry Anna, Irene is okay." The words came from Ruth

Bar-On, who a year earlier had founded Selah. Ruth understood that many new immigrants lacked a network of family and friends who could help in crisis situations. Selah was then among few volunteer organizations that expressly sought to care for victims of terror. During the intifada, as the number of victims multiplied, so did the number of new groups wanting to help them, many similar to Selah.

Nine months after the attack, when Anna was still undergoing painful treatments, a suicide bomber blew himself up at a busy intersection near Netanya. Several casualties were taken to the burn and plastic surgery unit at Rambam Hospital. Anna, though still wrapped in a burn suit and barely able to move her arms, went to the unit to visit the victims and their families. She told them that she had spent many months where they were. "I saw in the eyes of the parents that they would rather believe me than somebody who was healthy and fit, when I said their sons will be okay."

In the midst of her suffering, Anna began to help others, and she has worked as a volunteer for Selah ever since. She still has bouts of physical pain and sometimes feels a need for psychological support. "You don't wake up one sunny lovely morning and get rid of it," she said, referring to the memory of the event. Even eleven years later, in 2005, this tall, expressive woman allowed that she is occasionally seized with panic. A loud noise or finding herself in a crowd might set it off, she said. But under Selah's auspices she has received psychological treatment and, equally important, has gained strength by helping other terror victims. She has connected especially to immigrants from the former Soviet Union, including those affected by the Dolphinarium attack in 2001. In counseling sessions and four-day healing retreats, Anna's warm guidance has eased the way for those more recently affected.

Not all survivors have been able to deal with the challenge of their altered conditions. Some remain irreparably scarred emotionally as well as physically. But Natan, Elad, Kinneret, Maytal, and Anna typify a surprising number who have achieved a sense of equanimity and fulfillment. Kinneret told me that among the dozens of terror survivors she knows, almost all have shed the deep anger they felt immediately after their experience. The support system in Israel has evolved into a remarkable network for recovery. With the help of family, friends, and counselors, many survivors have embraced new lives, some with gusto. But even those who have successfully dealt with their trauma may never feel fully repaired. The memory of physical wholeness and life experiences in their pre-terror years cannot be erased. Still, with personal determination and support from others, many have not only come to terms with their condition, but have gained a greater appreciation for life.

5

Families

The wounds of terrorism commonly affect not only the victims of an attack, but their families. For those who have lost loved ones, coping often includes activity to perpetuate and protect their memories. In 2005, four years after her two daughters were killed in the suicide bombing at the Dolphinarium, I spoke with Ella Nelimov. Our meeting was arranged by Micha Feldmann, who knew her from his work with Selah. Ella graciously invited us to dinner.

Micha and I climbed two flights of stairs to her compact apartment outside of Tel Aviv. The walls of the small kitchen and living room were covered with pictures of her daughters, Yuli and Yelena, and their brother, Sasha, now 18. Ella pointed to a painting of a hypnotic swirl of red rose petals atop a green-yellow stem. A faint pencil outline of additional petals suggested that the artist was not finished. "Yuli's teacher gave me the picture after she died," Ella said. The teacher's inscription at the bottom read: "2001, Uncompleted Rose Painting by Yulia Nelimov, of Blessed Memory."

Sasha joined us as we squeezed around the small table in the dining alcove. Ella had prepared a sumptuous mix of Russian and Israeli-style dishes—herring, olives, sliced hardboiled eggs on black bread. The culinary highlight was a mountain of "kreplach," dumplings, a mainstay of European-rooted Jewish dining. Ella's mother, who had lived with them until her death in 2004, made kreplach regularly. "The girls loved it, and their grandmother loved making it for them," Ella said.

I asked if it was hard for the family to adjust after they immigrated to Israel from Russia in 1995. "No," she replied. "It was as if we were born here." Ella found work as a cook in the cafeteria of the Ministry of Education. Her three children quickly made new friends and integrated easily into school life. The hardest problem for Ella, she said, was to learn Hebrew. Her soft, round face was bracketed by three-inch-long gold earrings. Relaxed and unassuming, she recounted the night of the Dolphinarium attack: the unanswered calls to her daughters' cell phones, the fruitless search at the hospitals, the visit to the morgue. At first, Ella visited their graves every few weeks. Now she goes less often, "just whenever I feel I have to," she said.

What gives her the urge to visit the cemetery? I asked. "It's hard to explain," she answered. "It's a feeling as if I'm missing something, so I go."

What else has helped her cope? "From the beginning, it was easy to speak to the people from Selah," she said. "They understood. They would hold my hand, and just by doing that, sometimes without words, they helped me to feel better."

How about now, did she still need someone to hold her hand? I asked. "Well, time has passed. I take care of myself, and it's very important that I work." Ella paused. Her eyes were sad. "There are days when I still need help, especially during their *yahrtzeit* [the annual commemoration of their deaths]."

Had she spoken with other families who suffered terror attacks? "First of all, when a terror attack happens, I cannot watch anything about it on television. I can only talk to families that lost their children in the Dolphinarium attack." Ella said that she had never felt the need for professional psychological help. She valued the support she received from people like Micha Feldmann and the Dolphinarium families, but mostly, she said, she helped herself. She looked at Sasha and said, "We are basically optimists."

I asked Sasha if he also helped himself. He laughed, "Yes, I don't like psychologists."

Coping may take many forms, and for the Nelimovs it is clear that being surrounded by memories of Yuli and Yelena is key. The most prominent piece of furniture in the apartment is a 6-foot-tall cabinet with a glass door. Its five rows of shelves are crowded with memorabilia about Yuli and Yelena. Their necklaces are neatly arranged beside small blue jewelry boxes. Artificial flowers lie beside stuffed cloth animals, including a cartoon-like chipmunk. An eye-level shelf supports a satin heart inscribed, "I Love You This Much." A glance at the heart prompted Ella to say that she missed her daughters very much. "The noise and music in the morning. The laughter. Now it's quiet."

Did the loss of her daughters affect her feelings about the Palestinians? I wondered.

"After it happened, in the beginning, I looked at them differently. At first I was angry. But then I felt sorry for them, the Palestinians, because they send their children to be suicide bombers. I'm not a politician. I speak as a mother."

* * *

For Debra Applebaum, the widow of David and the mother of Nava, coping has taken the form of increased activity. When we met at a Jerusalem hotel in 2006, nearly three years after the bombing of the Café Hillel, she had just finished teaching a session at Matan, a women's institute for Torah studies. She began studying there eighteen years earlier. Now she spends hours at the institute almost every day, exploring the meaning of the Bible and its commentaries.

Is she doing things now that she had not done before their deaths? I asked. "I probably do things more intensely," she answered. "I try to keep even busier, whether it's Matan, or the museum, or whether it's political." For as long as she has been with Matan, she has served as a volunteer docent at the Israel Museum.

There she shares with visitors her expertise about archeological exhibits and their relationship to the Bible. As for politics, she half smiles as she explains her dismay about government policies. She and David opposed the 1993 Oslo agreement from the outset. "Over the years since then, I've been out demonstrating a few times a week." The Applebaums felt that relinquishing territory to the Arabs was neither just nor wise. The Jews have a biblical right to the land, they believed; and in any case, Palestinians would not accede to the existence of a Jewish state. "When Oslo was signed, my husband said this would lead to shooting in the streets," she sighed. "He certainly was right."

Despite her strong words, Debra's demeanor was neither harsh nor graceless. She spoke with calm about her politics as she did about the loss of David and Nava. When I noted her emotional restraint, she grinned and said it was a family trait. Her husband had been famous for his self-containment even in the midst of chaotic hospital emergencies. "Maybe I got it from him by osmosis," she quipped.

Debra's beret and long black sleeves signaled the modest attire of an Orthodox woman. Other than tiny diamond earrings, her only jewelry was a silver bracelet etched with a statement: "In memory of Dr. David Applebaum and his daughter Nava, who were killed by terrorists on September 9, 2003." The bracelet was produced by the OneFamily Fund, which sells such memorial items to raise funds on behalf of victims of terrorism. Debra and her family had long been friends of Marc and Chantal Belzberg, who founded OneFamily in 2002. The organization sponsors retreats for affected families, camp experiences for youngsters, counseling, and direct financial aid.

Had Debra or her five children participated in any of these activities? I asked. She shook her head. "No, my kids were not interested in this." She said they preferred to spend time with friends and cousins "rather than with other victims and their kids."

When I spoke to Natan, the oldest of her five children, he was even more definitive. He felt no need for "victim therapy," he insisted. Declaring that he was not a particularly emotional person, he echoed his mother's description of their family. As if to underscore the point, he added, "Right after the *shiva* [the week of mourning], I went back to work."

We met in early 2006 at Columbia University, where he was studying for a master's degree in business administration. Following his father's death, Natan, then 24, became the chief financial officer of Terem, the network of private clinics that David had founded. On leave from the company for sixteen months, Natan planned to return in 2007, after completing his studies.

Natan is beardless and thinner than his late father was. But David's broad smile and famous accessibility are no less characteristic of his son. While rejecting displays of excessive sentimentality, he admitted to feeling random moments of sadness. What prompted those moments? I asked.

"Something may remind me of my father or sister and I think, 'How would it be if they were here?'" Natan said that he and his father were alike and that they would often talk about family, business, or politics. He adjusted his frameless glasses as he acknowledged missing those conversations. Then he said, "Eight months after my father died, my son was born. His name is David."

Toward the end of my conversation with Debra Applebaum, she mentioned that she wrote an article that would soon appear in a religious literary magazine called *Megadim.* The article compares the biblical tales of the "binding of Isaac" and the "ascension of Elijah." Both stories, she said, depicted a sanctification of God. In the first, at God's command, Abraham prepared to sacrifice his son, Isaac, by binding him to an altar. (Upon Abraham's display of devotion, God intervened before Isaac could be harmed.) In the second, Elijah is provided a fiery chariot ride to heaven because of his devotion and obedience to God.

Although the two tales are different, Debra said, the overriding theme in both is the same. From this she drew parallels to the loss of both her husband and daughter. "I'm dealing with two deaths that are totally different stories, yet in many ways are the same."

Debra spent more than a year writing the article, which concludes that there is no clear-cut division between the living and the dead. She believes in the soul, and that David and Nava somehow still know what is taking place on earth.

Does that belief give her consolation? I asked. "Yes," she answered. "I believe in resurrection. It gives me a sense of continuity." She paused. "And comfort."

* * *

Stephen Flatow, an American, knows his way around a courtroom. Not only is he a lawyer, but he has testified frequently on matters concerning terrorism. His interest in the subject was prompted by the loss of his daughter Alisa, who in 1995 was killed by a Palestinian suicide bomber. But ten years later, an impending court appearance left him uncharacteristically sleepless. For the first time, he would be facing alleged accomplices to Alisa's murder.

On June 16, 2005, after walking past rows of cement barriers and security agents, Flatow entered the courthouse in Tampa, Florida. The prosecution had subpoenaed him to testify in a trial presided over by Federal District Court Judge James Moody. When he took the witness stand, in front of him sat Sami Al-Arian and three fellow-defendants. Al-Arian had taught computer science at the University of South Florida, where he openly advocated for Palestinian causes. He and the others were charged with conspiracy and providing material support for Palestinian Islamic Jihad. The organization, which was on the U.S. State Department's list of terrorist groups, claimed responsibility for many attacks against Israelis, including the 1995 bombing of Egged Bus 37 in Gaza. In his opening statement, federal prosecutor Terry Furr described Islamic Jihad as "dedicated to the annihilation of Israel through the killing and maiming of its inhabitants."[1] The bombing of Bus 37 killed seven Israelis and one American—20-year-old Alisa Flatow.

After being sworn in, Flatow, 56, recounted his last conversation with his daughter, on Saturday night, April 8, 1995. Sighing frequently to maintain his composure, he said that around 11:30 PM, he and his wife, Rosalyn, were on the phone with her. Alisa had called their New Jersey home from Jerusalem, where the time was 6:30 the next morning. The oldest of five children, she had finished three years at Brandeis University and was on leave to study at a seminary in Israel. In a few months she planned to return to Brandeis and complete her degree in sociology. "I'm going with a couple of girlfriends to a hotel on the beach," Alisa told her parents. They would be leaving in a few hours and planned to stay for three days.

"Where's the hotel?" her father asked. "In Gaza," she answered, assuring them that she would be in good hands. That spring was only two years after the signing of the Oslo Accords, and traveling in Gaza on an Israeli bus did not seem alarming. Stephen simply urged his daughter to stay close to her friends.

A few hours later, while the Flatows slept, six thousand miles to the east, their daughter boarded Bus 37 and slid into the seat behind the driver. One of her friends, Kesari Ruza, sat next to her. Kesari, like Alisa, was studying in Israel temporarily and would be returning to the United States to attend law school. En route to their destination, the bus approached the Gaza settlement of Kfar Darom. In 1930 a Jewish citrus farmer purchased Kfar Darom, a 65-acre parcel of land, and developed it into a fruit orchard. In the late 1930s, Arab marauders destroyed his holdings, and he sold Kfar Darom to the Jewish National Fund. Egypt gained control of the Gaza strip during the 1948 battle for Israel's independence and held it until 1967. Then, after victory over Egypt in the Six Day War, Israel established a military outpost at Kfar Darom, which later became a civilian community of four hundred. By the 1990s, local beach resorts were drawing vacationers like Alisa and her friends. Visits to the area ended in 2005, when the Israeli government ordered the evacuation of all the Jewish settlers from the Gaza strip.[2]

At the trial in 2005, Kesari followed Stephen Flatow to the witness stand. She told the court that ten years earlier, as the bus reached the outskirts of Kfar Darom, she was dozing. But she was jolted awake by noise, as if the bus was being pelted with rocks.

Her narrative assumed a staccato rhythm: "The bus continued to drive. . . . Blood was everywhere. On us. On our bags." A 24-year-old Palestinian man had crashed a Volkswagen van loaded with explosives into the bus.

Now a trial lawyer in New York City, Kesari's voice was steady throughout her testimony. "As soon as I woke up," she said, "Alisa's head kind of fell toward me. Her eyes were rolled back in her head, and her hands were sort of curled in." The courtroom was stone silent. "I realized something very bad had just happened. She wasn't conscious."[3]

When the scorched bus came to a stop, Kesari and others ran to a nearby field. Alisa remained on board motionless, in her blood-splattered T-shirt and denim skirt. Kesari looked back and saw someone carry her off the bus. It was around noon, Israel time.

That morning in New Jersey, at around 7:45, Stephen Flatow heard a radio report about a bus bombing in Gaza. "My heart sank," he told the court, thinking that Alisa could have been involved. During his twenty minutes of testimony, he paused frequently to hold back tears. But what he told the court, and more, he had shared with me months earlier.

In January 2005, we sat in the den of his comfortable West Orange home, where Alisa had grown up. Photographs of the Flatow family adorned the walls. In one picture, Alisa's dark hair and looped earrings framed her easy smile. Her turtleneck collar accentuated the arc of her chin. Another photograph showed Yitzhak Rabin in the Flatow home weeks after her death. Then prime minister of Israel, he paid his respects during an official visit to the United States.

Flatow ushered me to a seat across from a fireplace. His stocky figure sank into the leather couch a few feet away, and he stretched his arm across the backrest. "Calls went back and forth all that morning," he said, referring to April 9, 1995. He and Rosalyn were on the phone with worried friends, relatives, and government officials. The State Department informed them that Alisa was in Soroka

Hospital in Beersheva. At around 11 AM, a doctor from the hospital phoned Flatow to say that Alisa had undergone surgery and was in intensive care.

"What's her condition?" Flatow asked.

The doctor hesitated. "I suggest you come right away."

With the help of a travel agent, Flatow and a friend, Paul Wolf, boarded the afternoon El Al fight to Ben-Gurion Airport. After ten hours in the air, they landed early the next morning. American Embassy aides met them at the airport and drove them to the hospital, 60 miles south. As they approached Beersheva, an aide called ahead to the hospital, and Dr. Chaim Reuveni, a lead physician at Soroka, went out to the parking lot to wait for them.

Reuveni greeted Flatow and led him to the intensive care unit. "I was still pretty numb," Flatow recalled. There were six beds in the room, five of them empty. He walked to the corner bed where Alisa lay. Her hair had been shaved, but otherwise she seemed almost untouched, just a few scratches and a small bandage toward the back of her head. She was breathing with the help of a ventilator, she was warm, and her heartbeat was strong. "I whispered to her and picked up her hand, but when I let go, it just fell back onto the bed," Flatow said.

After a few minutes, Reuveni took Flatow to sit with a social worker and the surgeon who had operated on Alisa. They explained that a piece of shrapnel had entered the back of her head and that essentially, she was brain dead. At first, Flatow wondered why, if her condition was irreversible, she was being kept on the respirator. "Then the reason began to sink in as Dr. Reuveni said he had a question to ask me." Reuveni wanted to know if Flatow would permit Alisa's organs to be donated for transplantation.

Flatow reflected, and said he needed to speak to his wife. He was aware that Israelis, whether religious or secular, often were reluctant to donate organs. The disinclination was prompted in part by the religious admonition to bury all parts of the deceased body. It also hung on varied definitions of the end of life. For many, the cessation of brain activity was a sufficient indicator, but some still held that the heart must stop beating. Flatow, an observant Jew, knew of varied rabbinic determinations that placed organ donation in a different context. According to some, a transplanted organ could fulfill the supreme Jewish value of saving life, enshrined in the Talmudic passage: "He who saves a life, saves the world."

When he called Rosalyn, they spoke of how much Alisa loved Israel and the friends she made there. They recalled the many times that people invited her to their homes for dinners and for celebrations. "We figured that if there was a way to pay back the people of Israel, this would be a way. So we said yes."

Flatow's trip from Beersheva to Tel Aviv, where he would spend the night, was uneventful until he reached the hotel. While Israeli officials were helping him register for a room, they told him that the hotel had been notified that President Bill Clinton wanted to speak with him. When he reached his room, the phone rang and it was the president extending his sympathy. He alluded to the Flatows' decision to permit the transplantation of Alisa's organs. Flatow marveled at how quickly the word spread about his and Roz's decision. Clinton said to him, "My wife and I were talking this morning about what you've done, and we're not sure we could've done the same thing."

"You'd do anything for your daughter, right?" Flatow asked.

"Of course."

"Just because my daughter's not here on earth doesn't mean we stop being parents." The president listened attentively. Flatow said that he and his wife were still looking out for Alisa's best interests, "even though there's no tangible kid anymore."

"God bless you," Clinton said.

Alisa's organs were quickly matched to potential recipients. During the next day, her heart, lungs, kidneys, and pancreas were transplanted into six people. By Tuesday night, her body was prepared for the return flight to the United States with her father. When Stephen arrived at Ben-Gurion Airport, he was surprised to find a claque of Israeli reporters and television crews in the lounge. They asked about his decision to donate Alisa's organs and kept chattering in Hebrew among themselves. Flatow asked what they were saying, and one explained, "What you've done was something we don't do for ourselves." Another said, "You don't know what you've done for us. You've taught us a lesson." The story received continuing attention throughout Israel. The following month, in May, Prime Minister Rabin spoke publicly about the fact that "Alisa Flatow's heart beats in Jerusalem."

Some rabbis remained uncertain whether, according to Jewish law, brain death alone could signify the end of life. But since the Flatows' decision, organ donation has become more common in Israel.[4] "Alisa's case kind of jumpstarted the issue there," Flatow said, and waved his arm in a gesture of surprised satisfaction.

Another issue of public interest drew even more of Flatow's attention. In April 1996, a federal law was enacted that allowed American victims of terrorism to bring legal action against a terrorist state responsible for the act.[5] As early as 1993, Fathi Shiqaqi, then leader of Islamic Jihad, confirmed that Iran was providing money and arms to his organization.[6] On behalf of Flatow and his family, Washington attorney Stephen Perles instituted a federal lawsuit against the Iranian government. In March 1998, Judge Royce Lamberth of the D.C. District Court ruled for the plaintiffs. He ordered a judgment against the Iranian government of $22.5 million for compensatory damages and $225 million for punitive damages.

Winning the judgment did not necessarily mean collecting the money. Diplomatic relations with Iran had ended after the Islamic takeover of the country in 1979. Afterward, Iran's property in the United States, including its embassy, was maintained by the U.S. State Department. When Flatow sought to have Iranian assets sold to satisfy the court order, the State Department refused. Its position was that such action would jeopardize U.S. diplomatic assets in other countries. According to department spokesman James Rubin, the United States did not believe in judgments against foreign countries, but in negotiations with them.[7]

Similarly, in 1999 the State Department objected to a federal court judgment of $187 million against Cuba. The suit was brought by relatives of three American pilots shot down by Cuban fighter pilots the previous year. They had been flying unarmed aircraft over international waters for Brothers to the Rescue, searching for refugees trying to flee Cuba.

In both cases, the Clinton administration effectively nullified the court decisions in the name of national security. Flatow was especially dismayed since the president had seemed so solicitous on the phone after Alisa's death. He and his attorney, Stephen Perles, began to consider how the law could be strengthened. "Basically, we would walk up to Capitol Hill, knock on doors, and try to make appointments," Flatow told me. They met with scores of congressional representatives and aides who unfailingly expressed sympathy. Eventually, their efforts led to hearings on a new bill, titled the Justice for Victims of Terrorism Act.

In April 2000, Representative Bill McCollum of Florida typified the mood at a House hearing. He noted that besides Flatow and the families of the pilots, journalist Terry Anderson had also received a court judgment. In 1985, while working in Lebanon, Anderson was kidnapped and held for seven years by Hezbollah, an Iranian-sponsored organization. The court ruled that Iran must pay him $340 million for damages. McCollum contended that the administration's block on these payments was an "abusive interpretation of the law." The proposed bill would allow for appealing the president's interpretation. Furthermore, to defuse concerns about overseas U.S. assets, the legislation would only affect assets of countries on the State Department's terrorist list.[8]

The president signed the bill into law in October 2000. I asked Flatow if he considered its enactment a victory. Partially, he said. "We won to the extent that we got ten percent of our judgment, as did other families and victims." The government agreed to pay the compensatory, though not the punitive court awards. But even those funds would come from the U.S. Treasury, not Iranian assets, and Iran essentially went unpunished.[9]

Flatow's major satisfaction, he maintained, was not about the money. When he started the suit, he said, "we never thought we would collect a nickel." He and his attorney "just wanted to show the world what kind of bastards the Iranians were."

I asked if the years of effort were therapeutic for him. He stroked his chin and considered the range of his activities in the past decade—the court cases and meetings with elected officials, the organ transplantation issues, speaking about Alisa to religious and civic groups. He mentioned the Alisa Flatow Memorial Scholarship Fund that he and Rosalyn had established to help American youngsters who want to study in Israel. Then he considered the underlying impetus for all this. "I basically said to myself, you know, most families in Israel have been touched by the sudden loss of a loved one, or a neighbor's son or daughter, or somebody from the synagogue." He was sure they continued to feel the pain. Yet, he observed, they found the strength "to get up every morning and face the day. They didn't climb into a shell." Over the years, thoughts about the loss of his daughter have moved him to tears. But in considering how Israelis have coped, at least by outward appearances, he became determined to adopt a similar course of life.

No single formula for coping fits all. Unlike her husband, Rosalyn has avoided public attention. She helps select the winners in the memorial scholarship fund but rarely speaks about Alisa. When Stephen mentioned his wife's reluctance to talk about Alisa, his voice lowered.

In December 2005, the jury in the Sami Al-Arian case acquitted him of eight of the seventeen charges against him and deadlocked on the remaining nine. Rather than retry the case, prosecutors accepted a guilty plea from Al-Arian of "conspiracy to make or receive contributions of funds, goods or services for the benefit of the Palestinian Islamic Jihad." The arrangement also included expulsion of Al-Arian from the United States. The presiding judge, James Moody, then sentenced him to nineteen more months in prison, the maximum allowable under the sentencing guidelines, followed by deportation. Judge Moody described the horror of the bombings in Israel and said to Al-Arian: "Anyone with even the slightest bit of human compassion would be sickened. Not you. You saw it as an opportunity to solicit more money to carry out more bombings." To Al-Arian's claim that his funding went to the political wing of Islamic Jihad to help Palestinian widows and orphans, the judge responded: "The only connection to widows and orphans is that you create them."[10]

* * *

On a spring afternoon in 2005, a slight, chic figure mounted the stage at the community center in Nahariya. "My name is Smadar Haran Kaiser," she announced in halting English to an audience of American visitors. Smadar's fashionable black leather jacket and pants reflected her artistic background. Her short dark hair framed a face with deep-set, melancholy eyes.

"When I was asked to bring to you my story," she told her listeners, "I was at first in a slight panic." It was difficult enough to describe her experience in Hebrew, and she wondered whether she could handle the retelling in English. But her self-doubts quickly seemed to evaporate. "I have come to understand that my story is, in a way, the story of the Jewish people and the Jewish nation. I don't think my story has an end. It goes on." Hardly glancing at her handwritten notes, Smadar never veered from the calm flow in her narrative.

Nahariya is a northern coastal city six miles below the border with Lebanon, where residents enjoy a relaxed tempo and cool summers. Vacationers near the shore can hear the lapping of the Mediterranean surf. Smadar had grown up on a kibbutz, but during a visit to Nahariya in 1976, she and her husband Danny "fell in love" with the city. Smadar was 23 and Danny, 25. They decided to live there, and soon after, moved into an apartment on Jabotinsky Street, one block from the beach. Three years later, Smadar, an artist, was still entranced by the beauty of the shoreline and the inland fields of flowers. On a Saturday afternoon, April 28, 1979, she and Danny picnicked at a seaside park with their daughters, Einat, 4, and Yael,

2. "It was a beautiful Shabbat [Sabbath] day," she recalled. "Spring all over, flowers everywhere." That evening, as she and Danny went to bed, Smadar felt full of life.

Shortly after midnight they awoke to the sound of gunfire. Four armed Palestinians had traveled in a rubber boat from Lebanon to the Nahariya beach. They ran inland, killed a policeman, and burst into the Harans' apartment building, shooting guns and exploding grenades. Smadar opened the door to her apartment and pulled in a neighbor from the hallway as the terrorists were running up the stairs. Just before the hallway light went out, Smadar and the gunmen glimpsed each other. "Our eyes met for a moment, and then there was darkness," she said. Smadar bolted the door shut and Danny helped the neighbor into a crawl space above the ceiling. Smadar grabbed Yael, who was crying hysterically, and Danny pushed them up into the space. Before he could climb in with Einat, the terrorists blasted the apartment door open. "They broke in with grenades, shooting, yelling, looking for us," Smadar said. The gunmen held Danny and Einat while they searched.

Fearing that Yael's cries would reveal their hideaway, Smadar put her hand over her daughter's mouth. Smadar, Yael, and their neighbor remained motionless as the terrorists moved from room to room firing into the walls. Smadar heard Danny beg the gunmen to take him hostage and leave Einat. They ignored him and continued their hunt for the rest of the family.

As the terrorists searched, Smadar thought of her own parents. Her mother had lost her entire family in the Holocaust. Smadar recalled the painful stories about how her mother, then a youngster in Poland during World War II, hid from the Nazis. Now she crouched in fear and disbelief at her own situation. "This is just what happened to my mother," she thought. But her mother had survived, made her way to Israel to build a new life and a new state. How would Smadar and her family endure this ordeal?

The terrorists never noticed the panel covering the entry to the crawl space. After some time, the police arrived, and the gunmen fled to the beach with Danny and Einat as hostages. When the terrorists reached the beach, one of them, Samir Kuntar, shot Danny before Einat's eyes. "His death would be the last sight she would ever see," Smadar said. "Because then he smashed my little daughter's skull against a rock with his rifle butt." Moments later, the police killed two of the terrorists and captured the other two, one of whom was Kuntar. And then the unbearable coda: By the time the frightened figures in the crawl space were rescued, Yael too was dead. "In trying to save all our lives, I had smothered her," Smadar said.[11]

She paused, perhaps to maintain her composure, perhaps for the sound of sobs in the room to abate. When she resumed, she recounted the limitless despair that enveloped her. She felt lifeless. "I had lost my beloved family. I had lost my world." Afterward, she moved in with a girlfriend, but she kept to herself. One afternoon she walked to a large field of daisies and stood in the middle. She took in the smells, the colors, the buzz of nearby bees, the soft breeze against her face. It was a place that she had often visited with her daughters. "They never picked the flowers because they said, 'This is the flowers' house so we should leave them where they belong.'"

Smadar lingered in the field and sensed that she was receiving a message. The myriad surrounding sensations meant she was still alive. "At that moment, I let myself hope that I could build my life again." Somehow the pain and the hope would have to coexist. "I became determined not to give up, not to emotionally die. I will do my best to have a good life."

With the help of friends who were ever-present to care and listen, Smadar was able to rebuild her life. In the course of the next year, she met Yakov Kaiser, a clinical psychologist who had been gravely wounded in the 1973 Yom Kippur War. In 1980, Smadar married Yakov. Together they had two daughters, and they recently became grandparents. Their twenty-five years of marriage is a testament to their success in creating a new life. But Smadar, now a psychotherapist with a master's degree in social work, acknowledges that her past is always part of her present.

"I still miss Einat and Yael," she said. "I loved them very much. But I see life now, sometimes very happy, sometimes sad." With this she returned to the analogy between her experience and that of the Jewish people. Her mother emerged from the Holocaust alone, without family. Like so many survivors of the Holocaust and other tragedies that befell the Jewish people, she opted for life. After Smadar lost her family in 1979, she was determined to do no less. Her conviction was reinforced by what she also saw as a defeat for the terrorists. She would not allow them to murder her soul, she said.

In the quarter-century since then, Smadar's experience has occasionally prompted her to speak publicly. She led a campaign for the nation to honor the victims of terrorism just as it does its fallen soldiers. Her efforts were realized in 1997 on Israel's Memorial Day, when a memorial wall to terrorism victims was unveiled at the military cemetery on Jerusalem's Mount Herzl. Perhaps her most forceful presentment was her opposition in 2003 to a demand by the leader of a terrorist organization. Hassan Nasrallah, the head of Hezbollah in Lebanon, announced willingness to swap captives: the kidnapped Israeli businessman, Elchanan Tannenbaum, and the remains of three murdered Israeli soldiers, in exchange for 420 Palestinian and Lebanese terrorists in an Israeli prison. Nasrallah demanded that the freed prisoners include Samir Kuntar, the admitted killer of Danny and Einat Haran.

Smadar was reminded of a comment the imprisoned Kuntar once made to a reporter. "He said he didn't realize that Danny and I were 'peaceniks' who supported Palestinian rights. If he'd known that, he wouldn't have killed my family." She was disgusted by his attitude, which suggested justification for murdering another family whose politics he found less agreeable. "Nobody has the right to kill for any ideology," she said.[12]

The families of Tannenbaum and the murdered Israeli soldiers were pressing the Israeli government to agree to an exchange. At the same time, Smadar publicly urged that Kuntar, who was serving a life sentence for murder, remain in prison. Nasrallah insisted that excluding Kuntar would negate the entire arrangement. But the government remained steadfast. Foreign Minister Sylvan Shalom, speaking on behalf of Prime Minister Sharon, said that Kuntar's release was out of the question. The murder of a family in Israel, he said, was unforgivable.[13] In the end, Nasrallah backed down. The prisoner release did not include Samir Kuntar.

Smadar's disdain for Kuntar's action did not translate into hate for Arabs. She would never wish that a Palestinian child die because of what happened to her, she said. Her thoughts are not about revenge, but about hope. "Every year I hope next year will bring peace," she told me. "I think it would be good to have peace and find out how it is. Because I really don't know."

* * *

Losing a loved one is emotionally wrenching under any conditions, and even harsher when caused by a bloody act of terrorism. But if the aim of terrorists is to create fear and weaken morale, the reactions of Ella Nelimov, Debra and Natan Applebaum, Stephen Flatow, and Smadar Haran Kaiser suggest that those goals have not been met. They live with the pain of their losses, and their responses have not been uniform. Ella's and the Applebaums' manner of coping has been more private than Stephen's or Smadar's. Stephen has sought retribution more than the others have. But like most others who have suffered from terrorism, each has found a level of activity that has helped them manage their grief.

Ruth Bar-On's organization, Selah, has ministered to more than 12,000 victims and family members whose experiences were no less wrenching than those recounted in this chapter. Even the strongest, she said, can suffer from a reminder long after the event. A television report of a terror attack might be too much to bear, or perhaps the smell of burning meat would trigger a memory. But the overwhelming majority live normal lives. They work, they laugh, they take care of their families.

6

Doctors and Nurses

Terrorist attacks can affect a medical community in unanticipated ways. In 1991, after Iraq invaded Kuwait, a U.S.-led coalition undertook military action to force Iraq's withdrawal. During the six-week conflict, which began on January 17, Iraq launched thirty-nine Scud missiles at Israel even though Israel was not part of the coalition action. Fearing that the missiles might carry chemical or biological agents, the entire Israeli population was instructed to don gas masks during air raid alerts that sometimes lasted several hours. An exception was made for women giving birth because of the restrictive breathing imposed by the masks.

During the initial alerts, several women became panicky upon seeing others in the delivery room wearing gas masks. They felt singularly vulnerable to a gas or germ attack. Their delivering doctors, like other Israelis, had been expected to wear gas masks, but some began to ignore the instruction. By not wearing gas masks, the physicians helped reduce their patients' anxiety, though at the risk of toxic exposure to themselves.

A decade later, in the early 2000s, the frequency of terror attacks in Israel provoked another source of anxiety in the medical community—worry that their own loved ones could be among the victims. Dr. Esti Galili-Weisstub, a psychiatrist, would, like others who worked in hospitals, go to the emergency department after an attack. "We would draw back the curtain and wonder, Will it be someone we know?" She spoke of her efforts and those of her colleagues to control their emotions. It was a challenge, she said, to remain professional and give heart to others.

In March 2005 Yoav Mintz, a trauma surgeon at Hadassah, amplified his feelings. A child's crayon drawing hung from the wall of his spare office. It depicted a girl on a swing beneath two oversized blue butterflies. The artist was his seven-year-old daughter, Rotem, the middle of three children. Dr. Mintz, 39, glanced at the picture and spoke plaintively about his inability to spend more time with his wife and children. A trauma surgeon faces huge demands on his time, and this was all the more true during the intifada. "It's like you don't have a life other than being in the hospital and treating your patients. It's pretty hard."

Mintz was thankful that the number of terror attacks had dropped in recent months, though his schedule remained intense. "You can do it for a few years, but if you want to keep your family together, you know, you have to let go for a while," he said. He was looking forward to a two-year hiatus at the University of California in San Diego, where he would be performing minimally invasive laparoscopic surgery. There, he hoped, he would be far away from bombs and other explosives.

Meanwhile, Dr. Mintz maintained his dedicated pace seven days a week. We met at his hospital on a morning after he had made his rounds. Attired in a black turtleneck sweater, he sat back and traced his Jerusalem roots back nine generations.

Have the years of terror attacks affected Dr. Mintz in a personal way? I asked. His response came slowly. "You have to understand that every time there's a suicide bombing, the first thing you think is, 'Okay, where's my wife, where are my kids? What's my mother doing right now?' If the attack was on a bus, you worry, 'Which bus was it?' and you can't always know, because they may not have announced the number." He sighed. "It's like you're stressed all the time, thinking you'll have to treat someone that you know."

I asked what kind of thoughts he had while performing surgery on a victim of a terrorist attack. "You have to shut down all your feelings," he answered. "You cannot take care of patients if you look at them like you look at a regular person." Mintz likened his behavior during surgery to that of a robot. "You look at the internal organs and treat them. You look at the face, the chest, the legs. You don't connect them all together. Otherwise you can crack up."

Do most surgeons think the same way?

"We don't talk about that. Everybody deals with it his own way. I think you're the first one I'm telling about it."

Nor does Anat Globerman usually discuss her personal feelings about her work. Like Dr. Mintz, she is a surgeon. And like others at hospitals throughout Israel, with word of an attack, she reaches for a cell phone to contact her family before the victims start pouring in.

Dr. Globerman's route to her specialty began as a medical student at Ben Gurion University in Beersheva. There, in the 1990s, she became enchanted with vascular surgery. Recreating pathways for the vessels that carry a person's lifeblood seemed like poetry, she said. "Until I saw this work, I didn't know that there was such beauty in medicine."

Following medical school, in her early 30s, Globerman started her surgical training. The intifada had just begun, bringing a crush of patients. In 2005, when we spoke, she had taken a short leave from formal training to conduct research on the causes of atherosclerosis. We met in her laboratory, down the hall from a collection of experimental rats. The arterial walls of these specially bred animals were laden with fatty deposits, and she was seeking to understand the genetic basis of their condition.

I asked about her feelings during the height of the Palestinian attacks. "It was hectic all the time," she answered. Her smile seemed labored. "You didn't ever feel like going out for fun."

Did she recall any particular incidents? I asked. "I remember a young girl, maybe 17, who was brought here after a terror attack," she said. "The blood vessels to her lower limbs were all torn. Fractures, shrapnel, nails and bolts throughout her body, unbelievable numbers of bolts. The director of the vascular surgery department said she wouldn't survive." Initially, the doctors only packed her wounds to stop the bleeding. Her lungs were filled with blood. With many of the badly wounded, "you just try to sustain vital systems. You postpone surgeries because these patients couldn't survive the trauma of surgery itself."

Optimal treatment, including the resetting of broken bones and the repair of nonvital organs, is often postponed for severely wounded victims. The challenge is to see those patients through intensive care during the early crucial hours—and hope they survive.

Globerman's patient received singular care. Under ordinary conditions, Globerman believed, the surgeons would have amputated her legs. "Textbook knowledge would have suggested that," she said. But the experience gained from so many terror attacks taught the doctors to hold back. In fact, the youth and strength of that patient enabled her to survive through the first days, as vascular surgeons painstakingly began to reattach her torn vessels. In the end, the young woman and her legs were saved.

Globerman believes that, with the benefit of so much experience, Israeli medical approaches have saved numerous lives. Any other examples? I asked. She mentioned the work of Dr. Yoram Weiss, an anesthesiologist and intensive care specialist. He helped to perfect a technique to treat lung injuries called "alveolar recruitment." Ordinarily, a mechanical ventilator can help someone breathe by flowing oxygen under slight pressure into the respiratory tract. But under some conditions, this technique might cause damage. At the end of the branches of the bronchial tree, deep in the lungs, lie 300 million microscopic sacs called alveoli. It is in the alveoli that inhaled oxygen is exchanged with carbon dioxide, the gas that is exhaled as waste. If the alveoli are collapsed or weakened, the pressure caused by the flow from the ventilator might cause them to burst.

Weiss was called in to see a young man whose lungs were severely damaged. "You wanted to put him on a ventilator, but you didn't know how many alveoli were remaining," Globerman said. The patient was unable to breathe in adequate amounts of oxygen and was accumulating dangerous levels of carbon dioxide. Very few alveoli could have been intact, she believed. "I didn't think he had a chance. It was devastating." Then she watched Dr. Weiss place a disposable resuscitator, called an Ambu Bag, over the patient's nose and mouth. Globerman balled her hand into a fist as she replicated Weiss's next move. He gently squeezed the soft plastic bulb at the end of the Ambu Bag. She had never seen such prolonged gradual squeezes before. Each one lasted 30 seconds, she estimated.

Globerman's eyes widened. "I'm telling you, what happened then was dramatic," she said. After ten minutes, the patient's carbon dioxide levels began to decrease. She was still awed by how this simple manual application offered a solution that more advanced technology did not. "It was just out of knowledge and experience from the many blast lung injuries he saw before that Yoram Weiss decided, okay, let's start manually."

How did the patient do afterward? I wondered.

"He survived and eventually went home."

She had a personal story to tell. Two years earlier, in March 2003, a suicide bomber blew up Bus 37 in Haifa, the picturesque port city in northern Israel where she grew up. Seventeen people were killed and more than fifty wounded. It was on the eve of Purim—a holiday that celebrates the preservation of the threatened Jewish community in ancient Persia. The biblical tale tells of Queen Esther's intervention with her husband, the King of Persia, to save the Jews from a plot by the king's adviser to exterminate them. The holiday is celebrated with song and merriment. Children march about in costumes, much as Americans do during Halloween.

"Route Number 37 was my childhood route," Globerman said. It took her to school, to the movies, to see her friends." "A joy ride," she called it. "And now, twenty years later, Bus 37 was blasted when kids were coming home from the school that I attended." These children would have celebrated Purim in outfits like those that Anat Globerman and her young friends had once worn—the gown of a fairy princess, a clown suit, a doctor's white jacket. Immediately upon learning of the bombing, she phoned her relatives in Haifa. They were safe, but the destruction of Bus 37 still darkens her memories.

* * *

Yoram Weiss, the physician extolled by Dr. Globerman, is a modest man. He speaks with reticence about his own accomplishments and emphasizes team efforts. In April 2005, he led a group of medical residents and nurses through the intensive care unit during routine hospital rounds. Several patients wore clear plastic masks attached to ventilators. They were also tethered to intravenous drips, though none because of terror-related injuries. By then, the wave of attacks had receded. Despite the roomful of seriously ill people, the atmosphere was less intense than in previous years. Weiss led his team from bed to bed, reviewing the medical condition of each patient. He smiled and waved at one who showed surprising energy after a surgical procedure. "Are you sure you just had an operation?" he quipped.

Weiss graduated from medical school at the Technion Institute of Technology in Haifa. In 1990 he began his residency in anesthesiology and intensive care at Hadassah. Twelve years later, as acting director of the intensive care unit there, he oversaw the treatment of mangled patients during Israel's most trying period of terrorism.

In 2005, as he reviewed his experience, he emphasized the categorical difference in the nature of terror attacks before 2000 from those after. Previously, the major injuries were blast injuries from bombs that caused a severe wave of pressure. Victims largely suffered damage to their eardrums, lungs, and intestinal tracts. In the more recent assaults, bolts, screws, and other pieces of shrapnel were added to the explosives. Patients often bled excessively from the dozens of penetration wounds. Some tests suggested that anticoagulants had also been mixed in with the explosives.

As the number of attacks climbed, Israeli responders gained remarkable, if depressing, experience. They learned to respond far more quickly, efficiently, and independently than before. "Now, we hardly even have to talk about what to do," Weiss said. Everyone understands his role from the moment an alert sounds—whom to notify, whom to call to the hospital, what each person's assignment is.

After the first triage at the site of an attack, patients are triaged again upon entry to the hospital. "Now we start intensive care the moment someone arrives in the emergency department," Weiss said. "In the beginning, we did it much less well." Early in the intifada it might take an hour to sort out the influx of victims after an attack. "Now," Weiss said, "within twenty minutes the emergency room is empty. The patients have been moved to surgery, to intensive care, to the burn unit, or whatever. It means that people really know what to do now."

* * *

Dr. Todd Zalut, the head of the emergency department at Shaare Zedek, Jerusalem's second largest hospital, offered similar sentiments. Recent experience has taught Israeli responders to deal with a few hundred casualties "probably better than anybody else in the world," Zalut believes. He was less sure about managing a large-scale terror attack, especially with biological or radiological agents. "If you're talking about a mega-event with 10,000 casualties, nobody in the world has that kind of experience."

Zalut, 47, acceded to his current position after his mentor, David Applebaum, was killed in the suicide bombing at the Café Hillel in 2003. Zalut, like Applebaum, grew up in the United States, where he received his medical training. He went to Israel in 1991 as a volunteer doctor during the first Gulf War and later decided to stay. While working at Shaare Zedek and the Terem clinics that Applebaum founded, the two men grew to be close friends. Later, Applebaum become director, and Zalut assistant director, of the hospital's emergency department. At the first word of a terrorist attack, they both acted as if a rapid response was a personal challenge. "We would phone each other and see who would get to the scene first," Zalut recalled. But on September 9, 2003, when Zalut made his call, no one answered. He frantically began to phone area hospitals and intermittently to redial Applebaum's cell phone. But to no avail. Eventually, he reached someone at the attack site who told him several victims had been killed instantly and were placed to the side. One was David Applebaum.

Zalut was shattered. When we met early in 2006, his sense of loss was still palpable. "David planned this whole area," Zalut said, as we walked through the hospital's new emergency department. Recently completed at a cost of $30 million, the size was triple that of the previous department. It now included a shock and trauma unit and an isolation room for victims of infectious diseases. The impetus arose in part from the increased threat to the country of biological and radiological as well as conventional terrorism.

A large digital tracking board hung in front of the nurse's station. "This is a novel system that also was David's idea," he said, though Zalut also helped develop it. Glowing from the monitor were bright colors that indicated the status of every patient in the department. The color codes revealed the reason for the person's admission, how long he had been there, the doctors who had seen him, the status of laboratory tests.

Dr. Zalut has frequently made presentations on terrorism preparedness based on Shaare Zedek's experiences. On September 12, 2005, he spoke at the third annual symposium on emergency preparedness at New York University's Downtown Hospital. Two years earlier, nearly to the day, David Applebaum had spoken there on the same subject.

* * *

Nurses and other medical workers have also been deeply affected by the intifada. Sarinha Shapira, an operating room nurse, agreed that the barrage of attacks heightened her efficiency and that of her colleagues. "We work like robots and are more proficient," she said, but "another part of us has become more sensitive." Her husband is Dr. Shmuel Shapira, Hadassah Hospital's deputy director. Most of their family and friends live in Jerusalem, where many of the attacks have taken place. Like other hospital caregivers, Sarinha works with the added anxiety that every terror victim could be someone she knows. "It is very difficult," she sighs.

In 1971, when she was 15, Sarinha's family emigrated from Brazil. Her parents were Zionists who believed that the life of a Jew could best be fulfilled in the Jewish state. Six years later she completed her nurse training at Hadassah, where she has worked ever since. Slightly built, bespectacled, she presents an air of calm. But she admits to the emotional strain wrought by the repeated attacks. She recalled a June morning in 2002 when she was serving as head nurse of the hospital's operating wing. At 7:30 AM, patients who had been scheduled for surgery were wheeled in to prepare for their operations. Minutes later, word came that a bus was blown up near the Jerusalem Mall and many victims would be arriving at the emergency department.

She rushed to each operating room and found that a half-dozen patients had already been anesthetized. Except for one actually undergoing surgery, she halted the procedures in mid-action and had the patients removed from the rooms. "We had to make way for more critical casualties from the attack." Her voice softened. "It was very complicated," she said. In the end, the bombing left 19 dead and 74 injured.

Shapira remembers that day in particular because of one young victim whose sister was a medical student. The patient, Michal (not her real name), was critically injured and brought to an operating room. Soon after, her sister arrived and wanted to go inside. Shapira blocked her, insisting that hospital policy forbade family members from witnessing an operation. The sister complained bitterly. "We argued, and there was a lot of tension," Shapira recalled.

Michal had undergone a laparotomy—an exploratory opening of her abdominal cavity and chest to examine her organs. The surgeons were struggling to save her severely damaged heart and lungs. But less than an hour into surgery, she died. Her body was then cleaned, though the burned flesh and numerous penetration wounds remained visible. Shapira had to inform the sister that Michal had died. She felt overwhelmed by sadness as she led Michal's sister in to see the body. "At that moment I didn't know if I was a nurse or someone else, a friend, or what. I just cried with her."

Months later, Shapira encountered the medical student in a hospital corridor, and the young woman again expressed anger about being blocked from the operating room. Shapira told her that hospital rules were not the only reason she kept her out. After seeing Michal's decimated organs, Shapira knew there was almost no chance for survival. She did not want the medical student to see her sister die. The trauma to her would have been worse, Shapira said. Shapira then told her that she had lost her own brother in 1989 to a terrorist attack. "I always think about him. I know how difficult it is to cope."

Both of them began to weep again. The medical student's resentment softened, and she expressed appreciation for Shapira's good intentions.

* * *

In 1979, two years after Sarinha Shapira completed her training, Nava Braverman also graduated from Hadassah's school of nursing. But Braverman's subsequent career path was very different. She acquired a master's degree in public health and became coordinator of the Hadassah's women's health center. In the spring of 2005, behind a desk covered with documents and pamphlets, Braverman reflected on the recent years of violence. Her fondest hope, she said, was not that the Palestinians and Israelis would love each other, but that "maybe some day we'll learn to live without killing each other." This yearning, she conceded, seemed unlikely to be realized any time soon.

Braverman seemed amazed at what her job had become. She is in charge of the nursing team in the family information center. Commandeered by nurses and social workers, the center becomes the hub of traffic for anxious people who descend on the hospital after each event. Whether by phone or in person, the center can expect hundreds of inquiries from friends and relatives. It is bad enough that someone may be critically injured, but the agony is compounded when the identity of a patient cannot be established.

Under Braverman's direction, the nurses' team lists characteristics for each unidentified patient—hair color, eye color, special marks or scars. The information is immediately shared with other hospitals and with inquiring families to try to match the patients with the families. Even so, she recalled times that frantic families could not at first find loved ones, as when Ora Cohen was separated from two of her children (recounted in chapter 4).

There were also converse instances of too many claimants for a single victim. In July 2002, a suicide bomber exploded himself in the cafeteria at Hebrew University in Jerusalem. Eight people were killed and 85 injured. "One of the seriously wounded was a girl around 22," Braverman said. Two men arrived at the hospital apparently in search of her. Braverman's eyes turned quizzical as she explained that one was a father and the other a boyfriend. "But they were looking for two different girls," she said.

The injured woman was in surgery, and both men waited hours to see her. Finally, each man was led separately into the recovery room, but the patient was hardly recognizable. She was unconscious, her hair was burned, her body pocked with wounds, her face swollen into a balloon. "Both men said, 'She's mine,'" Braverman said. At first no one could decide what to do. Then the father said that his wife was with their daughter at the time of the explosion but that she was in Bikur Cholim, a small Jerusalem hospital. Braverman thought the man should take the patient's pink blouse to his wife for identification. An aide pointed out that the blouse was really white, having been colored by blood. Braverman found a small white section, cut it out, and drove with the father to Bikur Cholim. "Yes, it's my daughter's blouse," his wife said without hesitation.

I asked about the other man. Did he find the woman he was

seeking? "No, she had died," Braverman replied, without elaboration. Does Braverman remember these people's names? I asked.

"No, no. I can find them if you want, but usually I forget. It's one way to cope, I think." No need to find the names, I said.

Our conversation turned to recent terror attacks outside Israel, including those on 9/11, the restaurants in Indonesia, the train in Madrid, the subway in London, the numerous suicide assaults in Iraq. These all occurred after the wave of murderous bombings against Israeli innocents had begun. Braverman offered a brief though provocative observation: "Well, maybe they're the result of what's happened here." I wondered whether the contagion of terrorism had been enhanced by the failure of world leaders to consistently condemn the targeting of innocent Israelis.

* * *

Rony Berger, a clinical psychologist, would seem an unlikely hero to members of ZAKA. He is not religious, and they are ultra-Orthodox. His literary interests range from Henry Miller's *Tropic of Cancer* to Freud's *The Interpretation of Dreams,* while theirs are largely found in the Bible and rabbinic literature. Berger's politics are to the left, and that of ultra-Orthodox Jews typically to the right. But as recounted in chapter 3, ZAKA workers expressed great affection for the man who had done much to ease their emotional stress.

Berger is the director of community services for Natal, the Israel Trauma Center for Victims of Terror and War, a nonprofit organization established in 1998. Natal's services were enlisted after Yehuda Meshi-Zahav, the head of ZAKA, recognized that responding to the repeated terror attacks was taking a toll on his workers.

Scores of ZAKA members have benefited from Berger's therapy. They know little about his personal life. Would they be as receptive to his counsel if they knew his political inclinations? I asked. Berger was uninterested in the question. "Look, I have my preferences," he said during an afternoon at his home in Tel Aviv. "They certainly are not my people ideologically." But he harbors empathy for them, and not only because of the emotional stress they have endured. Some Israelis have little patience for the parochialism of the ultra-religious minority. "ZAKA are mainly strange birds, but they are underdogs," Berger said, unfazed by his mix of animals and metaphors. "And I like to help the underdog."

It was April 2004, a cloudless warm day, and Rony Berger, 54, looped his legs across a low glass table in front of his chair. We were on the outdoor veranda of his home, surrounded by semitropical foliage. He had just shown me his home office, a compact room near the front entrance. "That's where a patient sits," he said, pointing to a short couch whose back was covered with embroidered fabric.

Dr. Berger received his training in Israel and the United States—his Ph.D. is from the Florida Institute of Technology. He is contemplative, serious. Berger's focus is on people suffering from emotional trauma. In the 1980s, while in the United States, he worked with victims of domestic violence and rape. In the mid-1990s, encouraged by the Oslo Accords, he returned to Israel to contribute to reconciliation between Israelis and Palestinians. "I thought if we were to have peace, we needed to materialize it," he said. "So I came with the intention of getting involved with Palestinians and helping them to heal their wounds."

By 1997 Berger was, as he put it, "in the PLO (Palestine Liberation Organization) system." He had approached leaders of the Arab-run Al Quds University to help develop a trauma center, and they had accepted. Berger was soon commuting to the university's campuses in Abu Dis, on the edge of Jerusalem, and in Ramallah, the West Bank headquarters town of the Palestinian Authority. He was the only full-time Jewish professor on the faculty. In 1999 he and Al Quds psychologist Eyad Hallaq started a two-year study on school-based violence among Palestinians.

The Palestinians had no professionals in the mental health field, Berger said, and he wrote a mental health program for them. "Really bizarre," he chuckled, "an Israeli designing most of the first mental health program for the Palestinians. Come on." And then, he said with sudden gravity, the intifada started. "After September 2000, they let me know that if I wanted to remain alive, I'd better stop coming to the university. They could not assure my security." He has not been back since, though he remains in e-mail contact with a few former Palestinian colleagues.

Even while employed at Al Quds, in 1999 he was approached by Natal to develop stress management workshops in Israeli communities. For a brief period, until the intifada began, he was working simultaneously to reduce stress in both the Israeli and Palestinian populations. Then, after the intifada began and his ties to Al Quds ended, increased Israeli needs claimed more of his time. The police asked Natal to help Israeli front-line responders who were showing increased stress. Thus did the organization, and Berger, become counselors to ZAKA.

Berger has never been at the scene of a terrorist bombing, but he has lived the experience vicariously through clients from ZAKA, the police, and other responders. He reflected on the odd coping mechanisms that people develop. A young mother told him that if a terrorist came into her house, she planned to hide one of her children in her washing machine. Berger considered the notion irrational but kept silent. "In terms of helping her cope, the plan was helpful to her, so I would not criticize it." His own manner of dealing with the stress was to come home and hug his children and his wife. "If they're not home," he said, "I hug my dog." Some of Berger's colleagues have less benign ways of contending with the increased tension. He mentioned a medical professional who, after a day of dealing with victims of terrorism, heads for the refrigerator and gorges himself—and later vomits it all up. Berger interpreted this reaction as a symbolic riddance of a terribly distasteful experience, a cleansing ritual.

Whether the bulimic behavior was a consequence of interaction with victims or of other underlying causes can only be conjectured. Still, few therapists doubt that the wave of terrorism has taken a toll on victims and their caregivers, and to some extent on the entire society. In 2002, psychologist Danny Brom left Israel for a brief visit to the Netherlands. When he landed in Amsterdam, he was surprised to find that "the constant buzz that I was used to hearing had disappeared." The noise, he explained, was not a literal sound but a metaphor for the stress that had become endemic in Israeli society.

* * *

For Yehuda Hiss's institute, the repeated suicide bombings created a particular type of stress. Dr. Hiss has directed Israel's National Center of Forensic Medicine since 1988. Located in Tel Aviv, it is the country's lone forensic center, where medical knowledge is used to solve criminal and other legal problems. As with such institutions elsewhere, the Israeli center assesses the human remains of homicide, suicide, traffic accidents, drowning, and other unusual or suspicious causes of death. Techniques range from autopsies and DNA tests to analyzing dental records and fingerprints.

The center is also a principal forensic location for fallen soldiers. Thus, in wartime the workload surges as analysts seek to identify the bodies and body parts of military victims. But Israel's wars against its neighbors have been brief—six days in the 1967 conflict against Egypt, Syria, and Jordan; a few weeks of intense fighting in both the 1973 Yom Kippur War against Egypt and Syria, and in the 1982 battle against the Palestine Liberation Organization in Lebanon. In contrast, the terror attacks that began in 2000 produced a stream of casualties for more than five years.

In May 2005, Dr. Hiss, 59, lean and white-bearded, reflected on the effects of these new conditions on him and his staff. "For days on end, the media would bring the faces and the stories of the victims to the public," he said ruefully. The exposure brought greater attention to the work of his institute. In the past, the forensic specialists rarely spoke with the next of kin. "Now, with suicide bombings, families come to us and demand detailed explanations of what happened." They were often impatient and angry, as the staff struggled against a mounting backlog of body parts. "This was a new stress for the center," Dr. Hiss said, while maintaining that his own psyche remained intact. "As soon as I leave the premises, I really don't think about it," he said. "I keep myself busy, and I never discuss my work with my family," he told a newspaper reporter.[1]

Another leading member of the center, Tippi Kahane, 46, had a different take. She holds a Ph.D. in forensic anthropology and has worked at the forensic center since 1990. Her expertise is in assessing the skeletal and decomposed remains of victims. In the past, she and her colleagues worked with scientific dispassion. "We were tough," she said. But that changed with the rash of suicide bombings. "As victims were brought to the center, their cell phones kept ringing from family members: 'Where are you?' the callers asked." Kahane's voice nearly broke as she recalled that in 2002 this seemed to be happening almost every day. "Everybody felt, 'This is just too much to take,'" she said.

Yet she and the others at the center persevered. Whether denying that the bombings affected them emotionally, as did Dr. Hiss, or acknowledging a profound affect, as did Dr. Kahane, they stuck to their tasks. Still, as past experience suggested, there could be a breaking point for everyone, including medical examiners.

* * *

A conference titled "Tracking Terrorism in the 21st Century" was held in October 2004 at Duquesne University in Pittsburgh. Among the participants were three of America's best-known forensic scientists: Michael Baden, Henry Lee, and Cyril Wecht. For more than forty years their work included investigations of high-profile cases such as the deaths of John F. Kennedy, Martin Luther King Jr., Elvis Presley, and Vincent Foster. More recently, Baden and Lee had testified in the O. J. Simpson trial, and Wecht was a media consultant for the O. J. Simpson and JonBenet Ramsey cases. Their presentations at the conference dealt with their approaches to forensic medicine, though little of their work had involved terrorism.

In contrast, another medical examiner at the conference had long experience with terror victims. Dr. Maurice Rogev was the director of Israel's forensic center until 1988, when he was succeeded by Yehuda Hiss. Rogev had been invited to the conference by one of its sponsors, Cyril Wecht. Rogev, 77, and Wecht, 74, were longtime colleagues. But unlike Wecht, who was still the coroner of Pennsylvania's Allegheny County and routinely conducting autopsies,

Rogev had not touched any human remains in fifteen years. Rogev's lecture to the two hundred attendees was on "The Potential Use of Biological Extracts by Terrorists." He discussed plants and animals that generate poison—the caster bean, which is the source of the toxin ricin; the rattlesnake, lionfish, and poison arrow frog, all of which produce venom. But he said nothing about his role as a leading medical examiner in Israel. After his presentation, I asked Rogev if he would tell me about his experiences.

We moved to a small room down the corridor and sat across from each other. His South African accent indicated his country of origin and where he had trained in medicine and forensic science. Rogev had done autopsies on victims of unusual cruelty as far back as 1960, when, under sponsorship of the British government, he was posted to Kenya. Before Kenya gained independence in 1963, Mau Mau insurrectionists had hacked to death hundreds of whites and blacks. The bodies were in ghastly condition, Rogev recalled, "but emotionally, I remained disconnected." After independence, he served in Kenya's ministry of health as director of its medical research laboratories.

A decade later, encouraged by an uncle who was a scientist in Israel, Rogev immigrated there. In 1978 he joined the Israel Defense Forces as chief forensic officer and later received a simultaneous appointment to direct the national forensic center in Tel Aviv. "Then," he said cryptically, "it all caught up with me in 1989." Rogev peered through his thick-rimmed glasses and hunched forward. Silence. "I broke down, actually," he finally said. "I had a reaction to the large numbers of dead bodies I was examining."

In 1982, in the wake of Palestinian attacks from bases in Lebanon, Israeli troops invaded the country. After forcing the Palestine Liberation Organization to leave, the Israelis stayed in southern Lebanon in hopes of maintaining a buffer zone. But assaults against the remaining soldiers, principally by Hezbollah militants, took a continuing toll. By the time Israel withdrew completely in 2000, around nine hundred Israeli soldiers had been killed in Lebanon. Israeli citizens had increasingly questioned the value of keeping a military presence on Lebanese soil, and some analysts likened Israel's departure to America's from Vietnam.[2]

Long before Israel's withdrawal, the mounting casualties were having an effect on Maurice Rogev. "It was the numbers who were dead, but even more, the seriously wounded," he recounted. "Extracting bullets, seeing so many men wounded and blinded, it got to me." Rogev spoke his wrenching words with measured cadence. "I was having nightmares," he continued. "I would see an infinite number of bodies—no faces, just bodies and bodies. It would wake me up in a state of terror."

He received psychotherapy but knew he could never return to work on human remains. Since 1990, Dr. Rogev's forensic evaluations have been limited to reviewing reports and testifying at trials. I asked if he had difficulty with the media's recent coverage of terror incidents and their numerous victims. "I don't watch the news, even now," he answered.

* * *

Before the establishment of the state of Israel, as after, terrorist attacks against Jews in that area occurred with regularity. During some periods, stress among the citizenry became a norm. Still, Israelis always made room in their lives for the pleasures, sorrows, and routines that people around the world think of as normal. Only for a few, like Dr. Rogev, did the stress become too much to bear.

The eruption of nonstop terrorism after September 2000 prompted the Israeli government to employ extraordinary means to protect its citizens. Some, such as the building of a separation barrier between Israelis and Palestinians and the assassination of leaders of terrorist organizations, are controversial. Meanwhile, the rash of attacks has created a remarkable, if joyless, base of knowledge about rescue, response, and care of victims. This knowledge has given rise to a new field: terror medicine.

7

Terror, Medicine, and Security

In 2002 an Israeli medical journal reported a novel finding. A 31-year-old woman, a survivor of a terrorist attack, had suffered a combination of injuries increasingly being seen among recent victims of suicide bombings—multiple skin lacerations, severe burns, fractures, and damaged eardrums. CT scans also revealed bone fragments in her chest, groin, arms, and legs. But further assessment revealed that the bone was not hers; they were pieces from the bomber. Israeli doctors were coming to understand that suicide terrorism had expanded the scope of blast injury. Besides nails and bolts packed with the explosives, a bomber's bone could also act as flying shrapnel.

In this case, the embedded fragments signaled an additional concern. Laboratory tests revealed that they were positive for Hepatitis B, the first reported instance of flying bone acting as a vector for an infectious agent. The article described the finding as a "novel and gruesome way of disseminating infectious disease."[1]

As a result, the Israel Ministry of Health ordered that every injured patient in suicide attacks receive vaccinations against Hepatitis B. The experience had introduced a new dimension to the threat of bioterrorism.

In the next three years, Israeli physicians began to recognize more medical phenomena distinctly associated with terror attacks. The range of syndromes and responses prompted Dr. Shmuel Shapira, the deputy director of the Hadassah Medical Center in Jerusalem, to describe them as "terror medicine." Shapira's responsibilities included overseeing his hospitals' preparedness and responses to terror attacks. His burgeoning expertise was reflected in the numerous articles he wrote about injuries to victims and hospital management of terror attacks.

In May of 2005, I was part of a twelve-member delegation of Americans hosted by Dr. Shapira that met with Israeli experts on the subject of terror medicine and domestic security. For nearly a week, we heard from Israeli professionals who described their years of experience. The proceedings began with an overview by Dr. Meir Oren, director of the Hillel Yaffe Hospital. Located in Hadera, north of Tel Aviv, this hospital had received hundreds of victims during the intifada. In fact, the patient with the hepatitis-infected bone fragments was treated there, and Oren was a coauthor of the article about her case. Besides his Israeli medical training, Oren holds a degree in public health from Johns Hopkins University. A former director of Israel's Ministry of Health, he has written and spoken frequently about the challenges of terrorism.

Oren began his remarks with a review of the modes of recent terrorism. Airline hijackings in the 1960s gave way in later decades to car bombings and then to suicide bombings. Only through readiness and international cooperation, he emphasized, can terrorism be curbed. Accordingly, he was troubled to note that the United States lagged in preparedness and response capabilities. Oren was polite but unflinching. The sessions ahead offered plenty of opportunity to hear out Israelis on terror medicine and security, on incident management and the psychological effects of an attack.

Dr. Shapira's presentation to the group reached to the core of the subject. Terror medicine, he said, encompassed different mechanisms of injury and distinctive psychological effects. His conviction was informed by five years of experience with the intifada. Shapira's baritone resonated as he stated that around 2,500 of the 7,500 Israelis wounded in terror attacks since September 2000 had been treated at the two Hadassah hospitals in Jerusalem. His position as Hadassah's lead overseer of terrorism preparedness lent authority to his words.

In the next days, some of the Americans also made presentations. Dr. Pete Estacio explained the multibillion-dollar BioWatch program that he oversaw at the U.S. Department of Homeland Security. Dr. Nancy Connell reviewed the activities of the biodefense center that she directs at the University of Medicine and Dentistry in Newark, New Jersey. Dr. Clifton Lacy, president of the Robert Wood Johnson University Hospital in New Brunswick, described the intrastate communication system that he implemented when he was the New Jersey Commissioner of Health. I spoke about the anthrax letters that released lethal bacteria in the U.S. postal system soon after 9/11.

But the bulk of presentations came from Israelis whose expertise had been sharpened by the recent nonstop terrorism. In the first five years of the intifada, Palestinians had launched some four thousand attacks against Israelis. Most were thwarted, but those that were not killed some 1,100 Israelis. The murder weapons ranged from bombs and mortars to knives and stones. Although suicide attacks during this period comprised only 0.4 percent of all assaults, they were associated with 47 percent of all deaths from assault.[2]

These statistics were the beginning of the delegation's understanding that when viewed as a whole, the medical aspects of terrorism were unique. The distinctive qualities of terror medicine lie in four broad areas: preparedness, incident management, mechanisms of injuries and responses, and psychological consequences.[3]

* * *

Preparedness ranges from the development of standard operating procedures to the stockpiling of supplies at accessible locations. These stored materials should match the needs of casualties not only from explosives but from other potential weapons, including biological, chemical, and radiological agents. They include antibiotics to treat threat agents like anthrax and plague, antidotes for sarin or soman nerve agents, and potassium iodide to block the effects of certain radiation. Like Israel, the United States is well positioned in this regard. Its National Pharmaceutical Stockpile includes 50-ton packets of medical materials stored at eight secret locations around the country. As happened within hours of the attacks on the World Trade Center, a packet was flown to the New York area to enhance local stockpiles.

Preparedness also requires the ability to handle surges in the number of casualties. The government of Israel mandates that on brief notice every hospital be able to handle at least 20 percent more emergencies than its usual capacity. Several Israeli hospitals developed backup plans that even exceed this minimal requirement. In 2005 a newly built Center for Emergency Medicine was opened at the larger Hadassah Hospital in Ein Kerem. In minutes, the emergency bed capacity can be doubled to more than one hundred. The center's 4-foot-thick cement walls can withstand massive explosive impact. Two sets of shatterproof glass for each window can confine indoor air to a recirculating ventilation system for more than a week. Other hospitals, including Tel Hashomer in Tel Aviv and the Western Galilee Hospital in Nahariya, have underground rooms with hundreds of empty beds and IV stands at the ready.

Finally, preparedness requires educating health care workers about conventional and non-conventional agents and their implications for medical management. The Israeli government mandates that all hospitals engage in frequent citywide and regional exercises that build on lessons from actual events. A practice drill may involve hundreds of simulated "casualties" from a variety of weapons. In the United States, in the absence of a federal mandate, hospital exercises are less frequent and often less comprehensive.

As Dr. Meir Oren concluded from his many visits to the United States, most U.S. hospitals lack the capacity to deal with a sizable terror event. He blamed the problem largely on the failure of the federal government to offer adequate direction. "In the United States, preparedness is bottom up rather than top down," he said.

"It is too much to ask hospitals to generate their own protocols, especially when dealing with unconventional agents."

A second defining area of terror medicine relates to *incident management.* In Israel, distinctive procedures begin when Emergency Medical System responders arrive at a scene and a pre-assigned triage commander assesses the condition of each victim.

Since the modus operandi is "scoop and run," only minimal treatment like maintenance of an airway and pressure to stop external bleeding is provided at the attack site. The most severely injured survivors are triaged to a "level 1 trauma center," a hospital with advanced equipment and special expertise in trauma therapy. The less seriously injured may be sent to level 2 or 3 trauma centers, with efforts made not to overload any single hospital. Israeli approaches now assure that ambulances begin to arrive at hospitals within twenty minutes after an attack.[4]

A second triage occurs at each hospital, where patients may arrive as often as one every 20 seconds. At the emergency area entrance, the designated surgeon-in-charge assesses each new arrival. Patients are triaged to one of three admission sites according to severity of injury: (1) severe and critical, (2) moderate, (3) mild.

When I met with Dr. Yoav Mintz, the Israeli surgeon, he had no doubt that the intifada had generated a different kind of medicine. The casualties were more severe than those from ordinary traumas like auto accidents, falls, or stabbings. Scores of victims might arrive at the hospital in a matter of minutes. Terror medicine, he said, prompted a different way of thinking. "You have to make the quick decision about who goes first to the operating room, who goes first for a CT scan, who will suffer less from having to wait." He reiterated the frequent consequences of a suicide bombing: blast injury to the lungs, exploded intestines, burns. "And then you have secondary blast injury from shrapnel—nails, screws, bolts. Maybe a hundred small holes in different areas."

Terrorists have also sought to exploit the medical system. Since the discovery in 2003 of arms and gunmen in some Palestinian ambulances, all ambulances, even if conveying critically injured victims, must pause for brief inspection at the perimeter of a hospital's grounds.[5]

Another ingredient of incident management is the Israeli system of radio and computer connections among hospitals, police, and the military. Inter-hospital communications have been essential to helping family members, separated after an attack, quickly learn of each other's locations.

The third area of terror medicine encompasses the *nature of injuries and manner of treatment.* The worldwide spate of attacks with explosives has signaled the need for physicians and other health care providers to become familiar with the effects of blast devices. These effects fall into four categories. Primary blast injuries arise from a sudden increase or decrease in air pressure that can rupture the eardrum, the intestine, and other organs. Secondary blast injuries include penetrating wounds from fragments and other uneven projectiles. Tertiary blast injuries arise from compression caused by the collapse of buildings and the hurling of victims or surrounding objects. The quaternary category covers all other injuries from blast, including burns, crush injuries, and damage from the inhalation of toxic particles.[6]

Accepted forms of treatment for each type of injury generally predated contemporary terrorism. But a close-quarter bombing generates a combination that is otherwise rarely seen in a single individual. A victim may at once suffer from a breathtaking assortment of injuries: penetration wounds from small projectiles that damage soft tissues, vital organs, bone, arteries, and nerves; blast effects on the lungs, the eardrum, and intestine; and severe burns.

This expansive list of injuries experienced by large numbers of victims prompted Israeli trauma surgeons to modify their response protocols. Dr. Mintz spoke of how the seemingly endless stream of shrapnel wounds changed standard operating procedures: "At the beginning we said, 'Oh, you know, they're only small holes. The patient has a spleen injury and that's much worse.' But you learn that it's wrong to consider the small wounds that way because while you're treating the bigger injury, they can cause a patient to bleed to death." Now, even if small wounds are not visibly bleeding, each one demands careful investigation to see if they have lacerated a deep blood vessel.

Dr. Anat Globerman had a similar reaction. Like her fellow surgeons, before the intifada she thought of trauma typically in terms of a stabbing or gunshot wound. A blood vessel might be severed or the intestine punctured. A road accident could result in more extensive wounds. But none of these generated the effects of a close-proximity bombing. Globerman was insistent: "I'm telling you that it's a different type of casualty when it's civilian terrorism coming from a bomber just across the street. The victims are very, very wounded." She also underscored the difference from wartime casualties who might receive early first aid but not reach a hospital until much later. Such common delay meant that desperately wounded soldiers often died before being seen by top-line surgeons. Now, victims of terror attacks in cities can be taken to first-class treatment centers in minutes.

Moreover, doctors were seeing these more severely wounded survivors in rapid succession. They had to make quick assessments of each individual's needs in the context of the needs of all the new arrivals. Now, multiple penetration wounds were simply packed to avoid excessive bleeding while patients were operated on for more serious injuries. But as Dr. Mintz stressed, patients who seemed stable were sometimes suffering from severe injury that was not initially obvious. Thus, repeated reassessments are warranted, which makes more likely the discovery of critical injuries not at first apparent.

Beyond injuries from explosives, terror medicine includes understanding and treating the effects of nonconventional agents. If recognized in time, infection from deliberately released bacterial agents can be treated with antibiotics. In the case of smallpox, vaccination may offer protection even if administered a few days after exposure to the virus. The Israeli experience also suggests interest by terrorists in delivering lethal combinations of conventional and nonconventional agents. Organizations such as Hamas and al-Fatah have sought to detonate explosives mixed with the anticoagulant rat poison warfarin, with AIDS-tainted blood, and with the chemical hydrogen cyanide.[7]

The fourth component of terror medicine involves the *psychological effects* of terror assaults. Terror incidents have been described as a new kind of traumatic event that combines features of criminal assaults, disasters, acts of war, homicide, and political violence. As manifested by survivors of the 9/11 jetliner attacks, the sense of rage, grief, and despair becomes compounded.[8] The Israeli experience has also shown that initial psychological reactions after a terror attack are more intense than those from other traumatic events like road accidents. Accordingly, early psychological intervention is essential. If not appropriately treated during the first six months after an incident, patients may suffer irreversible stress disorders.[9]

Hospital workers faced added stress from unanticipated consequences of terrorist attacks. Julie Benbenishty, a critical care nurse, recounted how the proliferation of cell phones in the past decade created a new kind of challenge. Upon word of a bombing, Israelis commonly call friends and family to seek assurance of each other's well-being. But cell phone communications in a hospital may be blocked if there is suspicion that an incoming call might detonate a bomb planted in the building.

Furthermore, the general system may become overloaded, and thus calls do not go through. "The worst thing about this," Julie said, "is you don't hear a busy signal." When the system is overextended, the caller just hears the line continue to ring. "You don't know if the signal is not reaching the person you're calling or if the call is going through but the person can't answer." Thus, worried caregivers might work long hours without assurance about the safety of their own family members.

The psychological aspects of terror medicine also encompass heightened emotional effects prompted by certain weapons. Biological weapons in particular can generate frightening reactions. People experiencing more common forms of attack, such as the bombing of a bus or building, tend to assess the immediate situation rationally.

But lethal bacteria and viruses might not produce symptoms for days or weeks after exposure. The extended period of uncertainty about whether a person is infected can be highly stressful.

The anthrax attacks in the United States in the fall of 2001 underscored the profound psychological effects that can be prompted by a bioattack. Perhaps a half-dozen letters containing spores of Bacillus anthracis had been mailed to government and media offices. As a result, twenty-two people became infected, five of whom died. After postal workers and others learned that they might have been exposed to anthrax, many became fearful and unable to work. Because of leakage from the letters, some 30,000 people were considered at risk of exposure and were treated with prophylactic antibiotics. But anxiety reached far beyond, as evidenced by the fact that people in all parts of the country became afraid to open mail. The particularly stressful effect of biological agents is attributable to their being invisible, odorless, potentially lethal, and hard to avoid and control.[10]

* * *

Every terrorism incident generates anxiety, and no amount of rehearsal can replicate the stress of a real event. Still, tension can be sensed even during a drill, as ambulance drivers, police, doctors, and other responders rush about in a scene of induced pressure. During their time in Israel, the members of the American delegation observed a citywide exercise. It was May 29, 2005, and military, law enforcement, and medical authorities knew that a mock attack would be launched in Jerusalem that afternoon. But they were not informed of its scope or the kind of weapons that would be used.

At 2 PM Hadassah Hospital received a call that an "attack" had just taken place in the city and that casualties would soon be arriving. The Americans joined other observers in the large courtyard outside the emergency entrance, while the hospital staff began to prepare for the influx of patients. Within minutes, scores of medical personnel appeared in the courtyard, some in facemasks, rubber boots, and protective outerwear. Lettering on brightly colored vests labeled each individual's role—doctors in red, nurses green, ambulance drivers orange, administrators purple. Decontamination experts and stretcher-bearers were also milling about.

In front of the emergency entrance, Dr. Shmuel Shapira shouted into his bullhorn that ambulances were nearing the hospital. Dr. Avi Rivkind, the chief trauma surgeon and the triage commander, paced restlessly about the stone driveway. Suddenly, a white ambulance emblazoned with a red Star of David appeared down the road. But 30 yards away it came to an abrupt halt. A guard there opened the ambulance doors, leaned inside to make sure that no terrorists or weapons were present, and waved the driver on.

As the driver pulled into the courtyard, hospital aides leaped to the rear door and wheeled out the victim, who was strapped to a gurney. She was a young woman in military uniform with prominent red stains on her face, arms, and bare feet. An accompanying card described her mock injuries. In seconds, Rivkind assessed her condition and directed that she be taken to the emergency department. Moments later two more ambulances arrived, this time with dummies rather than live victims. Three naked mannequins—two adults and one child—were shifted to metal stretchers next to the ambulances. Their descriptive cards indicated a spectrum of symptoms, including generalized pain and reddened skin. The victims evidently had been exposed to some sort of chemical during the attack. An emergency physician later evaluated the information and concluded that the chemical was an acid, a corrosive material. Dr. Shapira raised his bullhorn: "We've identified the toxic agent. It's hydrofluoric acid." Aides in full protective gear began to hose down the "contaminated" dummies with water, as called for by the protocols.

More victims (both live actors and dummies) continued to stream in during the next thirty minutes. They were triaged according to the injuries listed on a card that came with each individual. Some were required to undergo wash-downs, while others went directly to the emergency department, to an operating room, or to intensive care. Medical personnel then began to simulate care, taking x-rays, dressing wounds. By the time the drill ended, 68 victims had been treated at the hospital.

Later, about fifty of the hospital's senior staff convened to assess the performance. As they crowded around a long conference table, Shapira, at the head, invited comments. Dr. Rivkind spoke first. He noted that several ambulances blocked the thoroughfare, that more personnel should have had hands-free walkie-talkies, and that the drill was elementary. "It was too easy for us to figure out that there was a chemical attack," he contended. Dr. Yoav Mintz said that communication between the staff outside the hospital and inside was difficult, and he also called for more walkie-talkies.

Dr. Koby Assaf, head of the emergency department, said his department had difficulty taking care of so many casualties. Sending a patient for x-ray imaging meant losing personnel from his department, since they had to accompany the patient. "After awhile, we stopped having x-rays taken," he said. The new Center for Emergency Medicine had been completed two months earlier, and this was the first drill that included use of the facility. Dr. Esti Galili-Weisstub observed that for all its advantages, the new emergency department was farther from the outside entrance than the old one was. As the number of patients increased, she said, the hallway became jammed.

The critiques continued for an hour. In wrapping up, Shapira suggested that in a real event, the performance would probably have been better because "people would have more adrenalin flowing."

Soon after this debriefing, Shapira conducted another one, this time with army officials. During the exercise, military and government health authorities had been present to assess the hospital's response. An observer sent by the government indicated that the patient entry area was overly crowded, that too many staff members had been posted outside, and that there was unnecessary delay about which department a patient should be sent to.

These comments echoed those I had heard earlier from Danny Laor, the director of national emergency preparedness for the Health Ministry. In the midst of the drill, he was leaning against the wall in the emergency department, watching. He had previously spoken to the American delegation about the need for repeated education programs to maintain preparedness. When I asked how he thought this exercise was going, he shook his head. "Too much confusion," he answered. "There needs to be a single commander, which does not seem to be what's happening here."

To an untutored observer, the stream of unsparing criticisms might have signaled that the drill was unsuccessful. In fact, every stage, from triage to treatment, went quite smoothly. Perhaps to save time, few of the critics belabored the positive aspects. Only at the end, when Dr. Shapira summarized the assessments, did he indicate that despite the noted shortcomings, the general feeling from the military observers, as from the Hadassah staff, was that the drill went well.

American experts who witnessed the exercise were impressed. Drills in the United States were based on planning and training, Dr. Clifton Lacy said, but the Israeli practice sessions benefited from being "based on real life experience." Dr. Pete Estacio, who had planned and participated in many drills in the United States, felt the Israeli exercise was very effective. A product of "a great deal of preparedness and experience," he said.[11]

Dr. Jeffrey Hammond agreed with some of the self-criticism he heard from the Israelis and wondered whether the response at the hospital could not have been better organized. But after some contemplation, he said, "You know, that's okay. Because it works for them."

* * *

Throughout the week in Israel, members of the delegation were considering which Israeli practices might be applicable to the United States and which not. The question reached beyond terror medicine to that of security, the other key subject on our agenda. In this regard, some Israelis questioned the wisdom of practices they had seen in the United States. Dr. Meir Oren, head of Hillel Yaffe Hospital, recalled witnessing an elderly wheelchair-bound woman in an

American airport undergoing a pat down. As the inspector's hands moved to sensitive areas, the woman became distressed. "Unnecessary," Oren said about the procedure. Unless there was reason for suspicion, a careful interview would have been more valuable, which is how the Israelis do it. Other Israelis wondered why passengers at American airports were checked randomly, while passengers who fit the profile of most terrorists go unchecked.

The American visitors listened with respect, though they were largely unfazed by such questions. Major John Hunt of the New Jersey State Police, who was deputy director of the New Jersey office of emergency management, was asked about profiling by a reporter. He responded that Americans had come to believe that singling out a person based on race or ethnicity violated his constitutional rights. But he acknowledged that the inability to profile "makes our job more challenging."[12]

Like Hunt, Dr. Pete Estacio of Homeland Security was convinced that Americans largely accept the current manner of screening at U.S. airports. His work on preparedness and security in the United States positioned him to be especially sensitive to both matters. But ironically, Estacio, of all people, was singled out toward the end of our trip for an unexpected lesson about Israeli scrutiny.

As our luggage passed through the x-ray detector, I stood chatting about the past week with Pedro Luis "Pete" Estacio. We were checking in at Ben-Gurion for our return flight to the United States. Like the rest of us, Estacio had just been asked a series of questions by airport inspectors: "What was the purpose of your trip?" "Where did you stay?" "For how long?" But after Pete's suitcase emerged from the machine, one of the inspectors, a trim young woman, approached him. "Please come with me." A curious smile formed beneath Pete's gray mustache. The son of Spanish immigrants to the United States, he had grown up near San Francisco. At 60, he bore a statesman's reserve.

Estacio's American passport carried stamps from countries in Africa, Asia, and Europe. Now, at the end of his first trip to Israel, was he being profiled for special scrutiny? The inspector ferried his baggage to a metal table.

Estacio followed the inspector, as did I and another member of our group, Leonard Posnock, co-chairman of the New Jersey-Israel Commission. The commission, part of the state's Department of Commerce, had helped organize the delegation. The inspector hoisted Estacio's luggage onto the table and asked him to open the larger piece. As her latex-gloved hands slid between the neatly folded layers of clothing, she continued to pepper him with questions: "Where were you born?" "Where did you grow up?" "What places did you visit while you were in Israel?" She rubbed a wand along the suitcase frame and delivered its cloth tip to a chemical sensor machine 30 feet away. She made a notation, and returned to the table.

"Now, please open the briefcase." Estacio snapped the latches and revealed an odd-looking computer amid a tangle of wires and accessories. The inspector asked him to place the contents on the table and turn on the computer. "What is this?" she asked, about the large detachable glass screen.

"That's the writing tablet," Pete answered. The computer could convert longhand into print letters. The design was evidently not in her database.

"And this?" she asked about a box the size of a wallet.

"A back-up for more computer memory," he said. The young woman slowly rotated each item. She rubbed the surfaces with the wand and, as before, delivered the cloth to the chemical sensor. When she came back she announced, "I'm sorry, we'll have to check further."

Pete's lips tightened, his first hint of irritation. The inspector glanced at the stack of business cards next to his computer accessories. "How did you get this one?" she asked with a half-smile. It read: Zeev Sarig, Managing Director, Ben-Gurion International Airport. Before Pete could answer, I interjected that Sarig had briefed us the day before. We were part of a delegation that included terrorism and security experts and had met with Israeli counterparts during the past week. The previous day, we had been treated to a security tour of the airport, including a demonstration of chemical sensors like the one used to assess Estacio's luggage.

In fact, Estacio was a lead official in the U.S. Department of Homeland Security. A physician and research chemist, he had previously helped develop methods of detecting biological and chemical agents. At the new department, created after 9/11, he was overseeing the nation's BioWatch program, a $6 billion initiative begun in 2002, to improve biosensor and surveillance techniques.

Slightly flustered, the young inspector simply said, "Excuse me, I'll be right back." She returned with her supervisor, who apologized for the inconvenience but insisted that Estacio's luggage required more testing. The supervisor then wheeled his bags down the corridor behind a curtain.

Pete Estacio, soft-spoken and laid back, had for days been immersed in the subject of our trip: Terror Medicine and Domestic Security. Now he seemed bemused. "This is silly," he whispered as we waited for the inspectors to return. He surmised that his unfamiliar computer raised the inspector's interest and that the chemical detector must have picked up a reading for nitrite or nitrate. Explosives are often based on compounds like amyl nitrite or ammonium nitrate. Airport detection devices are designed to sense them as well as other chemical agents.

He guessed that the cloth on the inspector's wand was probably used in previous inspections. The more often used, the greater the likelihood of a false positive reading. This is especially true if the sensor apparatus is calibrated very finely. In that case, benign items like shoe polish, inhalants, or even video head cleaners, which contain trace amounts of nitrite, might set off an alarm. Estacio's knowledge in this area was an extension of his expertise in both occupational medicine and biosecurity.

Eventually the inspector returned with the luggage. "Well, it's okay," she said with a big smile. "I'm really sorry, but. . . . " Estacio interrupted, "No problem." He grinned and said he understood the need for thoroughness. In fact, he had just lived out a generalization he had made three years earlier while being honored as a distinguished alumnus by the Center for Occupational and Environmental Health at the University of California. On that occasion, Estacio spoke of the need to consider chemical, biological, and radiological detection to be just as important—and as normal in everyday life—as fire alarms. "There will be false alarms," he said, "but the occasional false alarm is the price we pay for safety."[13]

As he boarded the plane for his return to the United States, Estacio reflected on the past week's experiences and his new appreciation for terror medicine and Israeli screening for security. But he knew his most poignant last-day memory would be of the young inspector's expression when she came upon the airport director's business card. "When she saw that card, her eyes almost fell out of her head," he chuckled.

* * *

At the outset of the 2005 meetings in Israel, some members of the American delegation wondered whether terror medicine was a truly distinctive field. Initially, Pete Estacio questioned whether trauma from terror was much different from other trauma. But after learning more about the Israeli experience, its approaches to readiness and response, he became convinced that it was.

Dr. Jeffrey Hammond, chief of trauma surgery at Robert Wood Johnson University Hospital, similarly, before visiting Israel thought of blast injury, surgical care, and psychological responses as forms of disaster medicine regardless of whether the cause was terrorism. But during the presentations he began to think differently, especially about the psychological effects. "And not just the psychological aspects of taking care of victims, but also taking care of the staff," he said. Several Israeli caregivers emphasized that they personally knew victims who had worked at their hospital.

Hammond also thought about organizational differences required for terrorist events and other types of mass casualty incidents. "It's one thing to prepare your facility for a natural catastrophe, and quite another to harden it against terrorism," he said. He mentioned the blast-resistant walls in some hospital facilities, their protective ventilating systems, the outer ring at which ambulances must stop for inspection before proceeding to the emergency department. It was clear that the threat of terrorism had prompted new ways of thinking about preparedness and security.

What Estacio, Hammond, and others on our trip had begun to absorb was already well understood in Israel: coping with terrorism was different from coping with other forms of trauma. Although aspects of terror medicine overlap with emergency and disaster medicine, several characteristics are distinctive. Those core areas have been discussed here—preparedness, management, nature of injuries, psychological effects. But other features are also relevant, such as the intentionality behind an attack, the threat to health care providers, the need for new approaches to security. Thus, terror medicine integrates medical management with knowledge about the spectrum and pattern of injuries to terror victims. It serves as a basis for developing curricula and standard operating procedures toward prevention, treatment, and rehabilitation of both individuals and communities.

During the American delegation's meetings with the Israelis in 2005, Dr. Shapira and Dr. Lacy signed an agreement between their two institutions to establish an International Center for Terror Medicine (ICTM). The purpose of the ICTM, under Shapira's directorship, would include the dissemination of information on best practices for caring for victims of terrorism and other mass casualty events. The vision for the center included a host of initiatives. One was to share lecturers and clinicians regularly between the two countries. Another was to establish a repository of medical information on terror victims in order to enhance knowledge about treatment and recovery. A third was to create a videoconferencing capability to enable real-time information exchange between countries during an actual or simulated attack.

Whether terror medicine is treated as a stand-alone discipline or part of a larger enterprise, like public health, seems less important than that its parameters be understood and taught.

8

American Rehearsal

Nearly two months before the meetings in Israel on terror medicine and domestic security, several members of the American delegation had been engaged in a weeklong drama. It began on Monday, April 4, 2005. On that day, Pete Estacio, Nancy Connell, and I sat in a large conference room packed with people riveted to a television screen. A VNN newscaster was reporting that police had traced an abandoned sports utility vehicle in Union, New Jersey, to a team of terrorists. A commercial sprayer inside the vehicle apparently had been used to release plague bacteria. Meanwhile, hundreds of people with flu-like symptoms were showing up at hospitals in Middlesex and Union counties. Hospital authorities, the newscaster said, had confirmed that the newly admitted patients were infected with pneumonic plague.

A dreaded killer through much of human history, the plague wiped out one-third of the population of Europe in the mid-fourteenth century. The disease, which is caused by the bacterium Yersinia pestis, may be transmitted by fleas from infected rats or by infected humans. With advances in public health, the plague largely disappeared from developed societies. Perhaps half-a-dozen cases a year are recorded in the United States, almost all in the Southwest, resulting from contact with an infected rodent.

The observers of the newscast were in the Sheraton Hotel in Iselin, a central New Jersey town. One floor below the conference room, the hotel ballroom had been transformed into a control center. Hundreds of government officials were tapping on laptops perched on long rows of tables covered with maroon cloth. They were monitoring the unfolding event and communicating with police, hospitals, and other agencies around the state. Meanwhile, VNN continued its somber minute-by-minute reports. By the end of the day, the number of cases had grown to more than one thousand and the state's borders had been closed.

The next day, as the toll continued to climb, VNN reporters spoke gravely of a population under bioattack. At the request of New Jersey health officials, ten million doses of doxicycline, an antibiotic used against plague, had been shipped from one of the national emergency supply stockpiles for distribution to state residents.

New Jersey's acting governor, Richard Codey, appeared on camera, as did other state officials, to urge residents to obtain the antibiotic without delay. They explained that although the disease could be deadly, taking the medication soon after exposure to the bacterium could offer protection. The network announced that designated community centers and other locations were providing free antibiotics along with medical screening and counseling. These sites were called PODs (Points of Dispensing).

Meanwhile, victims and the "worried well" continued to pour into area hospitals. To accommodate them, beds were squeezed into emergency areas and hallways. The overflow at Union Hospital required shifting one hundred patients to the nearby Elks Lodge. At Robert Wood Johnson University Hospital (RWJ) in New Brunswick, two hundred extra beds were rolled into the hospital's decorative atrium. Doctors and nurses in masks and protective outerwear moved through the makeshift area, quickly tending to one patient after another. Initially, the staff seemed to be coping with the usual load of patients along with the large emergency influx. But in a conference room that had been converted into the hospital's command center, the sense of urgency was palpable. Two dozen administrators and security officers were on their telephones, tapping computer keys, announcing updates. "Eleven more people just admitted to the emergency department," one voice announced. Another reported a bulletin out of the state's capital: "Trenton repeats that the state's borders will remain closed."

In the following few days, RWJ joined other hospitals in a national disaster medical plan to free up beds by shipping uninfected, moderately ill patients out of state. From Holy Name Hospital in the north to Riverview Medical Center near the New Jersey shore, patients were transported to Newark airport and flown to Dallas, where they were triaged to local hospitals.

In the midst of the siege in New Jersey, VNN reported that mustard gas, a chemical poison, had been released in New London, Connecticut. Federal and state officials continued to appear on camera, assuring viewers that the events in New Jersey and Connecticut were being addressed. On Wednesday, the Secretary of Homeland Security, Michael Chertoff, flew to New Jersey and, with Governor Codey, toured several PODs and hospitals.

By the end of the week, the medical system in New Jersey seemed overwhelmed. Since the outbreak began, the number of plague victims had more than doubled each day. On Friday, April 8, the cumulative total had grown to 38,000. Eight thousand of them were dead and more were dying. Although most of the infected victims were located in the central part of the state, cases had been reported by hospitals throughout the state, from all twenty-one counties.

The next day the siege abruptly ended. No more deaths, no more illnesses. VNN, the virtual news network, was no longer broadcasting. In fact, VNN had existed only for a week, airing on a closed circuit to an audience of participants and observers of the largest anti-terror drill in American history. Titled TOPOFF 3, it was the first statewide mock attack sponsored by the U.S. Department of

Homeland Security. The exercise was part of a series mandated by Congress after 9/11 to simulate terrorist attacks involving biological, chemical, or radiological weapons. Two previous "topoffs" (an acronym for top officials) were more limited. They had been conducted in Seattle, Chicago, and a few other cities for shorter periods. Unlike the earlier drills, TOPOFF 3 was intended as a mass casualty event that would, as Secretary Chertoff said, stress the system to the breaking point. The scenario had been planned for two years and cost $21 million. Aside from the mock victims, the 10,000 participants included officials from the military, intelligence, law enforcement, fire, rescue, and medical services—virtually everyone who would be involved in a real attack.

After the exercise, Homeland Security officials said that a full evaluation would take months and that vulnerabilities would be addressed as they were discovered. Some findings would not be made public because "obviously, there's information in there that is sensitive."[1] But, several problems were already obvious. Even before the drill ended, emergency departments were complaining of fatigued staffs and shortages of biohazard suits and antibiotics.[2] In the following weeks, impressions continued to surface in advance of an official critique.

During the five-day event, federal and state officials briefed terrorism analysts and health and law enforcement experts who had been invited to observe. In addition to receiving updates at the control center, the observers were taken to PODs and hospitals as the exercise unfolded. One dispensing center was in a gymnasium at Rutgers University in New Brunswick. Beneath the school's long red and white banners, aides offered fake medicine, advice, and screenings to lines of recruited students, some feigning nervousness. (A side table full of doughnuts and hot coffee seemed an incongruous diversion during this ostensible crisis.)

At the nearby RWJ Hospital, the usual routines were maintained for truly ill patients even as hundreds of bioterrorism "victims" were being admitted. As in hospitals elsewhere in the state, notices were circulated to inform visitors that the heightened security during that week was part of a drill. I toured several hospitals on April 6, in the midst of the exercise, where some personnel were engaged with the drill along with their usual responsibilities. There was less commotion and less tension than at the Hadassah Hospital drill that we would witness the following month during our visit to Israel. Unlike at Hadassah, at the New Jersey hospitals no large gathering of staff and responders stood at entrances and in hallways, no rush of patients from ambulances.

Of course, the nature of the terror attack in Israel was different from the one in New Jersey. In Israel, a mock blast and chemical release resulted in an intense though short-lived period when victims poured into the hospital. Acute injuries needed to be identified and decisions rapidly made about imaging, surgery, bleeding, and burns. But in New Jersey, the biological attack generated a continuous stream of debilitated people with like symptoms. Their care was largely uniform—antibiotics, fluids, bed rest, and monitoring.

The difference in emotional intensity of the workers at the two locations may also have been affected by past experience. For the Americans, the experience was theoretical, an exercise about what *might* happen. Light-hearted asides by responders and other participants were not unusual. Several officials, including New Jersey's attorney general, Peter Harvey, wondered if people would act as rationally in a real attack as they did in the exercise. These observers underscored the absence of the fear factor in the simulated event.[3] For the Israelis, their drill simulated bloody events they had repeatedly experienced and would likely encounter again. Everyone there was dead serious.

Observers of TOPOFF 3 from the school of public health at New Jersey's University of Medicine and Dentistry in Newark concluded that the overall effort was successful, though flawed. They questioned, for example, whether the public had been adequately encouraged to visit the PODs. They found some sites disorganized and recipients given inappropriate amounts of (mock) medication. But they were most concerned about lapses in communication. State officials were slow to share with federal authorities information about body counts, key officials were unaware of the number of operating PODs, and cell phone communications were hampered by defective equipment.[4]

In November 2005, the Inspector General of the Department of Homeland Security issued a 78-page review of the TOPOFF 3 exercise. The report claimed that the overall goal of testing preparedness had been met but that better coordination was needed. Its recommendations included developing better "procedures to define roles" and better "systems to track and share information more openly and efficiently."[5]

One of the federal officials who had briefed the invited observers during the exercise was Homeland Security's Pete Estacio. He too had helped plan the attack and later review its effectiveness. When I spoke to Estacio six months after the exercise, he emphasized that the problems with it largely centered on poor communication. "When information was shared," he said, "often it was not timely or not interpreted properly by the people receiving it." The result of such miscommunication is that people make bad decisions. This problem was magnified again in August, he noted, with the nation's poor response to Hurricane Katrina. These difficulties are unlikely to be resolved any time soon.

The obstacles are twofold. First, bureaucracies are sluggish. Agency practices are grounded in habit and slow to react to emergent needs. A second difficulty lies with an agency's propensity to maximize its influence. This often leads to competition rather than cooperation among bureaucratic departments. An agency's leadership may hold back information from others to protect the prominence of its own role, even at the expense of the common good.

In reviewing the response by New York City agencies to the attack on the World Trade Center, the 9/11 Commission noted confusion about which agency was in charge. Effectiveness was impeded because the fire department and the police department "each considered itself operationally autonomous."[6] After Mayor Michael Bloomberg determined in 2005 that the police would have primary responsibility at the site of a biological or chemical attack, the leaders of the fire department were furious. They claimed that the new directive "jeopardizes public safety." Their rationale was that firefighters had greater expertise in handling hazardous materials and therefore should be lead commanders during such events.[7] But many observers considered their disagreement just a continuation of the "battle of the badges." Interagency conflict, in fact, is endemic in all levels of government.

* * *

The decision by the Homeland Security Department to hold the nation's first statewide terrorist exercise in New Jersey seemed especially appropriate. The state had been deeply affected by the attack on the World Trade Center and later by the release of anthrax into the U.S. postal system. Around seven hundred of the 2,752 people who were killed at the World Trade Center lived in New Jersey. Soon after the attack, New Jersey law enforcement officials and medics were brought over to assist at ground zero, and several New Jersey hospitals had been enlisted to treat survivors.

In subsequent weeks, when anthrax spores were sent through the mail, New Jersey was again very much involved. Between September and November, bacteria that had leaked from envelopes contaminated postal facilities, offices, and buildings from Florida to Connecticut. Four of the poison letters were eventually found, and all were postmarked "Trenton, NJ," which meant they had been mailed in the Trenton-Princeton area. Of the twenty-two people who became infected during that period, six lived or worked in New Jersey. (All the New Jersey victims survived, though five of the others did not.)

The state is also seen as an inviting target for future terror attacks. The five-mile corridor between Newark and Elizabeth is dotted with oil tanks. At the nearby seaports, nearly 80,000 tons of cargo arrives every day in massive containers, few of which undergo inspection. Two miles from the ports, Newark International Airport services more than a thousand daily flights. Moments before landing, a plane may pass over several of the state's 140 chemical plants.

A large-scale release of chlorine gas from one of the plants could endanger 12 million people in the New Jersey-New York area. All these circumstances prompted the *New York Times* in 2005 to muse that this stretch of land might be the most terror-vulnerable area in America.[8]

Thus, based on its location, past experience, and commercial and communications networks, New Jersey is more attuned to the threat of terrorism than many other parts of the United States. Indeed, when the federal government invited applications from the states to serve as venues for the TOPOFF 3 exercise, New Jersey was only one of eight to respond. Accepting the designation meant that the state would allocate more than $2 million dollars to the effort along with thousands of man-hours. And in fact, preparedness in New Jersey has progressed further than in many other states.

For example, Trust for America's Health, a nonprofit organization, issued a report at the end of 2005 on public health readiness to deal with disasters and terrorism. The report concluded that despite improvements since 9/11, national preparedness remained inadequate. The findings were based on a state-by-state evaluation of ten indicators that ranged from "enough lab scientists to test for anthrax or plague" to having an "adequate disease tracking system." New Jersey was among only eight states to receive a positive assessment on at least seven indicators.[9]

Also, a survey released in 2006 by the American College of Emergency Physicians recognized New Jersey's unique provision for helicopter transportation of trauma patients. The organization graded the state A+ for attention to patient safety, including its training programs for disasters and for biological and chemical attacks. (The state received lower grades in a few other areas; for example, for having too few board-certified emergency physicians.)[10]

Thus, in the matter of preparedness for terrorism, New Jersey can serve as a useful reference. Its leaders, more than in many other states, are sensitive to the threat and have made large investments toward protection and hospital responses. But is that enough? One indicator would be to match its level of preparedness against that in Israel.

Of course, no responders in New Jersey or elsewhere in the United States have endured anything like the flood of attacks experienced by their counterparts in Israel. Nor do American medical facilities engage in as many practice alerts or drills as do the Israelis. Some U.S. locations lack essential requirements for preparedness. The shortcomings range from inability to handle a large influx of victims to inadequate systems of communication between hospitals and law enforcement authorities. Still, a number of Americans, including New Jerseyans, have sought to strengthen domestic preparedness. None have been more dedicated to the effort than the leadership of the Robert Wood Johnson University Hospital.

* * *

In 1986, the century-old county hospital in New Brunswick, New Jersey, was named after its main longtime benefactor, Robert Wood Johnson. With an infusion of private and state support during the ensuing decades, services vastly expanded. In the 1990s the hospital became a level 1 trauma center, one of three in the state. The designation signified the staff's ability to perform microsurgery, neurosurgery, burn care, and a variety of other specialized treatments for trauma victims.

The indoor courtyard that connects the hospital and medical school buildings is decorated with hanging ferns and potted trees. Half a football field in size, it served as an expanded emergency area during TOPOFF 3 before reverting to its park-like ambience. In December 2005, interspersed among the plants, medical residents in green scrubs sat reviewing notes. Jeffrey Hammond pointed to a quiet area where we could talk about the influence that our trip to Israel six months earlier had on his thoughts about terrorism. That experience prompted him to wonder about the emphasis in the United States on biological, chemical, and radiological threats. "The reality is that we may not be paying enough attention to the most likely scenarios, which have to do with explosives and incendiaries," he said.

Hammond trained at the University of Miami to become a trauma surgeon and remained there to become co-director of that university hospital's burn center. But in 1990 he left to help build a trauma program at RWJ. Sixteen years later, with four full-time trauma surgeons and others on call, he headed one of New Jersey's leading programs.

I asked Hammond, now 56, when he became interested in terrorism issues.

"9/11," he answered at first. "Until then, disasters had been sort of a peripheral concern." But then he qualified his initial response. "Actually, I had an experience with disaster in May 1980, when I was the chief resident in surgery at Jackson Memorial Hospital in Miami." That incident foretold his broader concerns after 9/11, when he started writing papers and making presentations on disaster management.

The earlier episode began after a jury acquitted two white policemen of killing a black businessman. The verdict precipitated a four-day race riot in which eighteen people were killed. Jackson hospital was in the midst of the expansive riot zone, which was cordoned off by the police. "That's just great," Hammond laughed, "except if you're in the middle of it." He and others in the hospital worked nonstop amid the shooting and chaos. The chief of neurosurgery did reach the facility during the second day of the riots, though his life had been threatened and his car windows smashed while driving in. A medical student on the way to the hospital was shot in the neck and ended up a quadriplegic. "Absolutely frightening," is how Hammond characterized those four days.

As the senior surgeon present, though still a resident, Hammond had to make unusual command decisions. He placed a radiologist with little surgical training in charge of the emergency room. That allowed junior surgical residents to go to the operating rooms and begin surgery, he said. But they would wait for Hammond to do major parts of the operations. "I would walk into a room and the patient's abdomen would be open—they'd been shot or something. All I could see was their guts." He would operate and then move to the next room. "I was like a machine," he chuckled, comparing the experience to MASH.

Hammond had hardly thought about those days until September 11, 2001. Then he began having aversive thoughts, as he called them—flashbacks, trouble sleeping, maybe post-traumatic stress disorder. Talking about his experience with colleagues helped him overcome anxiety. But the memories rekindled by 9/11 sparked his concern about the need for preparedness. Because of his own experience, he was especially sensitive to the effects of such events on responders. So he positioned a group of the psychologists and social workers at RWJ to counsel doctors and other rescue staff. Termed a critical incident stress management team, the group developed ties with similar teams around the country. The biggest challenge has been to maintain interest as the sense of urgency recedes.

I asked Hammond how he rated American preparedness relative to Israel's. Apart from the influence of the different sizes of the countries, he sensed a difference in attitudes. "Americans see incidents as something that happens to 'someone else,'" he said. He mentioned the 1995 bombing in Oklahoma City and the shooting in 2001 of youngsters in a San Diego schoolyard. Though widely reported, these events seemed distant to most people. "It happened to the other guy, not part of my life." But our trip to Israel, he said, underscored how differently the Israelis feel. "There, it's not happening to 'someone else.' It's happening to me, or mine, people I identify with."

Finally, I asked how his RWJ Hospital would fare if suicide bombers exploded nearby and three hundred victims suddenly needed care. He offered an extended "hmmm." Then: "It would depend on the time and the day of the week." He thought a bit longer. "We're more prepared on some days than others, depending on the staff. Some people are more savvy than others." Hammond seemed to play out scenarios in his mind. He leaned forward and tapped his finger on the table: "We definitely would be pressed." He hoped that a triage system near the attack sites could direct patients who needed less complicated surgery to other medical centers. "Which is the Israeli approach," he said. Then he added with a skeptical laugh, "At least that would also be our plan."

Enthusiastic as Hammond is about an International Center for Terror Medicine at RWJ, the spearhead of the hospital's participation was Dr. Clifton Lacy. For Lacy, terror medicine was an outgrowth of his work before becoming president of the hospital. Beginning in January 2002, upon appointment by the newly elected governor, James McGreevey, Lacy served for three years as New Jersey's Commissioner of Health and Senior Services. With 9/11 and the anthrax attacks still fresh in his mind, he became "a student of weapons of mass destruction," as he put it.

Among the governor's early counterterrorism initiatives was the creation of MEDPREP (Medical Emergency and Disaster Prevention and Response Expert Panel). He asked Lacy to head the new panel, which consisted of the state's leaders in counterterrorism, law enforcement, trauma, and emergency medicine. After a few months, the group offered a series of recommendations. Many ultimately were adopted, including a statewide surveillance system for disease outbreaks and the incorporation of health care experts in rapid response teams. New Jersey also became the first state to implement an uninterruptible radio system that connected its eighty-four acute care hospitals and fifteen key state agencies.

When Lacy left the government in 2004 to head the RWJ Hospital, he remained deeply concerned about domestic vulnerability to terrorist attacks. Convinced that collaboration between American and Israeli experts could be mutually beneficial, he led the American delegation to Israel in 2005. At the end of the trip, he said the experience had more than met his expectations. "It was terrific," he told me.

Clifton Lacy, 52, has spent virtually all his life in New Jersey. After graduating from Rutgers University in 1975, he attended the Robert Wood Johnson Medical School, trained there in cardiovascular diseases, and eventually became chief of cardiology. At the time he was tapped by McGreevey to serve as health commissioner, Lacy was also serving as the hospital's vice president for medical affairs.

Tall and thin, Lacy is chronically energetic. His gray mustache and beard encircle a boyish grin. Although versed in U.S. state and national preparedness, Lacy admitted to surprise by what he learned in Israel. "It gave me a different perspective," he said. Echoing Hammond, he noted that he and others in the response community were often focused on "mega-terror." That is, planes crashing into buildings or mass casualties from biological, chemical, or radiological agents. "Israel gave me the perspective of 'multi-mini-terror.'" By that he meant incidents that might cause relatively few casualties but that occur frequently. "These events seem so effective now in Iraq, as they were in Israel, taking out twenty or thirty people with each bombing, maybe a hundred," he said. "But it's the drumbeat of frequency." He judged these repeated events to be very effective at causing disruption.

The sites of terrorist attacks in Israel are often discreetly memorialized. Modest displays are visible at Jerusalem bus stops and other public places where attacks took place. At some spots an unadorned plaque might list the names of those who were killed. At others a collection of photographs is posted, sometimes above a cluster of fresh chrysanthemums. Otherwise, the previously damaged location, whether a bus stop, restaurant, or shopping mall, appears much the same as before the attack. Visits to such sites left an impression on Lacy. "An event here, an event there," he said, "and how quickly they clean them up . . . so they can go on with life." Still, the scar persists. Somehow, the Israelis have balanced two competing impulses: the sad tug of loss, and the determination to move forward.

Lacy wondered how Americans might fare if faced with similar attacks. "Here, society is so intact that those kind of events would be completely disruptive," he said. The visit to Israel prompted him to think more about positioning New Jersey and the rest of the country to deal with this kind of threat.

After leaving the government, Lacy continued to consult with state and federal officials on preparedness planning. As a result of the trip to Israel, he began to press for stronger linkage between the medical response workers and law enforcement. The coordinated efforts in Israel between the police, military, and health officials were impressive. While there, he was struck by how much New Jersey lagged in that area. "We've gone a long way in integrating health care with public health and with emergency management," he said. "But not enough with law enforcement and with intelligence and counterintelligence."

* * *

Dr. Lacy is more focused on terrorism preparedness than many other hospital leaders. The many briefings he received on continuing threats during his tenure as health commissioner especially sensitized him to the issue. Still, despite the enhancement of preparedness at his hospital and others in the state, TOPOFF 3 demonstrated continuing weaknesses. Preparedness at other locations throughout the country appears even more wanting. A stream of recent assessments uniformly concluded that the nation remains under-prepared.

The Greater New York Hospital Association represents some 250 hospitals throughout New York, New Jersey, Connecticut, and Rhode Island. In 2004 Susan Waltman, a spokeswoman for the association, testified at a congressional hearing on "Terror Attacks: Are We Ready?" Her response to the question mirrored that of many others in public health, law enforcement, and counterintelligence: we are better prepared now than before, but much still needs to be done. The most important lesson from 9/11 and the anthrax attacks, she said, was the need for every hospital to have a "capability to respond to disasters of all types [including] biological, chemical, and radiological events."[11]

A year later the nonprofit, nonpartisan Trust for America's Health issued its report on federal and state readiness for bioterrorism and other disasters. The organization's president, Lowell Weicker, is a former senator and governor of Connecticut. Its board of trustees and advisory council include other political and business leaders, deans of schools of public health, and directors of state health departments. For public health and bioterrorism preparedness, they gave the federal government a grade of D+.[12]

Around the same time, in December 2005, members of the 9/11 Commission issued grades for compliance with forty-one recommendations in its 2004 report. The grades were mostly C or lower. In the five areas relating to emergency preparedness and response that the members appraised, they awarded two Cs, a D, and two conditional Fs.[13]

Soon after, in early 2006, the American College of Emergency Physicians produced a "national report card" on the state of emergency medicine. Its evaluation noted the "critical role of emergency medicine in times of natural or man-made disasters." Although the report was issued after Hurricane Katrina, its data about preparedness in Louisiana and Mississippi had been compiled prior to the devastating storm. Still, the authors cited the hurricane as highlighting the lack of surge capacity in those states as well as in many others. For the nation's emergency medicine system as a whole, the report rendered a grade of C–.[14]

In 2006 an article in the *Journal of Homeland Security* reviewed a dozen recent assessments of the nation's ability to address terrorism. The subjects included hospital preparedness, public health readiness, and school safety. Especially disquieting was the finding that 90 percent of American schools are "soft targets" for terrorist attacks and that schools often do not rehearse for emergencies. The article offered no grades for performance, but concluded that "there seems to be a critical need to develop assessments that link local, state, regional, and national preparedness."[15]

Deciding if an area of society is adequately secure or prepared to deal with a terrorist attack is in part subjective. Does a single fence around a chlorine plant offer adequate protection, or is a double fence necessary? Is one security guard sufficient, or should there be three? How much is enough? The answers depend on location, time, perceived risk, and an individual's sense of comfort. Thus, offering a grade for preparedness, as several studies have done, suggests that the evaluation is more definitive than may be warranted.

Still, virtually every recent study has concluded that security and preparedness in the United States are inadequate.

Some segments in American society are better protected than others. Since 2001, for example, federally mandated standards have improved screening at the nation's airports. But security at the seaports is a continuing issue. Of the six million ocean-borne cargo containers that enter the United States annually, only around 5 percent undergo inspection. Conditions also vary widely in hospital preparedness and response capabilities.

There are no federal requirements for hospital disaster planning, so the nation's nearly six thousand hospitals write their own protocols. Some states require hospitals to conduct disaster drills, and some do not. The closest approximation to national standards are guidelines set by the Joint Commission on Accreditation of Healthcare Organizations. Established in 1951, this commission is a private voluntary association that establishes performance standards for hospitals and other health care institutions. Although it is not a legal requirement, most hospitals seek the commission's stamp of approval. Accreditation now obliges a hospital to conduct two drills per year, one of which involves an influx of simulated patients. (The other can be a "tabletop" exercise at which scenarios are played out through discussion.) The only requirement for the hands-on drill is that there be enough "victims" to test a hospital's "resources and reactions under stress."[16]

As a result, the nature, quality, and frequency of exercises have been uneven. Some hospitals have held numerous drills involving attacks with conventional and unconventional weapons, but others have not. The congressional Government Accountability Office found in 2003 that most urban hospitals in the United States had never participated in a mass-casualty bioterrorism exercise.[17]

By 2006 the record of participation had doubtless improved, though gaps remained. Jean Smiley, the deputy commissioner of health for Onondaga County, New York, said that all four medical centers in her region had conducted drills in the past year, but of varied quality. One hospital had engaged in a large-scale exercise with thirty "chemically contaminated" patients who went through wash-downs and extensive monitoring. "That hospital definitely did a lot more than another one that just sent five people to a shower," she told me. The public health director for Cerro Gordo County in Iowa, Ron Osterholm, worries that Mercy Hospital in Mason City may not be well prepared. "They do self-evaluation after a drill, and it's not clear what they're really looking to accomplish," he said.

In mid-2006, the Joint Commission on Accreditation began to require the presence of an observer who would write a written critique of a drill. The observer could be from the hospital doing the test, though not him- or herself a participant in the drill. Apart from questions about the objectivity of someone employed by the same hospital, nearly one thousand hospitals do not participate in the commission's accreditation process.

By contrast, in Israel, uniform standards for preparedness, outside observers of drills, and evaluation by experts not affiliated with the institution under review are already mandated. This approach seems preferable to the more individualized and self-contained efforts that are common in the United Sates. Adopting such practices could mitigate some of the unevenness in current American disaster planning.

Americans and Israelis who work in emergency response as well as law enforcement, security, and intelligence have periodically shared views with each other. In the area of terror medicine and disaster management, Israelis have developed advanced programs that simulate realistic conditions of a terrorist attack. Some American institutions have begun to incorporate such simulation programs, often with the assistance of Israeli specialists.

These exchanges and interactions have benefited both societies. But their value to the Americans has been especially augmented by the knowledge born of Israeli experience.

9

Teaching from Experience

A semi-conscious figure lay on the ground, shaking violently. The victim's heavy cough and gasps flushed saliva to the corners of his mouth. Mucus began to puddle below the nose, and tears ran from both eyes. His blood pressure had fallen perilously, and he was in mortal danger. An approaching emergency responder, a paramedic in full-body protective gear, had been informed that a nerve agent had been released in the area, an apparently deliberate chemical attack. The paramedic jammed a needle into the victim's quivering thigh and emptied a syringe of atropine. Even with early drug intervention, recovery from nerve gas exposure is uncertain. But minutes after the injection, the violent heaving began to subside and the atropine seemed to be having an effect. The emergency worker stood back, took off his mask, and released a sigh of satisfaction.

The worker had never before ministered to a victim of a chemical attack, but the patient had been through the experience hundreds of times. In fact, the victim was a life-size mannequin that simulated with remarkable realism the symptoms of someone exposed to sarin or a similar agent. The mock chemical attack had taken place at the Israel Center for Medical Simulation, a three-story building on the campus of Sheba Medical Center in Tel Hashomer near Tel Aviv. The center, which opened in 2001, was the culmination of a decade-long effort by its director, Dr. Amitai Ziv. Convinced of the value of simulation techniques as tools of education, he developed numerous programs that replicated medical challenges for doctors, nurses, and paramedics. Truly sick or injured patients are not treated at the center, although it houses examination, operating, and intensive care rooms, and equipment that might be found in any hospital.

Six feet tall and athletic, the 46-year-old Ziv exhibits the controlled energy that might be expected in a former combat pilot. The mental and physical skills required of a pilot in the Israeli Air Force are so demanding that only one of every hundred recruits makes the final cut. After six years of full-time military service, Ziv went on reserve status in 1982. The next year he entered medical school, followed by a residency in pediatrics. A physician's clinical training is almost entirely drawn from treatment of patients, while that of a fighter pilot is largely based on practice under mock conditions. Ziv thought about the numerous simulation exercises that went into his flight training. Squeezed into a fake cockpit, he would manipulate a multitude of switches while being tugged and swiveled as if in supersonic flight. Computers assessed his every reaction. Why not bring such modeling to medical instruction? he thought.

In the mid-1990s, Ziv created an array of scenarios as teaching tools. Using both live actors and dummies as patients, medical personnel could learn to treat emergency victims of heart attacks and road accidents. In some situations, the mock patients might be abused children or women undergoing childbirth. With the increased incidence of terrorism, computer-driven mannequins were programmed to simulate symptoms caused by possible terror weapons. Victims might twitch from apparent exposure to a nerve agent, or leak mucus induced by a simulated anthrax infection. Lung sounds could be programmed to suggest injury from a blast. In the course of the intifada, virtually every Israeli army medical team visited the simulation center. "We trained six thousand physicians and paramedics in real-life emergency situations," Ziv said in 2005.

"They trained with the mannequins in real field conditions—under fire, smoke, and shooting."[1]

Delegations from many countries have visited the center. On the eve of the Gulf War in 2003, Ziv was invited to testify before the U.S. House Committee on Homeland Security. Subsequently, American army medical teams were sent to his center to witness various scenarios. Smoke that was piped into a mock battle area enveloped the legs of people at the scene. The sound of grenade blasts and machine guns echoed in the background as emergency responders rushed to the choking, bleeding mannequins. When the firing dissipated, the paramedics applied stethoscopes to the victims' chests, listening for irregular heart sounds and indications of lung injury. After inserting a breathing tube into the mouth and applying a tourniquet to a bleeding leg, the emergency workers would move the "patient" to a safer area. All the while, video cameras were recording the actions for later review.

Israel's post-2000 terrorism experiences prompted Amitai Ziv's center to develop more programs based on terrorist attacks. Although simulation programs are included in some U.S. training, none is comparable to the one at Sheba Medical Center, according to Dr. Jeffrey Ponsky, chairman of the American Board of Surgery, who visited Ziv's center in 2004. But that situation seemed likely to change. Ziv has since presented dozens of papers and workshops, many in the United States, including at the Mayo Clinic, the Greater New York Hospital Association, and the Department of Homeland Security. In 2006 Ziv told me that "multi-modality" simulation centers were being developed in other countries as well. He had been asked to help replicate the Israeli model not only at Case Western University in Cleveland and at the Mayo Clinic in Rochester, Minnesota, but at locations in Sao Paulo, Brazil, and Montreal, Canada.

* * *

Dr. Benjamin Davidson, 56 and silver-haired, is the director of Assaf Harofeh, a large hospital in central Israel. In early 2006, he was in

Washington, D.C., for meetings on computer-based simulation programs under a project called ER One. Initiated by two physicians at the Washington Hospital Center, Dr. Mark Smith and Dr. Craig Feied, the ER One Institute seeks to enhance medical preparedness for disasters and terrorist incidents. The institute is supported by the MedStar health care organization, which includes the Washington Hospital Center, Georgetown University Hospital, and five other area hospitals.

Unlike Amitai Ziv's simulation center in Israel, the ER One computer program does not use actors or mannequins. It is more like playing a Nintendo game. A player moves video images of hospital personnel and patients around in disaster environments. Davidson was asked to help develop these computer games because of his unusual expertise. Before joining Assaf Harofeh in 1998, he had served as Surgeon General of the Israeli Air Force.

When I asked what Israel and the United States can teach each other in the area of preparedness, Davidson spoke of his admiration for American orderliness. "We in Israel need more of that," he said, "because we tend to improvise all the time." His comment seemed an ironic contrast to an observation by others that American responders adhere too rigidly to written protocols. After a moment, he smiled and admitted that his personal preferences were irrelevant. The Israelis could never be locked into a plan. "We can't because that's the way we are," he said. With a big laugh he added, "It's genetically programmed in us."

In fact, Davidson fully understood that the Israeli tendency to innovate accounted for many military victories. Israel won wars not only because of advance planning but because of improvisations on the battlefield. Memorable examples occurred in 1973 after Egypt and Syria launched a surprise attack during Yom Kippur, the holiest of Jewish holidays. Israel was late to mobilize, and its forces initially were reeling. In the north, Syrian tanks forced a retreat from the Golan Heights, and in the west, Egyptian troops crossed the Suez Canal and decimated Israeli outposts on the opposite shore. By the second week, however, the tide had begun to turn. While taking huge losses, Israeli tanks slogged their way back up the Golan Heights. When facing concentrated firepower, tank commanders figured out new routes on the spot. Killed or incapacitated commanders were quickly replaced by other crewmembers, who continued the climb through unplanned pathways. After reaching the top, Israeli forces were poised to drive to Damascus.

On the Egyptian front, Ariel Sharon, then a field general, also led a stunning counterassault. In the second week of battle, his troops wedged a path back to the pre-war line along the Suez Canal. Then, using rubber dinghies and rafts, they ferried heavy equipment to the other side. Despite the absence of permission from his superiors, Sharon rushed his soldiers deeper into Egyptian territory, where they encircled large swaths of the Egyptian army. His actions and those on the Syrian front led Egypt and Syria to accept a ceasefire and eventual disengagement. Israelis' daring responses had served the country well. In fact, Davidson and others who are developing simulation programs for ER One know that disasters and terror events do not follow a script. Planning for the worst is necessary, but so are portals for creative responses.

When Dr. Smith and Dr. Feied conceived ER One in the late 1990s, they were not focused on simulation programs. Their aim was to build an unusual emergency department at the Washington Hospital Center. It would be equipped to handle not only the customary fare of illness and injury, but the consequences of terrorism, disasters, and epidemics. Their initiative gained traction after 9/11, when Congress funded a study by the ER One Institute to help design the new emergency facility. (The hospital's proximity, just two miles north of Capitol Hill, was hardly a liability to congressional interest in the project.) Subsequently, the hospital itself pledged at least $25 million toward building the new emergency department. The goal was to create a model that could be replicated around the country.

Meanwhile, the ER One Institute began to spawn a variety of programs that ranged from technology applications to enhanced nursing readiness. An ER One conference in January 2006 addressed the challenges that mass casualty incidents posed to hospitals. Presentations by experts from the United Kingdom, the United States, and Israel were especially revealing. The British and Americans noted the dismal condition of preparedness in many of their countries' hospitals. The contrasting level of advanced readiness in Israeli hospitals was striking.

James Ryan, who heads the Center of Conflict Recovery at the University College of London, was the first to speak. A former professor of surgery at the Royal Army Medical College, he served on a citywide team that assessed the response to the terrorist attacks in London on July 7, 2005. "We refer to it as 7/7," he said. On that day, four suicide bombers exploded themselves almost simultaneously, one on a bus and three at locations in the underground metro. Fifty-two people were killed and hundreds injured.

Ryan's message to the two hundred conference participants carried unsettling themes. Planning for disaster and terrorism in the United Kingdom was hobbled by competing bureaucracies. The department of health and its various components—the emergency planning board, nurses and physicians, hospitals, the military—all "have their fingers in the pie," he said. Only recently have these various groups agreed to work toward a common approach to prepare for and respond to disasters.

Ryan was professorial, but his delivery was leavened by a slight Irish brogue. British planners, he maintained, were inhibited by a national trait not to share information between agencies. With one hand in his pocket and the other gesturing in wide sweeps, Ryan's pose symbolized conflicting impulses of restraint and alarm.

He spoke of the wave of self-congratulations for the response to 7/7 that initially washed over the country. "Our government ministers were patting people on the back," he recalled. "But just now, seven months afterwards, we're beginning to be honest with each other." Ryan ticked off a list of mishaps, beginning with the failure of the communications system. Strategic organizations could not talk to tactical groups, who could not speak to operational workers, he said. Even ambulance drivers were unable to reach the next level up by radio. "The phones failed, the two-way radios failed, the billion-dollar communications systems failed." Messages had to be delivered by human runners, and British investigators are still trying to understand why the system collapsed.

Because of inadequate communications, early reports about the bombings on 7/7 were wildly inaccurate. Information coming to officials at the control center in London indicated that a dozen attacks had taken place and that more were coming. "We're going to be hit continuously," Ryan and others thought at the time, "and this could go on for weeks." Only later did they realize that the failure of the system had given free reign to hyperbolic rumors.

Ryan's voice lowered when he said that not until fifty-seven minutes after the first blast did any victim actually receive hospital care. Some patients were still waiting for hospital care four hours after the blasts. The chaos around the attack sites caused delays that may have cost lives. If the incident had lasted longer and hospitals had been further backed up, Ryan concluded, "there could have been an absolute disaster."

Unlike in the United Kingdom where the terrorism experience was recent, in the United States nearly five years had elapsed since the last attacks. Memories of 9/11 and the anthrax letters had dimmed. But the disheartening response to Hurricane Katrina in the fall of 2005 graphically demonstrated the lack of readiness for a mass casualty incident. There was no reason to think the United States could handle a large terror event any better. At the ER One conference, Jeffrey Hammond, of New Jersey's Robert Wood Johnson University Hospital, contended that much disaster planning in America was based on wishful thinking. He noted that in 2006 communications between several New Jersey and New York agencies was still poor. "We actually have to position a New Jersey state trooper at the main police headquarters in New York City so we know what's going on in New York," he told the conference audience.

Similar concerns about readiness came from Dr. Paul Carlton, who in 2002 retired from military service with the rank of Lieutenant General. A former Surgeon General of the U.S. Air Force, he now directs the Office of Homeland Security for the Health Science Center of the Texas A&M University System. The system includes ten research and teaching facilities across Texas. With a dash of understatement, Carlton suggested that "the report card on Katrina has not been good." He then posted a series of slides that listed a dozen federal agencies and their ostensible responsibilities in the event of a mass casualty incident.

Carlton's close-cropped graying hair and straight-up posture reflect his military past. His laser pointer danced across the overhead screen, stopping at one agency after another. With each stop he issued a burst of commentary. The Department of Homeland Security has strategic goals, he said. The Department of Health and Human Services focuses on response. There is debate about how far the Department of Defense should be involved, he continued. He beamed onto the Federal Emergency Management Agency and a few other departments. Then he slowly turned his gaze at the audience from left to right. "There should be some concern in your minds as you look at this," he finally announced. He reiterated that no single agency was in charge of medical response—and even worse, "they give conflicting guidance and it's very confusing." A better approach, he concluded, would be to coordinate response teams at the state and regional level.

* * *

Although Dr. Shmuel Shapira from Hadassah Hospital recapitulated Israel's experiences, other Israelis then working in the United States offered informed perspectives about both countries. Dr. Asher Hirshberg, 49, is short and theatrical. A renowned vascular surgeon, he founded the trauma service at Sheba Hospital near Tel Aviv in 1994. Six years later he accepted an appointment at the Baylor College of Medicine in Houston and subsequently began working with the ER One Institute's project on computer modeling. When he spoke at the conference about internal hospital planning, his sonorous voice echoed the concerns of previous presenters. He focused on two issues. The first built on James Ryan's criticism of the misplaced self-congratulations after the London bombings. On the overhead screen, Hirshberg flashed an e-mail message circulated by a London trauma surgeon the day after 7/7: "It is difficult to overemphasize how impressive the response was." That inflated compliment, Hirshberg said, typified the "piece-of-cake attitude" that overrode any inclination to be critical. "Had any of the victims suffered a preventable complication or could any treatment have been done better?" he asked rhetorically. "We don't know," Hirshberg answered, "because that information was not reported."

He cited similar tendencies after the terror attacks in Madrid in 2004. Simultaneous bombings on the railway system killed nearly two hundred and injured two thousand. Several surgeons wrote about the experience, indicating that their hospital received 312 casualties in three hours.[2] That is an extraordinarily high casualty load, Hirshberg noted, yet "the impression from the article is that it was just a busy day at the hospital." No mention of preventable deaths, complications, or errors. In fact, such issues, though unpleasant, are commonly detailed after traffic accidents and other localized trauma events. But in assessments of terrorist incidents, emotion and a misplaced sense of patriotism tend to overtake careful analysis. The result, according to Hirshberg, is that the true capabilities of an institution to respond are grossly exaggerated.

Hirshberg's second critique involved hospital disaster plans, which commonly presume that severely wounded patients will receive treatment as if "on a normal working day." Such an approach, he said, would overwhelm the trauma service. In large casualty events, severely wounded victims should not necessarily receive optimal care as they arrive at the hospital. Patients not facing immediate life-or-death issues can be kept waiting, Hirshberg advised. A trauma team should provide full care to them only after the most urgent cases have been treated. Emphasizing each syllable, Hirshberg said that a hospital must be prepared *not* to treat a hysterical Mrs. Jones who has multiple lacerations, but rather a subdued Mr. Smith with a ruptured spleen. (Of course, lacerations must be inspected as possible gateways to deeper injury, but a burst spleen, leaking blood into the abdomen, clearly is life-threatening.)

Hirshberg's comments reflected Israeli practice. In Israel, assessments of performance after each terror event are conducted with unsparing rigor. Trauma services in a large casualty incident are framed there so that Mrs. Jones would not receive optimal care initially, but Mr. Smith would. Not that Hirshberg views all Israeli approaches to disaster planning as exemplary. He thinks hospital capabilities to handle a chemical attack are overstated. "Look, to work in a contaminated environment you have to be training daily to do it, like a fireman trains for his work," he told me. Hospital drills in Israel, even though held several times a year, would not provide enough experience to perform well in chemically soaked surroundings, Hirshberg believes.

When I asked him what Israeli experience could teach Americans about terror medicine, he spoke of the attitudes in the two countries. "I think one key lesson from Israel is . . . commitment." Unlike in American hospitals, commitment to preparedness and security permeates the staff in every Israeli hospital, he said. "In Israel, everyone has a role, from the CEO of the hospital to the cashier in the cafeteria. Everyone participates in disaster drills and takes them very seriously." Doubtless, the seriousness is rooted in their many experiences with real events.

He emphasized another difference as well. In Israel, the protocols for planning are mandated by the government, including by the Ministry of Defense and the Ministry of Health. The approach is "top down," though with leeway for on-the-spot creativity. In the United States, disaster preparedness is largely "bottom up": hospitals draw up their own disaster plans in the absence of federal requirements. Like other Israeli observers, he believes the absence of federally mandated standards to be a large weakness in hospital planning. Herein lies a paradox: Israel, with its nationally mandated requirements, allows wide latitude for improvisation. But in America, where plans are written by each hospital, practitioners are reluctant to stray from the written protocols.

Hirshberg also sees commercial interests as having undue influence on American practices. He views the military-industrial complex and the health care complex as driving forces both in commerce and politics. Unlike in Israel, these forces have shaped an expensive agenda that, in his judgment, is unwarranted: to prepare for all conceivable hazards and disasters.

Hirshberg's economic and political interpretations may be arguable, but his observation about Israeli commitment is not. It is a theme picked up by another Israeli now working in the United States, Yuri Millo.

Dr. Millo was hired in 2003 initially to direct the ER One Institute's computer-based simulation program. He is a slight figure seemingly in constant motion. "I get three or four hours of sleep a night," he admitted to me between sessions of the 2006 ER One conference on hospital preparedness. Millo had developed the conference agenda, secured the speakers, and was now gauging reactions of the disaster planners and administrators in the audience. "I'm getting good feedback," he told me, sounding both pleased and relieved. At 43, bookish and unostentatious, he enjoyed a pivotal role at the institute.

Millo came to the United States in 2001. Trained in plastic surgery at Shaare Zedek Hospital in Jerusalem, he took leave from his practice in Israel to develop an online medical tutorial for a Virginia-based company called the Internet Academy for Continuing Medical Education. Two years later, while preparing to return to Israel, he received an offer from Mark Smith and Craig Feied at the ER One Institute to work on computer modeling for hospital training. With their encouragement, he also began to plan a hands-on program for disaster management unlike any other in the United States.

* * *

One-and-a-half miles east of the Capitol, rows of attached homes along Massachusetts Avenue give way to a complex of large buildings. The sprawling gray structure to the right, encircled with barbed wire, is the city jail. To the left is a six-story red brick building whose portico identifies it as the D.C. General Hospital. The jail is full, but the hospital is empty. Since 2001, when Washington's mayor, Anthony Williams, determined that the city could no longer afford the upkeep for the deteriorating structure, the hospital has stood as an empty monument. Its origins reach back to the city's first public hospital, which was established in 1806 and moved to the present location in 1846. Whether the current ghost hospital will be refurbished or replaced remains uncertain. But in October 2004, portions of the facility took on an unusual function. Under the supervision of Yuri Millo, the defunct emergency department and other sections of the building became the location of an ER One Institute training project.

A two-day course is held there at least once a month and is open to around thirty medical and security personnel at a time. By mid-2006, some five hundred people from every part of the country had participated in hands-on exercises involving mock biological, chemical, radiological, and explosives attacks. The course is offered under the auspices of the training and exercise division of the ER One Institute, known as the Simulation and Training Environment Lab (SiTEL). Insofar as the facility is devoted entirely to these exercises, it resembles Amitai Ziv's Medical Simulation Center in Israel. But Ziv's center focuses on the treatment of victims, whereas the ER One project concentrates on the interactions of hospital personnel. And unlike drills in other U.S. hospitals, in which real patients are simultaneously being cared for, the emergency department and other sections of D.C. General can be devoted exclusively to the event.

On a cold afternoon in February 2006, in the midst of a training course, thirty-two participants were assigned roles for a mock terror attack with conventional explosives. They assembled in the emergency department and were told that two buses in downtown Washington had been bombed and that victims would soon be arriving. The participants—physicians, nurses, administrators, security personnel—were assigned roles compatible with their usual professional responsibilities. Each wore a bright orange vest with bold lettering that identified his or her role in the exercise. Those wearing TRIAGE vests headed for the entrance to assess the severity of injury of incoming victims. When a victim arrived, a triage officer was to quickly assess the severity of injury and attach a colored tag to the victim's shirt. Red signified need for immediate care, yellow indicated that treatment could be delayed, and green that the injury was minor.

A second group was led to a room 150 feet down the corridor that became the Emergency Operations Center (EOC), which was the command headquarters. These individuals wore vests that identified them variously as INCIDENT COMMANDER, SAFETY OFFICER, LIAISON, and OPERATIONS CHIEF. They took seats at a long table equipped with laptop computers, walkie-talkies, and phones, about to become the hub for information and coordination as the incident unfolded.

A dozen clinicians remained in the emergency department and were given vests that read PHYSICIAN, NURSE, RED AREA LEADER, and more. Dr. Steven Chin, one of five Californians taking the course, was designated TREATMENT AREA LEADER. The assignment fit nicely with his actual position at Presbyterian Intercommunity Hospital in Los Angeles, where he was medical director for preparedness and response. At 2:15 PM, he received notification that ambulances were arriving at the hospital. "Everyone get ready," he announced with gravity.

Minutes later, the first patient appeared at the hospital entrance, where she was screened by a triage official and tagged red. A heavyset woman, she was escorted into the emergency department, screaming, "I can't hear, I can't hear." (The patients were actors covered with red and black dye. Some feigned hysteria, and others appeared unconscious.) The screaming patient was moved to the bed in the fourth bay, where a nurse grabbed her wrist and tried to take her pulse. The Red Area Leader, Dr. Brendan Furlong, who in fact chairs the Department of Emergency Medicine at Georgetown University Hospital, moved in close. He faced the patient eye-to-eye as she continued to yell, "Help. I can't hear." Furlong, attired in a blue scrub shirt and khaki pants, peered through his small dark rimmed glasses. His high forehead reached back to a shock of dark hair. With exaggerated lip movement, he yelled back, "Did you get knocked out?" The patient evidently saw, if not heard, what he asked. She shook her head no, but continued to register distress. "Please help me," she repeated urgently.

Furlong read aloud from the written description of injuries that were clipped to the patient's shirt. "Penetrating chest injury. Shock." The nurse lowered her stethoscope and announced, "We have odd sounds on her left side," evidently injuries from the "blast."

Furlong responded firmly, "We need an x-ray of her chest and an x-ray of her cervical spine." "Okay, move her out," he ordered, as three more patients were being wheeled into the emergency area. He approached a young man in the second bay just as someone near the front of the emergency area shouted, "Red. Red. A red patient is dying in the hallway." A man in a vest labeled PHYSICIAN, ran to the patient.

Just then, another female victim, this one apparently unconscious, was wheeled in. Her medical description indicated she had been intubated at the attack site. (Intubation involves placing a tube through the mouth into the trachea to maintain an air passage to the lungs.) The beds in all eleven bays were now occupied. Seven of the patients had penetration wounds from metal fragments and were waiting turns to be moved to the imaging department. There a CT scan, a computerized form of an x-ray, could help detect the depth and severity of injury. Meanwhile, a voice from one of the bays kept yelling, "Where's my wife? Where is she?" A NURSE ran to him and said, "Don't worry, we'll find out."

A twelfth victim was carried in, and then a thirteenth, who was curled up in pain. He was placed on the floor next to a patient already in the third bay. An urgent call came to Dr. Chin from the triage group at the hospital entrance: "We have several critical patients and no transport. Can you help us get patients into the emergency department?" Chin turned to Dr. Furlong: "Can you send some people out there and get those patients?"

"No, I can't spare anyone," Furlong answered abruptly. Chin was frustrated. As leader of the treatment area, he could order Furlong to act, but he knew that would increase the tension. To his relief, Chin spotted someone at the end of the room taking notes but who agreed to put his pad aside and relieve the overload at the entrance.

As more patients arrived in the emergency area, some crying, some yelling, Dr. Furlong and the rest of the staff felt overwhelmed. The station nurse desk grabbed her walkie-talkie, pressed a button, and said, "EOC? This is the emergency department."

Dr. Victor Freeman, past president of the Washington D.C. Medical Society, now acting as LIAISON in the Emergency Operations Center, took the call. He interrupted the INCIDENT COMMANDER, Ann Marie Maddon, who was sitting across the table. "It's the emergency department and they need two more physicians and one nurse," Freeman said. Maddon, who is director of Critical Care and Emergency Services at the Washington Hospital Center, was not sure how quickly the request could be filled. "Tell them we'll try," she replied. Minutes later, Freeman received more bad news. "Uh oh," he announced to Maddon and everyone else at the table. "Two of the hospital's CT scanners are down. Only one is functioning."

Back in the emergency department, a nurse stood over a semiconscious patient with a swollen forehead, and wounds on his chest and lower abdomen. The attached description of the injury indicated shallow, labored respiration. The nurse called to a physician outside the bay, "This one needs to go to the OR (operating room) quickly."

By the time the exercise ended at 3:30 PM, twenty-eight patients had been brought to the emergency department. Eighteen were routed out for x-rays or surgery or to the intensive care unit. But ten patients were still in the bays. In the course of the drill, several walkie-talkies and telephones stopped functioning, and two of the hospital's three CT scanners were still down. Urgent requests that eight additional physicians and four nurses be sent to the emergency department had been only partly fulfilled.

In the debriefing afterwards, participants expressed appreciation for the experience. Most had never previously worked in a terror-disaster environment like this one. Dr. Furlong offered an unflinching critique of his and the others' performance: "By the end there was mayhem as patients kept coming in. I wasn't able to delegate efficiently, and the phones failed." He spoke rapidly, eager to list all the weaknesses. "We did not tag patients well, so there were repeated assessments, which wasted time. I'm used to having more support staff, so when I say 'take an x-ray,' someone is there to do it." Then he nodded appreciatively and said the exercise had been valuable by showing what did not go well "and what we should do better."

Standing behind the cluster of participants, a small figure in a midnight blue jumpsuit listened intently. She had quietly observed the exercise from beginning to end. What did she think of the performance? I asked her. Dvora Hertz gently shook her head, a hint of disapproval. "They were too much slowed down by the system," she answered in accented English. As a member of Israel's National Committee on Mass Casualty Events, she had helped write that country's terror-response protocols and numerous scripts for mock attacks. Every Israeli hospital must use the national protocols as a basis for its own plans, and every hospital is evaluated by outside observers during these unannounced attacks.

Hertz's knowledge is based on more than thirty years at Sheba hospital, where she has served as trauma coordinator and head nurse in the emergency department. In fact, she and two Sheba physicians had been recruited by Yuri Millo nearly two years earlier to help design the disaster exercises for ER One. They were present at the first drill in October 2004. The model of the entire project was based on the Israeli experience.

I asked Hertz what the participants should have done differently. She realized that several of them had not worked together before, which contributed to their hesitations. But she felt they could have done better anyway. For example, the unconscious patient in the hallway, who was tagged red, should have been started on medical care earlier. Instead, the nurse was checking on the steps to take according to the disaster plan. "The nurse was working to protocol.

The doctor also. They should have together moved the patient for treatment. Immediately."

A month after the drill, I talked with Dr. Chin by phone and asked if the ER One course had been helpful. He said that none of the exercises in California that he previously participated in was comparable. "The ER One drill was really special, because you're actually in the hospital where everyone is part of the exercise." He wanted to replicate that realism for clinicians in his home state, but without a similar facility, he was unsure whether that was possible.

* * *

When I asked Yuri Millo to compare preparedness for terrorism in the United States and Israel, he answered: "It's all about people, not about technology or gadgets." He spoke of Israelis growing up in an environment where people help each other as a matter of course, especially in the face of an ongoing external threat. Political, religious, and economic tensions are omnipresent among Israelis. But the highest collective priority for the public, he said, was imposed on them: to survive. "Here in the U.S., we are living in a kind of materialistic society where there are no real threats perceived from outside." That perception, he believes, accounted for different attitudes about preparedness in the two societies.

Can the gap be narrowed? I asked. "Yes, if the health care provider or the protective service person in America is convinced that the threat is realistic. But that's really hard." Millo thinks that many Americans view the challenge of terror attacks as if it were a movie, not a real-life threat. People understand the challenge intellectually, but few seem to have absorbed it as a collective community threat.

When we spoke in 2006, Millo acknowledged that the devastation wrought by Hurricane Katrina the previous year prompted empathy from many Americans, though not a sense of national vulnerability or national unity. Furthermore, most people in New Orleans who were able to leave did so, and those without means stayed behind. "So each group minded their own business according to their own possibilities," Millo said. He was discomfited by these reactions and mused that in Israel, if someone is hurt, the entire society seems to become a zone of support.

He noted that volunteer neighborhood service was common throughout Israel. Whether in the area of public safety or health care, Israelis more readily engage in local service than do Americans. "You have a willingness there—after you come home from work, you patrol in the neighborhood or do other community service, without any payment," Millo said. "It's just a feeling that you should give some service for your friends, kids, anybody."

By contrast, he cited an initiative in 2005 by U.S. Surgeon General Robert Carmona to create a Medical Reserve Corps (MRC). The aim was to establish throughout the country local teams of volunteers to strengthen the public health infrastructure and improve emergency preparedness. A year later, the program was still trying to gain traction. By 2006, although some four hundred MRC units had been established across the country, few had attracted substantial numbers of volunteers, especially among physicians.[3] The limited number of doctors willing to join was "really discouraging," Millo said.

So, what specifically can the Israeli experience teach Americans? I asked Millo. Two things, he responded. First, for Israelis, responding to terrorism is not theoretical. The ordeals they have undergone can provide answers to questions that for others may be only speculative. Or, as Millo put it: "[In Israel] it's not a matter of, 'I think this or that is correct,' but rather, 'I did it and here is the outcome.'" Second, echoing a now-familiar theme, he emphasized the Israeli concept of flexibility within the rule structure. In America, he said, the tendency is to conform more rigidly to predetermined plans because people are afraid to make a mistake. But in mass casualty situations, applying common sense should trump adherence to a static protocol.

Millo paused, not wanting to seem presumptuous. "Look," he explained, "the next event will never be exactly like the previous one. You need good principles, but you can't be afraid to go a little bit beyond the rules. The purpose is not the rules; the purpose is to save lives." He realizes that the ER One drills can only be marginally helpful. But they engage health care workers, administrators, and security officials in exercises they otherwise would not experience. As a result, when a real incident occurs, these responders will have the lessons of the program tucked into their memories. As a result, Millo hopes, "they will at least have the instincts to move in the correct direction."

When ER One Institute co-director Mark Smith spoke to me in 2006 about Yuri Millo, his enthusiasm was unrestrained. Millo had become the institute's main Israel connection. In the past two years, Millo's expertise and that of others Millo recruited had markedly advanced the institute's efforts to enhance preparedness. "Yuri can do anything," Smith said with a large grin. "He is driven and talented. He's phenomenal!"

The value of Israeli approaches to preparedness and response had become palpable to Mark Smith, Craig Feied, and others at ER One. Similarly, Israel has much to teach about the emotional effects on a population that has been targeted with repeated terrorist attacks. But the psychological trauma wrought by the 9/11 attacks on America offered lessons in its own right. In fact, mental health responses to the terrorist attacks in both countries bore instructive parallels, as is shown in the next chapter.

10

Trauma: 9/11 and the Intifada

Adam Oestreich, 33, gazed out of the panoramic window from his office on the 38th floor of 2 World Financial Center. For the thousandth time, he thought about the Twin Towers that once soared from the cavern across the street. Now, nearly five years after September 11, 2001, aided by recollections that he put to paper at the time, Adam spoke about that morning with chilling clarity. "I was at my desk when the first plane hit," he said. It was 8:45 AM. "We shook a bit in our seats and didn't know what happened." Dozens of fellow workers in the Merrill Lynch office, where he is a sales analyst, ran to the window. Fiery pieces of the North Tower were cascading to the ground. Adam stretched to look upward and saw a huge hole at the impact site, surrounded by fire.

As television news was reporting the event, the phones began to ring. Wives, husbands, and friends were incredulous. "Did you see what happened?" "No, it wasn't us." "Yes, we know people in that building."

When the second plane hit the South Tower, 18 minutes after the first, the floor shook under Adam's feet. He reached for the desk to keep from falling. This time the crash was nearer his office's floor level, and the fireball seemed more threatening. Company workers were screaming. Above the din, the office manager yelled: "Everybody get out NOW!"

The stairwell was jammed with people from the floors above and below (the Merrill Lynch offices at that time were on the 24th floor). He eventually reached the lobby and exited to South End Street, parallel to the Hudson River. Once outside, Adam stared up at the burning towers. Surreal, was all he could think, as he turned toward the West Side Highway to walk north.

Moments later an audible gasp swept through the crowd. "I looked up and saw people falling and jumping," he said. "I wish I could say there was only one. It got worse as the fire spread." Adam continued north amid the exodus of "refugees." "And I mean *refugees.* People carrying odd stuff, crying, shaking, and in total shock."

Five blocks from his office, he came upon someone with a telescope aimed at one of the towers and asked to have a look. "It was an image I will never forget," he said. He squared his thumbs and index fingers to frame his own upper body and said this was how close the lens brought him to the figure in view. The man was leaning out of a window above the fire in the North Tower. "His face was chubby," Adam said. "He had brown hair and looked to be in his early thirties." He seemed within touching distance.

As Adam described the scene to me, we were sitting at a conference table in his company's offices. He rose, gripped the back of the chair with one hand, and leaned far forward. He held his other hand aloft and began to wave it. "The man was half-hanging out and waving his white shirt," Adam said, replicating the motion. After a minute of peering into the telescope, he could no longer bear to watch. "The man looked tired, as if he knew the situation was futile." Not far from his window, other people were jumping.

Adam, whose short compact frame is topped with dark hair, spoke soberly. Despite his poignant recollections, he said he never felt emotionally impaired by the experience or in need of counseling. His office building was closed for nine months of repairs, and then he returned without hesitation. Did the 9/11 episode have any continuing effect on him? I asked. "Not much," he replied. During the first year after the attack, occasionally he felt depressed. No longer, he insisted. Still, he admitted to a touch of apprehension at the sound of an airliner above the building.

For Nikki Stern, the tragedy of 9/11 was far more personal. Her husband, James Potorti, 52, was killed in his office on the 96th floor of the North Tower. In the aftermath, she immersed herself in advocacy for victims' families. Initially, she contacted support groups in New Jersey, where she lived, and in New York City where she was director of public relations for the architectural firm of Swanke Hayden Connell. After acquiring information about available services from the United Way, the Red Cross, and other community organizations, she helped connect them to affected families. Her activity caught the attention of New Jersey's governor, James McGreevey, who appointed her liaison to families of victims from New Jersey. In 2003 she became executive director of the New York–based Families of September 11, an advocacy organization for victims' relatives.

Nikki's exuberance and organizational talents seemed to fit well with the roles she had undertaken. But our conversation in 2006 made clear the depth of her pain and the importance of her advocacy as a coping mechanism. "It was either doing that or walking into the ocean," she told me over coffee in a café in Princeton. She still lived a few miles from the café in the house that she and Jim shared during their ten years of marriage. At first I did not assume her ocean reference to be literal. Then she explained that for months after his death, she drove repeatedly to Spring Lake, a shoreline town an hour from her home. "I would just look at the ocean and think about walking in," she said, her voice suddenly drained of energy.

Besides suicidal thoughts, Nikki's anguish translated into other symptoms of severe trauma. Previously, she had commuted to work by train with Jim; now she would sit only on the side that did not face the site of the World Center. After some weeks, just boarding the train became overwhelming, and she began to depend on friends to drive her into New York. At work she had difficulty concentrating, and although her employers kept her on for a while, she felt she had to leave. "I was just not much good there," she said. Only her activities on behalf of the families of victims seemed to give her solace.

As Nikki shared her thoughts, I thought of how large the gap can be between appearance and inner turmoil. She was fashionably, if informally attired—jeans and a black turtleneck pullover, thin silver necklace and earrings. She was composed and smiled often. Only when recounting her most dire moments did Nikki's head dip and her voice lose strength. Those brief lapses hinted at the anguish that engulfed her after 9/11.

I asked if she had sought professional assistance to deal with her grief. "Yes, and my husband's company was very helpful," she answered. Jim was among 295 employees of Marsh and McClellan, an insurance brokerage company, who were killed in the World Trade Center. The company provided survivors and loved ones with a list of therapists and agreed to help pay for counseling for a year or two. Nikki chose a psychologist in Princeton, Dr. Ruth Goldston.

"I feel like a freak," Nikki told Goldston in one of their early sessions. She lamented that being a 9/11 family member set her apart from the rest of the world. She had no children and little extended family. "I needed to be around people who were affected like I was," she said. Goldston knew three parents who had lost children in the 1988 bombing of Pan Am Flight 103 over Lockerbie, Scotland. She arranged for Nikki to meet them, and together they formed a group that in time drew around thirty others who had lost loved ones on 9/11. The Lockerbie parents gave strength to the rest by example. "We didn't have support groups like this," they said, according to Nikki. "But we did advocacy, and that helped us cope." For some members of the group, this message may have been news, but for Nikki it underscored the importance of what she was already doing. As she later wrote, her advocacy for victims' families was based not only on altruism but on self-preservation.[1]

In the aftermath of 9/11, traditional relief agencies like the Red

Cross were joined by dozens of newly formed organizations. Some, like Friends of Firefighters, aimed to help a particular segment of the affected community. Others focused on memorial projects, as did Hearts Across America Remember, whose volunteers produced 9/11 memorial quilts. Several people who lost loved ones established their own organizations. Patricia Quigley's husband, Patrick, and Susan Retik's husband, David, were passengers on two of the hijacked airliners. The women founded Beyond the 11th to offer emotional and financial support to widows of war and terrorism. Anthony Gardner's brother Harvey was killed in the North Tower. He founded the World Trade Center–United Family Group, which aims to protect the legacy of the victims and provide emotional support for their families.

When I met Nikki Stern in 2006, she had recently left her position with Families of September 11. After nearly five years of intense activity with victims' families, she was seeking work with another focus, perhaps in public policy or writing. Was she leaving behind an important coping mechanism? I wondered. Nikki seemed uncertain. Then she elaborated on the affectionate 7-month-old puppy that she recently acquired. Molly is a brown-eared, furry mix of Bichon and spaniel. Just the right size for her owner's lap. "And one of my coping mechanisms," Nikki grinned.

The impact of 9/11 on people who were directly affected, like Nikki, was of course more pronounced than on those who did not lose loved ones. But emotional residue remained near the surface for many in the New York area. Adam Oestreich's reactions are typical of many who were peripherally affected by 9/11. Although not so traumatized as to require therapy, certain cues still revive a sense of unease. Fifteen randomly identified New Yorkers were asked about their feelings four years after the attack, and they offered a common theme. Their daily lives were largely free of memories of that day, but every few weeks or months they might be transported back "by a sudden sound, or the sight of a police officer searching bags in the subway, or a certain hue in the sky."[2]

Surveys suggested that around half of New York's 8 million residents had suffered adverse emotional effects in the weeks after the attack. Heightened anxiety caused many to sleep poorly, impaired their concentration, or prompted them to stay home and not go to work or to other places.[3] For most, even those who were highly distressed, anxiety and depression diminished with the passage of time. Relatively few needed counseling or therapy. But around 11 percent of the New York–area population was thought to be suffering from post-traumatic stress disorder (PTSD) in the first two months. By the end of the year, the figure had fallen to one percent.[4] Doubtless several who had been severely traumatized, like Nikki, benefited from mental health therapy. In fact, the nature and parameters of PTSD have been defined only in recent years.

* * *

A review of Civil War medical records indicates that many Union Army veterans showed signs of "irritable heart," a nineteenth-century term for nervous or mental disease.[5] Psychological trauma associated with World War I battles was described as "shell shock." In World War II and the Vietnam War, it was called "combat fatigue." Beyond the immediate effects of trauma, the phenomenon of delayed stress reactions also became better understood after the Vietnam War. Veterans might exhibit symptoms for the first time months or years after their actual combat experience. The term "post-traumatic stress disorder" had not appeared in the American Psychiatric Association's manual of mental disorders until 1980. Then, PTSD centered on severe emotional reactions after exposure to a catastrophic event like war, natural disaster, or an airplane crash.

Subsequent versions of the manual broadened the range of causes to include personal traumatic encounters like divorce, serious illness, and financial reversal. The most recent edition, published in 2000, contains six pages on PTSD. Following exposure to "an extreme stressor," the expansive list of diagnostic criteria includes: intense fear, hopelessness, or horror; a sense of recurrence and imminence about the causative event; avoidance of activities, places, or people that might arouse recollections of the trauma; persistent difficulty sleeping, frequent anger, difficulty concentrating.[6]

The fighting in Iraq that began in 2003 has intensified interest in the relationship of PTSD to combat experience. A Web site of the U.S. Department of Veterans Affairs and the National Center for PTSD, intended for soldiers returning from Iraq, includes comprehensive information about the disorder. It describes symptoms and treatment, and it instructs veterans about where to find further help.[7]

An army study in late 2004 showed that one in six soldiers in Iraq reported symptoms of serious depression, anxiety, or post-traumatic stress disorder. The ratio surely understates the true numbers, since many troops do not readily admit to suffering emotional distress. "The warrior ethos is that there are no imperfections," observed Dr. Michael Kilpatrick, a health support official in the Defense Department. Still, the support system in Iraqi battle areas has been more advanced than in previous wars. Unlike in the past, the army has deployed "combat stress control units" in the field to help soldiers deal with emotional challenges through quick psychological intervention. On-the-spot counseling, rest, and assurances "that they are not crazy," often spur rapid recovery, according to Dr. Thomas Burke, an army psychiatrist in charge of mental health at the Pentagon.[8]

Besides active-duty troops with emotional problems who have not availed themselves of counseling, others in need first showed symptoms sometime after their military service. But a network of government-financed support is readily available for both troops in uniform and veterans.

In the case of civilian victims of terrorism and other disasters, nongovernmental organizations often need to become the lead supporters. Thus, attaining free or low-cost mental health assistance can be challenging for the general population. But after 9/11, both government and private initiatives sought to help people who were traumatized by that day's events. Families of September 11 was among several new groups formed in the weeks and months afterward. Five years later, its Web site continued to list dozens of organizations that provide counseling services and educational programs for 9/11 families in need of support.

* * *

Days after 9/11, the New York State Office of Mental Health and the Federal Emergency Management Agency established a free psychological counseling program. Titled "Project Liberty," it offered help to people directly affected by the attack on the World Trade Center as well as to their families, fellow workers, and members of their spiritual group. Notices about the project, including a call-in number, were widely publicized. The program was substantially reduced two years later, but it continued to provide services for the fire department and school children. By the end of 2003, thousands had received telephone or in-person counseling, or education services, under the auspices of the project.[9]

In 2006 a hotline was still available to steer callers to other relief agencies. Most of these agencies were branches of national organizations that were providing counseling services long before 9/11. In fact, several first became linked in 1970, with the creation of the National Voluntary Organizations Active in Disaster (NVOAD), which was founded to help coordinate the work of relief organizations for victims of earthquakes, hurricanes, and other natural disasters. Its thirty members include high-profile groups like the American Red Cross, the United Way, the Salvation Army, and Catholic, Protestant, and Jewish service organizations. At state and city levels, Voluntary Organizations Active in Disaster (VOAD) chapters often coordinate help to victims of crime and accidents as well as large-scale disasters.

Shelley Horwitz is the chair of New York City's VOAD. After 9/11, Horwitz participated in numerous meetings of VOAD committees on subjects ranging from disaster relief to mental health and spiritual care. Representatives of some forty local New York organizations participated. For many, the events of 9/11 also deepened sensitivity to the situation for Israelis, who by then were regularly enduring terror attacks.

"September 11 drove home to us what the Israelis were experiencing," Shelley told me in 2006. "Not just the Jewish community felt this way, but Americans in general." Shelley is also the planning director of the United Jewish Appeal–Federation of New York City, a nonsectarian organization that raises funds to help needy Jews and others domestically and overseas.

The New York UJA-Federation was already funding social service projects in Israel, including some organizations that helped victims of terrorism. These Israeli groups tended toward distinctive niches and worked independently of each other: Eran provided 24-hour emotional support by phone; Selah focused on helping new immigrants to Israel; Natal supported victims generally, but especially traumatized professionals in the mental health, rescue, and emergency services; and Amcha provided psychological support to Holocaust survivors and their children.

Prompted by the terrorist attacks in Israel and, on 9/11, in the United States, New York UJA-Federation leaders felt that integrating the expertise of such groups could be helpful in both countries. Coordination could enhance the delivery of services in Israel and facilitate the exchange of information between experts there and in the United States.

As a result, the New York federation provided funds for several Israeli mental health professionals to create the Israel Trauma Coalition (ITC). Formed in January 2002, the coalition brought together a dozen Israeli organizations. Groups like Selah and Natal, as well as several hospital-based trauma treatment centers, began to work on collaborative projects. They included sharing "best practices" and providing workshops to alleviate the stress for those who worked with victims. An estimated half-million Israelis suffered some degree of trauma from the terrorist attacks, and the ITC held forums for hundreds of primary care doctors to help them identify symptoms of stress disorders in their patients.[10] By 2006, forty-three Israeli organizations had become members of the ITC and another sixty were participating in some of its activities.

Psychologists Mooli Lahad and Danny Brom, who helped form the ITC, were especially focused on community preparedness and response. Dr. Lahad's work on stress and coping reached back to the 1970s, when rockets fired from Lebanon forced Israelis near the northern border to spend long hours in underground shelters. In 1980 he founded the Community Stress Prevention Center in the northern town of Kiryat Shmona. His techniques for developing community resilience have since been recognized internationally. Numerous countries have invited Lahad to share his expertise after terrorist events and natural disasters. In 2004–2005, his team was invited to Russia after the terrorist attack in Beslan, to Sri Lanka following the tsunami in South Asia, and to the United States after Hurricane Katrina.

Dr. Danny Brom, who has also helped trauma victims in these countries and beyond, had been a leading trauma researcher in the Netherlands before immigrating to Israel in 1988. In 1999 he founded the Israel Center for the Treatment of Psychotrauma, which became the first Israeli facility where people could walk in for free crisis counseling. Both Lahad's and Brom's organizations are members of the Israel Trauma Coalition.

The daily operation of the coalition is overseen by its director, Talia Levanon. When I met her in 2005, the ITC was approaching its third year of existence. A psychotherapist, Talia had all but given up seeing her own patients in order to work fifteen hours a day for the coalition. The intifada, she said, had turned Israelis into "crazy doers." The bombings prompted them to work longer and harder—not only to do good, but because "it makes us feel better, as if we have more control." About her overworked colleagues, she said: "We all have sleeping disorders. We wake up in the middle of the night and think of things we need to do."

Does she turn on the light and make notes? I asked. She responded with an elfish grin. "If I did, my husband would hit me on the head. I just try to fall asleep." Then she explained with a ring of pride what the ITC had accomplished. Fueled by the work of Lahad and Brom, the coalition had developed an approach to a community under stress. She might call on Natal or another ITC affiliate group to help students who were not performing well at school. Had they been traumatized by the wave of terrorism? Did they need psychological or medical attention? Had their families been affected? "We look at four systems in a community," she explained, defining them as education, welfare, health, and the network of informal volunteers. "We see what needs exist in each system and try to fill in the gaps." The object, she said, is to build a continuum so that services will flow seamlessly through all the systems.

This effort is an outgrowth of the National School Resilience Project, which was initiated in 2000 by Brom's psychotrauma center. The project sought to assess the long-term effects of terror on children. Schoolteachers were trained to screen for signs of depression, anxiety, and other possible post-trauma symptoms. A study of nearly four thousand youngsters found that at the height of the intifada, about 13 percent showed some symptoms of post-traumatic stress disorder,[11] far higher than normal.[12] The screening project has since included thousands more youngsters and the provision of therapy to those in need.

Talia Levanon speaks quickly. Propped on the desk of her Jerusalem office are pictures of her four daughters. Her smiling 20-year-old, Noga, is dressed in army khakis and draped in a flak jacket. She is posing with the German shepherd she trained. "They work at bomb detection," Talia said, rolling her eyes. "I worry sick about her."

Talia marveled at how she and the rest of the Israeli population were coping with the intifada. But she wondered how much was just habituation to the stress. "When you're in a survival mode, you don't fall apart," she said. She thought Israeli resiliency might weaken when the threat of terrorism declined. "When there no longer is outside pressure, people will need to deal with their anxieties and anger." She paused. Recognizing that in some sense the Israelis were engaged in a long unpleasant experiment, she simply mused, "It remains to be seen what will happen."

Shelley Horwitz was also a key leader in the development of the Israel Trauma Coalition. In the 1970s she had lived in Israel, where she taught English and worked in community services. "So I was familiar with the styles of operation in both countries," she told me. Despite similar values and goals, some approaches in the two societies were different. As many others noted, Israelis were good at innovation, especially during an emergency. Horwitz savored a description she once heard: "Israelis will figure out how to change a tire while the car is moving."

She explained that her American colleagues in human services are more proprietary than Israelis, more reluctant to deviate from standard procedures. "Here we do more evidence-based practices. We're more deliberate and committed to the plan." Does this mean the Israelis would be better off doing the same? I asked. Not necessarily, she said, because in the United States, "we have the luxury of reflective space. We're not under fire."

She was speaking about the provision of mental health services, but the basic premise about the Israeli approach was generic. It echoed Benjamin Davidson's reference to Israeli improvisations on the battlefield, Asher Hirshberg's endorsement of deviations from disaster plans, and Dvora Hertz on the value of skipping emergency room protocols that might delay medical response to a seriously injured patient.

I asked Shelley Horwitz about the state of readiness in the United States. "We're not disaster-prepared anything like the Israelis," she answered. When she was teaching in Israel, a 7-year-old boy once called her attention to an unattended package in the school playground. In the United States that would not happen, even with adults, she said. "People here are not educated to think that way." Then, with resignation, she concluded that Americans are unlikely to become more aware and responsive until the threat seems imminent or until there is another attack on U.S. soil. Horwitz was sounding the recurrent worry about this country by people who have worked in both societies. It is difficult for Americans to fathom life under a barrage of seemingly endless assaults. Even Israelis had not previously imagined the kind of stepped-up terrorism that befell them in the recent intifada. But by the time of 9/11, Israel had much to teach America about dealing with trauma spawned by a terrorist attack. Jonas Waizer, a mental health specialist in a nonprofit community agency, acknowledged as much. His organization, FEGS–Health and Human Services System, provided counseling to more than 200,000 New Yorkers during the first year after 9/11. That agency and others freely borrowed from Israeli practice. As Waizer later wrote: "Israeli colleagues, with experience in other terror attacks and disasters, taught us new approaches to staff training and a more flexible mix of mental health practice and public health outreach."[13]

The current Israeli approach to dealing with trauma has developed, in part, through the experience of volunteer groups. Many were started by dedicated individuals like Ruth Bar-On, who founded Selah, one of Israel's first such relief organizations.

* * *

After returning to her Tel Aviv home late in the evening of June 1, 2001, Ruth Bar-On clicked on the television. It was near midnight, and a suicide bombing had just occurred at the Dolphinarium dance hall. The newscast reported that many victims were young people from the former Soviet Union. Ruth felt a sudden emptiness and whispered to herself, "Heavens, not again." Earlier that evening she had visited with Sasha Sarokin, a six-year-old boy whose family had emigrated from Russia a year before. He was staying with his uncle while recuperating from a bombing two weeks earlier in the West Bank city of Hebron. Sasha's father had been killed in the incident and his mother was still in intensive care.

New immigrants to Israel often lack a network of relatives and friends, and are especially needy when faced with critical situations. Ruth's volunteer work began in the 1970s on behalf of Soviet Jews. Recognizing the special needs of new immigrants, she founded Selah, the Israel Crisis Management Center, in 1993. Beginning with a handful of helpers, the organization has since developed a countrywide roster of more than six hundred volunteers. Under Ruth's directorship, Selah has connected to thousands of new immigrants from Russia, Ethiopia, Argentina, and elsewhere. To help them cope with critical illness and other tragedies, the organization provides financial aid, counseling, and moral support. Only a few of the organization's volunteers are psychologists and social workers. The rest have been tutored by Selah's staff about how to help, how to relate to people in distress. As the number of terror attacks mounted, the need for support grew among new immigrants as well as among others in the society.

Moments into the newscast on the Dolphinarium bombing, Ruth grabbed her jacket and drove five minutes to Ichilov Hospital, a mile from the event. She knew that worried parents and other relatives would be rushing there. At the hospital entrance, she saw dozens of ambulances and emergency vehicles with lights still flashing. Hundreds of people in search of loved ones were already streaming into the lobby. Is my child here? Is he badly injured? Can I see him? Some patients were in the emergency department, and some were in the midst of surgery. Others had been moved to intensive care. Not all their names had been forwarded to the information desk, and harried aides could only urge patience.

The intifada was just seven months old, and Israeli hospitals had not yet refined information techniques for crowds of anxious visitors. That kind of efficiency would further develop with continuing experience. Ruth squeezed past the entrance and moved through the anxious crowd. She began phoning Selah volunteers. "I'm at Ichilov. We need you. Can you come here now or to Wolfsohn [a nearby hospital]?" Working through the night, she and, eventually, eighty Selah volunteers fanned out to all the area hospitals, lending comfort to the families.

"When I worked in the Soviet Jewry movement in the 1970s and 1980s, it was with a passion," she told me in 2005. Her passion now was to help these victims. Although she still lives in Tel Aviv, where she was born in 1940, she has traveled to every corner of Israel and many countries beyond. Her visits overseas often involve fundraising. Selah's annual budget of $1 million comes largely from private donations. The money is for beds and refrigerators, professional counselors, healing retreats—the array of needs of the wounded and the bereaved. The dedication of a half-dozen full-time staffers is reflected in their willingness to work for very little pay. Ruth's net salary, the highest in the organization, is around $30,000 per year. She, like the others, often labors around the clock.

Soon after Ruth arrived at Ichilov, she spotted a diminutive woman sitting quietly, oblivious to the surrounding frenzy. Ruth approached her and asked if she was all right. The woman said she was awaiting information about her two teenagers, Yelena and Yuli. Ella Nelimov spoke evenly. But when Ella said she was waiting to learn whether they were at this hospital or another, she seemed not to have considered the most tragic possibility. "The mind cannot comprehend . . . ," Ruth said to me, her voice trailing off. Then she resumed her narrative: "I smiled at Ella, patted her shoulder, and moved on to speak with others."

Some time after 1 AM, Ruth drove to the National Forensic Institute, where the bodies of twenty young victims had been sent. There she joined with other Selah volunteers who were trying to comfort families that had just identified the remains of their children. And there she again saw Ella Nelimov. She embraced Ella, as she and fellow volunteers had done for so many others. For Ella it was the first act in a lifeline of support. A day later, Ella received a visit from Selah's Micha Feldmann, who befriended Ella and the remaining members of the family—Ella's mother and her son, Sasha.

When I asked Ella nearly four years after the loss of Yuli and Yelena if she still sought help to deal with her loss, she said that when she feels the need, she calls a friend or someone at Selah. "We sit and talk. Sometimes we cry. Sometimes we laugh," she said. She recalled that before she met Ruth Bar-On at the hospital she had never heard of her organization. But since then, Selah volunteers had become like family to her.

* * *

Member organizations of the ITC like Selah, Natal, and the centers begun by Mooli Lahad and Danny Brom predated the onset of the intifada in 2000. But they soon became outnumbered by an astonishing array of new organizations. Elisheva Flom-Oren, an Israeli coordinator for the New York UJA-Federation services in Israel, told me that relief organizations established since 2000 numbered in the hundreds. Some are more equipped than others to help, but for almost all, the motivation was "to do good."

As happened in the United States after 9/11, new groups were often started by relatives of victims. After Seth and Sherrie Mandell's 13-year-old son, Koby, was killed in May 2001, they established a foundation to help others who also lost loved ones to terrorism. Koby and a friend were stoned to death near the West Bank settlement of Tekoa. His parents determined to "take the cruelty of Koby's murder and transform it into kindness," according to the Web site of the Koby Mandell Foundation.[14] Among its activities, the foundation sponsors summer camp programs that have been attended by hundreds of youngsters affected by terrorism.

Similarly, Arnold and Frimet Roth established the Malki Foundation after their daughter's death in August 2001. Malki, at 15, was among fifteen fatalities in a suicide bombing in Jerusalem's Sbarro Pizza restaurant. During her short life, she had been devoted to her disabled younger sister and was a volunteer counselor at a camp for teenagers with handicaps. The foundation in her name funds specialized therapy for disabled youngsters. The Mandells and Roths acknowledge that they also created their organizations as a means to help them cope. For the Mandells, it was "to fight against" their despair and pain. For the Roths, it was "a way to go on."[15]

Many other organizations arose from a sense of caring, even if no family members had been directly affected by terrorism. The extent of assistance provided by such groups was largely governed by their ability to organize, mobilize resources, and market themselves. No group excelled at this more than the OneFamily Fund.

* * *

Michal Belzberg, nearly 13, was eagerly anticipating her bat mitzvah. It was August 9, 2001, and in two weeks she would, according to Jewish tradition, symbolically enter adulthood through participation in a Sabbath service. Michal was the second of seven children, and her older sister had celebrated her bat mitzvah the previous year. Her father, Marc, was a successful businessman, and the family looked forward to hosting another large party. Marc and his wife Chantal would be paying for airfare and lodging in Jerusalem for their extended family from Canada, the United States, Belgium, France, and the United Kingdom.

That afternoon at 2 o'clock, a Hamas terrorist blew himself up in the Sbarro Pizza restaurant in downtown Jerusalem. The bomber was Izzedine al-Masri, 23, a resident of the West Bank Arab town of Jenin. It was the incident that killed Malki Roth and fourteen others. Among the dead were five members of the same family, Mordechai and Tzira Schijveschuurder, their daughters, Raíaya, 14, and Hemda, 2, and their son, Yitzhak, 4.

Although the Belzbergs did not know the victims, they anguished with other Israelis about the loss of so many innocents. Later in the evening Michal, Marc, and Chantal talked about the day's events. "Michal, do you really think now we should have a big party?" her mother asked. Marc wondered if they shouldn't be trying to help people affected by the attacks. As the family talked further, Michal agreed that she wanted to do something that would have meaning long after her bat mitzvah. When Marc suggested that money for the party could be given to victims and their families, she said, "Daddy, I think that's a good idea."

In the following days, Chantal made dozens of phone calls. The party is canceled, she told one guest after another. "We really don't think it's appropriate now." When she explained that money intended for the party would be used to help terror victims, the responses were uniformly supportive. Friends and relatives sent contributions, and in the weeks after Michal's scaled-down bat mitzvah celebration, the family had accumulated $150,000. Marc, Chantal, and Michal visited several affected families and asked how they could help. Some welcomed their offer of financial assistance and others refused. But all were grateful for their concern.

The Belzbergs concluded that despite the efforts of existing organizations, many victims and families were not receiving adequate support. They started a Web site that described the ordeals of affected families and how contributions could help. The Belzbergs named their project OneFamily Fund, hired a director, and with a growing staff began to solicit donations and to develop projects for victims and families. The fund began to support counseling services and family retreats.

On an afternoon in early 2005, in the Jerusalem offices supplied by her husband's company, Chantal Belzberg spoke of her 10-hour workday. She had recently become the organization's unpaid director, overseeing an eleven-member staff. "I'll tell you something. All I ever wanted was to be a full-time mommy," she chuckled, surprised at where the past three years had taken her. She sees her children in the evening, though after their bedtime she is back to e-mail and phone calls for the organization. When we met, Chantal showed me plans for an upcoming four-day retreat for a hundred families. She would soon be on the phone with supporters and new potential donors in the United States and Britain. Why does she devote so much time to the effort? I asked. Her silent half-smile provided a tacit answer. Helping others brings personal fulfillment. Then she added, "If you save $100 in salary costs, that $100 goes to a family in need."

In 2005, the annual budget for OneFamily fund approached $4 million. During its four-year existence, the organization provided $11 million in goods and services. Thousands of Israelis have benefited from its help.

* * *

In July 2004, the Losch family in Wyckoff, New Jersey, hosted Dana and Michal Eliraz, bubbly 14-year-old twin girls from a Jerusalem suburb. On most days, after a quick breakfast, the girls were off to the Teen Travel Camp run by the nearby Jewish Community Center. With ten other Israelis and thirty Americans, all teenagers, they went on day-long bus trips to museums, a comedy club, the New Jersey Aquarium, an outing at the beach. Midway through their stay in America, I met the twins and asked what they liked best so far.

"Everything," Dana replied. Giggles. Her dark ponytail bobbed about.

Okay, but what was really the best? I pressed.

"New York. The Empire State Building, when we went to the top," Dana said.

Do you agree with your sister? I asked, turning to Michal.

"No, it was sad," Michal answered. Had she misunderstood my question? She burst out laughing and assured me that she agreed with Dana.

Tall and thin, the Eliraz girls seemed perpetually upbeat. For their hosts, Sarah and Jorge Losch, and their 19-year-old daughter Jessie, evenings and weekends with the twins became addictive. Charmed by their warmth, the Losches found themselves looking forward to their return from camp every afternoon. The final morning of the girls' three-week stay in America was sad for everyone. "We were crying, they were crying," Sarah recalled. Before the bus pulled away to take them to the airport, the twins kept repeating, "We love you, we love you." Not that Dana and Michal's connection to their family in Israel had weakened. Two or three times a day, a call would come from their parents, their grandfather, or their older brother Guy. If the girls were at camp, Sarah or Jessie would assure the family that everything was fine. "When the girls were here, they would get on the phone," Sarah said, and then imitated their response to their grandfather: "Hellooo. I love you *saba.*"

July–August of 2004 was the third summer that OneFamily had connected Israeli youngsters to this camp program. The New Jersey community, which called the project Open Hearts–Open Homes, had partnered with OneFamily to bring over a dozen youngsters at a time. Since 2002, three sessions, each for three weeks, were held every summer. The program was one of many that were intended to provide a joyful experience for Israelis affected by terrorism.

When Michal and Dana unpacked their bags on the first day of their stay with the Losch family, they placed a half-dozen photographs on the bureau. "That's our mother and father," Dana said to the Losches, "and our two brothers, Guy and Roi." Roi, mirroring the expansive smile of his sisters, was 22 when he was killed the previous year. He was a victim of a suicide bombing of Bus 14 in Jerusalem. Without a hint of melancholy, Michal pointed to Roi's picture and purred, "He was so cute." In the weeks following, when the girls spoke of Roi, it was always with an air of cheerfulness. When Sarah asked about him, the girls just smiled and said he had many friends and everybody loved him.

Trained in early childhood education, Sarah wondered if their light-hearted response was a defense mechanism, perhaps a manner of coping. "I'm not a therapist," she told me, "but I wondered if they were living in a kind of time warp." Or perhaps emotions did not run deep in their family. After the twins returned to Israel, the Losches remained in contact with the girls and their parents. Phone calls and e-mails were suffused with pleasantries and rarely referred to Roi's loss. But after a few months, their mother, Irit, e-mailed Sarah that she felt so grateful and close to the Losches that she considered them family. Departing from the usual pleasantness, she wrote, "You can't understand how difficult it is. I try to put on a good face for the rest of the children. But Roi was also my best friend, and I'm really dying inside." As Sarah quoted Irit's words to me, her eyes became moist.

Two years later, in 2006, the Losches visited Israel, where they were hosted by the Eliraz family. Dana and Michal, now 16, were still relentlessly upbeat, as were their brother Guy, their father, and grandparents. Only their mother, Irit, would reveal a flash of sadness when she discussed Roi. But it was clear that Roi's memory was a continuing part of all their lives. Members of the family and friends of Roi frequently visited a small nearby park, now named Roi's Garden. It was on a bluff overlooking the cemetery in which he was buried.

* * *

Tens of thousands of Israelis have received help to cope with trauma wrought by the wave of terrorism. Survivors, families who lost loved ones, or people who were just stressed by years of assaults were freely assisted. Many Israelis actively sought help, while others responded to overtures from organizations. Although the Israeli government provided some financial assistance, private volunteer groups filled gaps to help nurse the survivors back to productive lives. They proved essential to the nation's well-being.

After 9/11, private groups in the United States also augmented government assistance to victims and families. As in Israel, new volunteer organizations emerged in the wake of the attacks. The most notable difference between the two experiences was that the American organizations were formed after a single mega-event. In contrast, Israelis continued to organize throughout the years of attacks as increased numbers needed help. Moreover, many more groups in Israel spontaneously sprang from the grass roots than in the United States. In part this was attributable to a profound sense of community among Israelis—"We're all in the same boat here," Israelis repeatedly emphasized to me. If Americans were subjected to continuing attacks, perhaps they also would coalesce around a core sense of common destiny. That question remains open.

Since this book is principally about the Israeli experience and how people have coped with terrorism, little has been said about the terrorists themselves. Their behavior is of course a key part of the overall subject. The next chapter is based on interviews with Palestinians who support or oppose the killing of innocent Israelis. It draws on the thinking of a former terrorist who was gravely injured in an Israeli reprisal and who later came to reject Palestinian violence against Israeli civilians and endorse a two-state solution. It also displays the views of unrepentant militants who remain committed to the destruction of the Jewish state. The net impression offers little hope for an end to terrorism in the Middle East any time soon.

11

Palestinians

In 1972, when Bassam Abu Sharif opened an innocent-looking book delivered by mail, the ensuing explosion nearly killed him. Two years earlier, Sharif had helped plan the hijacking of three passenger airliners that were forced to land in the Jordanian desert. He was a member of the Popular Front for the Liberation of Palestine (PFLP), a Marxist terrorist group that denied Israel's right to exist. After the hijackings, Sharif's picture appeared on the cover of *Time* magazine with other terrorists under the caption "Pirates of the Sky."[1] Israel's foreign intelligence agency, the Mossad, had sent the rigged book to Sharif, though the agency later stopped targeting terrorists with mail bombs. But Sharif's life since then has provided instructive parallels and contrasts to those of Israeli victims of terrorism.

Ten miles north of Jerusalem, in the West Bank city of Ramallah, is the compound of the headquarters of the Palestinian Authority, where Yasser Arafat was buried in November 2004. Sharif, who had been a longtime adviser to Arafat, lives just outside the compound. Three months after Arafat's death, on a chilly February afternoon, I departed Jerusalem for a meeting with Sharif. Foreign nationals, unlike Israelis, were permitted to travel from Israel to Palestinian towns. The travel restrictions against Israelis began in October 2000, when two Israeli soldiers inadvertently drove into Ramallah and were lynched by a local mob.

Ramallah also became a breeding ground for suicide bombers. But by early 2005, terror attacks had declined, and talks were revived between Israeli and Palestinian leaders. In fact, on February 7, a week before my visit, Prime Minister Sharon and the newly elected chairman of the Palestinian Authority, Mahmoud Abbas, met and pledged to seek an end to violence. A year later political conditions would be radically different: Palestinian voters elected the terrorist organization Hamas to a majority in the Palestinian legislature and Ehud Olmert became prime minister after Sharon suffered a stroke from which he never recovered. But in February 2005, the reduced tension and my American passport enabled me to travel into the West Bank unencumbered. My cab driver, Mohammed Rabiah, an Arab resident of Jerusalem, navigated us through the Israeli checkpoint just beyond the Jerusalem boundary. After a brief examination of our credentials, a uniformed Israeli waved us through.

The soft-spoken Rabiah, a trained accountant, had abandoned his profession fifteen years earlier in favor of more lucrative work as a taxi driver. Once past the checkpoint, we entered the ramshackle West Bank village of Kalandia. The contrast in road conditions was emblematic of life on the other side of the demarcation line. After smoothly paved surfaces, we encountered a battery of potholes that forced our cab to buck and jump like a rodeo steer. As we proceeded through other villages, billboard images of the recently deceased Arafat were plentiful. But there were just as many of Mahmoud Abbas, whose contested election the previous month seemed to be a welcome step away from the authoritarian rule imposed by Arafat.

As we approached Ramallah, the surrounding conditions improved. Driving was less bumpy, and homes appeared more spacious and attractive. A mile into town, we reached the stone walled perimeter of the Palestinian headquarters. Uncertain of the exact location of Sharif's home, Rabiah drove to the entrance of the compound and asked a Palestinian guard for directions. The young man in a black beret and khaki uniform began an explanation in Arabic. Cradling an automatic, he pointed back up the road. Rabiah turned the cab around, drove 100 meters, and parked near a stately three-story stone house.

I walked past a garden of low hedges and approached the large front door. After identifying myself through an intercom, a voice invited me to enter and climb one flight. At the top of the stairs two guards ushered me into an office. I was unsure if Bassam Abu Sharif was the man in dark glasses standing beside the desk until his raspy greeting echoed the sound I had heard in our phone conversations. A weathered windbreaker covered his turtleneck sweater, and gray sweatpants signaled an atmosphere of informality. Bassam beckoned me to the small couch in front of his desk. He pressed next to me, and only later did I understand that he moved so close because he was nearly deaf.

On the wall behind us hung a dozen photographs. One was of Sharif in the late 1970s, holding his then-toddler daughter, Karma. Another showed his son, Omar, playing a guitar. The gray-haired gentleman in a fine suit was his father. "That picture was taken in Monterey, California," Sharif said. His English, though heavily accented, has been refined by visits to the United States where his father and other relatives now live. The only non-family member in the pictures was Yasser Arafat, who appeared variously with Sharif and his wife and two children. The intended message was clear: Arafat had been close to Sharif and his family.

My interest in meeting with Abu Sharif, now 59, was not only to hear his political views but to learn about his experience as the target of an Israeli bomb. I asked him much the same questions that I asked Israeli victims of Palestinian bombs—about the circumstances of the bombing, the injuries, the psychological effects.

I had not realized the extent of the physical damage to him until we met. Various fingers from both hands were missing, and as he spoke, the right corner of his mouth drooped slightly. The blast had left scars across his face and much of the rest of his body. Still, his chin, though marred, retained the outlines of rugged good looks.

In 1972 Bassam Abu Sharif, then 26, was editor of *Al Hadaf,* the weekly newspaper of the Popular Front for the Liberation of Palestine. Based in Beirut, the PFLP was one of several terror organizations that had operated from Jordan before the hijackings. The PFLP's action in September 1970 catapulted it to world attention but aroused the ire of Jordan's King Hussein. The hijackers kept the terrorized passengers aboard while wiring the three airliners with explosives. After a week, the captives were released and the planes blown up. But King Hussein then ordered his troops to suppress all Palestinian activism in his county. Following bloody confrontations, the PFLP and the rest of the Palestine Liberation Organization were evicted from Jordan. In the end, Sharif recognized the events as "a catastrophe for the Palestinian cause."[2]

When I asked Sharif about the booby-trapped book, he said it was the size of a standard dictionary. His excitement about receiving the new volume was enhanced by its apparent subject matter. "I could make out the words, 'Che Guevara,' who was a big hero of mine." As Bassam Abu Sharif talked further, he went through the motions of holding an imaginary book and lifting its cover. "You know, you usually start by looking at the title, maybe going to the index, and then flipping through some pages." Then he issued a single clap of his hands as if simulating a blast. He threw his head back and sat motionless.

I broke the silence. After the explosion was he unconscious? I asked.

"Actually no. I remember everything."

What happened next?

"After the bang, I couldn't see anymore. And I couldn't hear anything, although I didn't realize that at first. Everything was black, but I could feel blood coming from parts of my body."

Sharif's unhesitant recollection suggested that he had replayed the incident in his mind over the years. I asked if he had been in pain. "No pain," he answered, "but I could feel cuts, openings." He drew his hand along his face and neck and the sides of his body.

Sharif had been in the archives room of his newspaper's offices when he opened the parcel. Through the blackness, he moved to the door by feeling his way along the shelves. When he reached the corridor, he felt hands on his shoulders. "I thought that someone was trying to kidnap me."

The hands were directing him down the corridor, and he asked who the person was. No response. "I didn't realize I couldn't hear," he told me. He began to reenact his desperation. "Why aren't you answering? Who are you?" As he was guided out of the building, he struggled for breath. The thought of being kidnapped heightened his fears. Returning to reenactment, he gulped for air and pointed to his open mouth. "The blood was all over me, and I felt it in my throat blocking my airway." He was guided into a car and driven to a hospital. "I couldn't see, but I could feel, and my breathing was becoming more desperate." He felt a tube being inserted in his throat, which provided some relief as it sucked out blood from his breathing passage. That was the last thing he remembered.

Unconscious for nine days, he remained in the hospital for three months. Recovery, such as it was, continued at home. His scarred body, severed fingers, and impaired sight and hearing were irreparable consequences of the blast. As Sharif spoke, he raised his dark glasses to his forehead. His right eye remained round, while his left eye squinted as if trying to focus. He pointed to the right eye and said, "It's glass." With his fingertip he audibly tapped the glass surface. "Can you see me all right through your other eye?" I asked. His left eye narrowed further. "Ohhh, I can see you with the eye and the mind, but not the eye alone."

I asked if he was angry at having been so badly injured. He cocked his head to the side. "I'll tell you, I was angry with myself to allow them to trick me. I said to myself, 'Stupid.'" The "them," of course, was the Mossad, the Israeli intelligence agency.

Through the years, however, Sharif began to shed his bitterness. Long before the 1993 Oslo agreement, he had urged Arafat to seek a two-state solution—one Israeli and the other Palestinian. I wondered about the basis of his changed attitude. What psychological effects, I asked, did the bombing have on him? "Look," he answered, "it has kept me from leading my life the way I did before. I loved reading, usually at night. Now I can't do that. After reading for a little while, I get pain in my eye and my head." He became contemplative. "And my hearing." He pointed to the right ear with the large hearing aid. "If you sat on my left side I wouldn't hear you at all. That side is deaf." He emphasized that these were physical annoyances. He seemed to be searching for a more direct answer to my question, and finally he said, "I have no psychological reaction, for example, when I see an envelope."

Did other things bother him such as a loud sound, a boom? I asked.

He dragged his answer: "Nooo." He linked his response to a political point. "When I hear a loud sound, it means the Israeli army is here." He said that Israeli tanks would park outside his office and shell Arafat's former office across the street. While acknowledging that the noise was disconcerting, Sharif surmised that it was no more disturbing to him than to others who had not personally been bomb victims.

Sharif then shifted his thoughts back three decades and spoke of how the bombing oddly boosted his self-confidence. "I was 26 years old, and I was in love. Before the bombing, I didn't dare go to her family. They were well-known Maronites, religious and very rich." He added plaintively, "And I was a Palestinian." His implication was obvious, that the difference in social rank prompted his reticence. "But after I was blown up, I went to her family. I had the confidence, a year and a half later."

I thought about Kinneret and Maytal and how their pain and injuries, paradoxically, also led them to enhanced confidence and strength.

And what happened to the young woman he was in love with? I asked. "She is my wife, Amal, the mother of my two kids," he offered with a smile.

A week earlier, on February 9, Sharon had met with Abbas, who promised to cooperate with the Israeli plan to evacuate the settlements in Gaza. At the same time, they called for a ceasefire and pledged to return to the "roadmap" toward a peace agreement.

I asked if Sharif was encouraged by the meeting and by the long-term prospects for peace. His chin jutted forward as he contemplated the question. "On the surface things might look better, but I am doubtful," he answered. He said the Israelis were continuing to confiscate land on the West Bank and build more settlements. "This will create a lot of grudges, a lot of reasons for people to revolt, and will not lead to peace. Leaving Gaza does not mean the end of the problem."

I returned to his earlier observation that he had long ago rejected actions like hijacking. When did that happen? I asked. As far back as 1972, he began to question the value of "special operations," and not because of the injury he suffered. "It became very clear," he said, "that the negative results of such operations had become more than the positive results." Sharif left the PFLP in the late 1980s to join with Arafat. By then he was convinced that Israel would not be liquidated and that peace could come with the creation of a Palestinian state in the West Bank and Gaza.

Sharif emphasized to me his scorn for the occupation, and he did not reject armed opposition by Palestinians in all circumstances. But he held no brief for the kind of terrorism that became rampant during the intifada. He said he had challenged Hamas and others, both in public debate and written articles, to end their attacks on civilians.

"Ohhh, these are unfortunate victims. What do you think? Do you think I'm happy when I see old men or kids on buses killed? This is stupidity. It's sick in the mind. I understand when you go to war, you are a soldier and you fight. . . . But I don't understand targeting civilians."

Sharif also condemned Israeli reprisals that included destroying houses of the families of terrorists. "I don't understand how you can leave a family in the wind and rain because one member—a son, a cousin, or whatever—is said to have a relationship with an organization." Still, he has not shrunk from publicly rejecting suicide bombing and random violence. "People have said, 'Bassam you must be worried about yourself, challenging Hamas and the others.' And I said, 'To hell with them.'"

Bassam Abu Sharif's reasons for opposition veer between the moral and the pragmatic. The path he envisions recognizes the national rights of two peoples. Not so with the groups he criticizes, like Hamas, Islamic Jihad, and Al Aqsa Martyrs Brigades, who glorify the killing of Israelis as an act of martyrdom.

* * *

Orit Stelser's blue uniform and gold leaf epaulettes identify her as a major in Israel's national prison services. Her slight frame and charming demeanor defy the stereotype of a tough prison official. On March 24, 2005, we met at the entrance to Ohaley Kedar, the high-walled prison near Beersheva, 50 miles south of Jerusalem. Behind the walls were eight hundred inmates, three hundred of them security prisoners. I had received government authorization to interview several prisoners, and Orit was there to escort me inside. She had arranged the visit to a section containing fifty-three Palestinians who were involved in terror attacks.

After passing through the fortified entrance, guards led us through a labyrinth of doors and hallways to an open area within the prison grounds. Fifty feet ahead stood a single-story building whose steel door opened into a whitewashed corridor lined with twenty-five cells. The upper half of each cell door contained a lattice of horizontal and vertical bars that permitted easy viewing from one side to the other. Each cell contained a pair of bunk beds with colorful blankets and a surprising array of household goods—a bureau, desk, television set, eating utensils, a hot plate for cooking. Shelves were stocked with bottles of orange and grapefruit drinks and other soft beverages. Each cell served as bedroom and kitchen, and each included a lavatory area. The door to cell number 6 was open, and under the relaxed watch of a few guards, its two occupants were affixing clothing hooks to a wall. Behind them, hanging from the wall, were pots, pans, and towels. Other shelves held stacks of books.

It was 2 PM and most prisoners were in the exercise yard, which was available to them for three hours a day. The enclosed yard was visible through the bars at the end of the corridor. Several prisoners were briskly pacing back and forth in exercise fashion, while others played table tennis. Some inmates had chosen to remain in their cells, reading, and a few stood chatting in the corridor.

Every prisoner in that section had killed or helped kill Israelis. But the atmosphere between guards and inmates seemed devoid of tension. Orit and the other guards asked if I wanted to meet with anyone in particular. I said that individuals who spoke English would make interviewing easier. I pulled out a list of questions I had prepared: "Do you consider yourself a terrorist?" "Are suicide bombers martyrs?" "What is the goal of suicide bombings or other attacks against civilians?" "Has being in prison changed your attitude about the Israeli-Palestinian conflict?"

A guard walked over to cell number 2 and asked Abbas Al Sayyed, age 39, if he would talk to me. Through the bars Al Sayyed greeted me in fluent English and said he wanted a few minutes to put on a clean shirt and neaten himself. Since he was still awaiting trial, he was not obliged to wear the brown jumpsuit of a convicted inmate.

Abbas Al Sayyed had been the Hamas leader in the West Bank town of Tulkarm, from which he allegedly directed at least two suicide attacks. The first, on May 18, 2001, at a shopping mall in Netanya, killed five Israelis and injured more than a hundred others. The second, and more notorious, was at a Passover Eve dinner of elderly guests at the Park Hotel in Netanya. On March 27, 2002, Muhammad Abd al-Basset Odeh, 25, dressed in woman's clothing, entered the dining hall and detonated himself. The explosion killed 30 and injured 160 diners, most in their 70s and 80s. The next day Arab television showed a videotape of Odeh somberly reading his will. The broadcast initially aired on Al-Manar, the television network of the Lebanon-based Hezbollah. Like Hamas, with which it works cooperatively, Hezbollah is on the U.S. list of terror organizations.

Soon after the telecast, a poster appeared in Arab media showing Odeh brandishing an M-16 assault rifle in one hand and a copy of the Koran in the other. The poster announced the death of the "martyr" Odeh and promised paradise to Muslim believers who kill infidels in the name of Allah.[3]

This attack prompted the Israeli military to reenter the West Bank and take control of the major cities that they had evacuated as part of the 1993 Oslo agreement. Through interrogations and captured documents, Israeli authorities learned that Odeh was driven into Israel from Tulkarm. The vehicle, a Renault Express with Israeli license plates, had been purchased for $4,000 by a Hamas operative with a false Israeli ID. In seeking areas where they could inflict heavy casualties, Odeh and his driver drove through several Israeli cities before entering Netanya. Upon seeing a crowd around the Park Hotel, Odeh waited nearby. At 7:30 PM, after hundreds had gathered inside the dining room, Odeh walked in and blew himself up.

Abbas Al Sayyed was charged with planning every detail of the attack, from equipping Odeh with an explosives belt to the videotaping of Odeh reading his will, which Sayyed helped him write. Before dispatching Odeh, Sayyed allegedly instructed him to shave his beard and mustache, don a wig of long hair, and dress in a full-length dark gown to conceal the explosives. As was later confirmed, Sayyed also planned to add a chemical poison to the metal shards and bolts mixed with the explosives. He had obtained a vial of cyanide from his pharmacist nephew, Tareq Zaydan, but decided to postpone its use for a subsequent bombing. He was apprehended before he could launch any further attacks.[4]

A sense of repugnance about the deliberate killing of innocent people at the Park Hotel was far from universal. Nine months after the attack, in January 2003, the official newspaper of the Palestinian Authority, *Al Hayat Al Jida,* carried the following item about Odeh, referring to him as a *shahid* (Arabic for "martyr"):

> . . . in Tulkarm's Abd Al Majid Tia School soccer field, under the auspices of Jamal Tarif, director of education; Sport Supervisor Jamal Odeh; and in the presence of school principal Jamal Ayat; the head of the Sports committee, and committee members; the Tulkarm Shahids Memorial soccer championship tournament of the Shahid Abd Al-Baset Odeh [the suicide bomber who attacked a Netanya hotel last Passover Eve], began with the participation of seven top teams, named after Shahids who gave their lives to redeem the Homeland. Isam, the brother of the Shahid [of the Passover eve Massacre], will distribute the trophies.[5]

It was Odeh's purported handler, the man behind the attack, to whom I was about to speak. A guard unlocked the door of Sayyed's cell and directed him across the hallway to a room the size of a walk-in closet. We squeezed into chairs opposite each other across a small table.

I was facing an individual whose neat mustache, carefully groomed hair, and freshly laundered shirt signaled concern about personal appearance. His vanity seemed uncharacteristic of the abnegation associated with Islamic fundamentalism. Sayyed had graduated from Jordan's University of Science and Technology as a mechanical engineer and later, in 1992, completed a program at Emory University in Atlanta on anesthesia equipment. There he became an expert on ventilators, medical gases, and anesthesia machines. He was educated, intelligent, and articulate. But he was also a man whose moral universe embraced the deliberate killing of Jews.

The guards left us alone. None could be seen past the open door of the room, though I had confidence that help would be available if needed. Sayyed spoke freely and expressed no bitterness at his incarceration, though plenty about "the Israeli occupation."

He had been arrested in Tulkarm during the Israeli reoccupation of the city soon after the Passover bombing. Before I could ask the reason for his arrest, he peremptorily announced, "I cannot go into the charges against me, and I neither confess nor deny any of them." Acknowledging that he was a Hamas political leader, he said he was willing to talk about "the resistance."

When I asked if he considered himself a terrorist, his answer was unsurprising: "I do not think of myself as a terrorist—I am a freedom fighter. I am ready to sacrifice all I have, including my life, for getting rid of the occupation."

What about suicide bombers, I asked, are they terrorists?

His quick response suggested the question was not new to him. "I consider suicide bombers to be martyrs." He then offered an assessment as if he were a teacher presenting a tutorial. "There are three kinds of suicides," he said, "altruistic, anomic, and egoistic." Dismissing the last two as inappropriate under any circumstances, he allowed that the first form could be justified because "the cause of martyrdom is altruistic."

His message was chilling, but his manner of speaking was calm and deliberate. I probed further: Is it ever right to purposely blow up innocent people?

"To be fair, we should look at the whole picture," he answered. The word "fair" foretold an attempt at justification. He leaned forward to underscore the importance of what he was about to say. "There is a conflict between us and the occupier. The martyrdom operations in the Palestinian-Israeli conflict are exceptional. But the exceptional occupation forces us to use exceptional means."

Challenging Sayyed was not my purpose, nor would it have changed his views. I had come to hear him. But his notion of "exceptional" sounded like an apology for the inexcusable. He had contended that Palestinian suicide bombing was "altruistic" because the bomber was giving his life to benefit others. Now he was summoning the word "exceptional" as if Israeli malice was so extraordinary that it deserved an inhuman response.

I told him I was struck that his use of the words "fair," "altruistic," and now "exceptional" had stretched their meaning to suit his purposes. I pressed him with a central question: What exactly did he think was being achieved by these killings? This time his answer was direct:

"The goal of suicide bombings is to deter the occupation."

If the past four-and-a-half years were difficult for the Israelis, they had been devastating to the Palestinians. During this period, around one thousand Israelis were killed, compared to nearly four times as many Palestinians. Poverty and unemployment had become far worse for the Palestinians than for the Israelis. Yet, echoing other Hamas spokespersons, Sayyed insisted that the suicide bombings had resulted in success. By what measure? I asked.

"Because of the resistance, the Israelis are fleeing Gaza. Sharon tried but failed to submit [*sic*] my people." Again, his choice of words like "fleeing" was tailored to what he wanted to believe. Contrary to Sayyed's interpretation, Israelis understood that the decision to withdraw the 8,500 Jewish settlers from Gaza and turn governance over to the Palestinians was ultimately based on demography. About 1.2 million Palestinians live in that small strip of 141 square miles between Israel and Egypt. Keeping them under Israeli rule presented two unpalatable alternatives. Granting them Israeli citizenship would nearly double the number of Arab citizens in Israel and threaten its identity as a Jewish state. But denying them citizenship would undermine Israel's status as a democracy.

It was this calculus rather than that of Sayyed or of his organization Hamas that led to the Israeli evacuation of Gaza. Indeed, if retreating in the face of terror attacks had been the main impetus, withdrawal from Gaza would not have been the priority. Almost every suicide bomber had entered Israel from the West Bank. The barrier fence between Gaza and Israel had largely prevented the entry of would-be terrorists from Gaza. The sharp decline in the number of attacks by 2005 was attributable in part to the new barrier being built in the West Bank. Thus, if terror attacks had been the measure, Israeli withdrawal would have been from the West Bank, not Gaza.

Had imprisonment influenced Sayyed's thinking? I asked. "My

three years here have not changed my mind," he replied. The essential notion behind Abbas Al Sayyed's behavior was his belief that Israel had no right to exist as a Jewish state. "Don't expect me to forget my homeland," he insisted. "All the Palestinians have had their homes taken away, and I don't think they can forget." After describing Israel as a terrorist state, he again justified suicide bombing—martyrdom operations—as an appropriate "exceptional response."

Midway through our conversation, a penetrating chant from the exercise yard summoned the Muslim faithful to prayer. Sayyed politely excused himself and said he would be back in a few minutes. He walked through the door to the courtyard and joined a dozen others standing shoulder to shoulder. In unison they prayed, first standing, then descending to their knees, heads bent to the ground, rising with arms extended and palms up. After several repetitions, the prayer was concluded and Sayyed returned to our small room. His entry into the courtyard and return to the room drew no special attention from the guards. During prayer, the area seemed to belong to the Muslim faithful.

Doubtless, Sayyed would kill every guard if he had the chance, which raised my curiosity about his cordial interactions with them. He acknowledged the seeming civility of their day-to-day relationship, shrugged his shoulders and said, "There are rules between us and the jailers." I asked what he could say about the charges against him. Without emotion he responded that they included overseeing the suicide attacks at the Park Hotel and at the Sharon Mall in Netanya.

The closest he came to acknowledging any association with the attacks was after I asked why he had not become a suicide bomber but only sent others. "We all have our responsibilities," he answered, "and mine were as a Hamas official at a certain level." Sayyed's two children remain in Tulkarm with his wife, Ikhlas. When he was arrested in 2002, his son Abdallah was 2 and his daughter Mawada, 4. Only recently had the children been permitted to visit. "For two-and-a-half years I didn't see them," he said plaintively. As he spoke, his voice lowered, a rare hint of emotion.

Six months later, in September 2005, the Tel Aviv District Court convicted Sayyed of killing thirty-five Israelis in the two bombings. He was sentenced to thirty-five consecutive life terms, one for each of the murdered victims, plus fifty years for other crimes, including attempted murder. The sentence was the longest in Israeli history. The court also found that Sayyed intended to use cyanide in a terror attack. Sayyed's arrest apparently saved Israelis from being targeted with a mass-casualty chemical weapon.

* * *

During my interview, Sayyed only toyed with acknowledgment of the charges against him, but other prisoners freely admitted their culpability. After speaking with Sayyed, I sat with two other prisoners in the little room. Thabit Mardawi, 29, and Haroun Nassar al-Deen, 35, both wore the brown jumpsuits of convicted criminals. Mardawi's English was weak, and Nassar al-Deen acted as translator when not speaking for himself. They both listened politely to my questions and answered softly. If gauged by manner and demeanor, they appeared entirely unthreatening.

That impression of geniality reminded me of an experience related to me when I was writing *The Anthrax Letters,* about the dissemination of anthrax bacteria by mail after 9/11.[6] One of the targeted areas was the office of a weekly tabloid, the Boca Raton, Florida, *Sun*. Gloria Irish, the wife of the paper's editor, was a real estate agent who showed nearby apartments to two Arab men during the summer of 2001. She found one of them to be particularly charming. "Marwan al-Shehhi always came in with a smile," she told me, and she even considered inviting him to a family dinner. After September 11, she was shocked to learn that Marwan al-Shehhi was the pilot of the plane that crashed into the South Tower of the World Trade Center.

How long have you been in jail? I asked Mardawi.

"Three years."

What was the reason?

"Resisting the occupation—after several actions against the occupation."

What kind of actions? I asked. Mardawi chuckled and responded matter-of-factly, as if describing a routine day at the office. "I sent a martyr to Wadi Ala. There were eight Israelis killed." When I asked the name of the "martyr," he could not remember. "There were so many of them, more than seven or eight other operations." Later, Orit Stelser, of the prison service, told me that Mardawi had been the operational commander for at least eleven suicide bombings.

So you helped prepare and encourage suicide bombers? I asked.

Mardawi shrugged and began to finger a string of prayer beads. His voice, though high-pitched, remained even. "I advised the operation."

I asked whether he considered becoming a suicide bomber himself. His answer flowed easily: "Not all of us choose how to die. Inside our organization one man has a particular role and another man has another role. I had the role to organize things as a leader for the operations. I headed the military wing for the operations. It's like the military, like General Abizaid, the leader of the U.S. army in Iraq who decides about operations there." (General John Abizaid was then commander of CENTCOM, which included the Iraq and Afghanistan theaters.)

It seemed incongruous that this thin, mild-mannered young man, whose wire-framed glasses suggested the appearance of a librarian, was actually a major Hamas figure. In the organization's terror structure, he would decide when, how, and which Palestinians would blow themselves up deliberately to kill Jews. He had done so, according to his own admission, more times than he could count.

I asked if he considered himself a terrorist, and Nassar al-Deen interjected to speak for both of them. As Sayyed did before, he insisted, "Of course not. We are freedom fighters."

Mardawi then explained that he considered suicide bombers to be martyrs, based on Muslim belief associated with an afterlife. This prompted me to ask about the often-repeated assertion that the bombers were greeted in heaven with seventy-two virgins. While granting that every martyr could expect seventy-two virgins, al-Deen insisted that was not the point of their suicides. "The first thing we look for in heaven is to see God and join the friends and family we have in heaven." He maintained that the suicide bombers were intelligent, accomplished, and not susceptible to being duped. "If you look for the reasons why these guys went and exploded themselves, you will find they finished university and had a wealthy situation. You can't come to someone who is highly educated and ask him, 'Do you want to go to heaven for seventy-two virgins?' This idea came only from the Israeli occupation, what they put in the media."

Blaming the Israelis for this idea belies the facts. In a televised statement, Mohamed Abu Tayun, an 18-year-old aspiring suicide bomber said he wanted to become a "martyr." He explained: "I want to go to Paradise where there is happiness and joy and I get to be with seventy [*sic*] virgins." In fact, the notion about the available virgins has been extensively purveyed by many Islamic theologians.[7] Nassar al-Deen's reference to the socioeconomic status of the bombers also calls for comment. Whether highly educated or not, they had been subjected to a culture of hate toward Israel that has infused much of the Arab world. The belief system within Hamas, Islamic Jihad, and other groups does not allow for compromise. "The story, in short, is that there is an occupation, and it is my duty to fight this occupation," Mardawi said. For Thabit Mardawi, occupied land includes all of Israel, and his duty includes employing methods that are beyond the realm of civilized behavior.

What is the goal, I asked, of suicide bombing, of going on a bus, seeing a pregnant woman and children, and killing them? Nassar al-Deen translated my question for Mardawi, and they went back and forth in Arabic before Mardawi finally answered. He seemed discomfited by the question. "We don't search on the bus for a pregnant woman or a child. . . . It's like this: Sometimes when you go to make this operation, it's not easy to reach there. Sometimes you can't be sure you can make it another time."

Apparently sensitive to the abhorrence felt by others about willfully targeting a child, Mardawi seemed to be saying that the bombers had no choice. Although children and pregnant women might not be his first choice of targets, better to kill them than not kill any Israelis at all.

I sought to broaden the nature of discussion and asked if they knew Bassam Abu Sharif. Surprised by the question, al-Deen said he knew who Sharif was. What do they think of him? I asked. Mardawi answered tersely and then validated his own activities. "He doesn't like the suicide bombs, the martyrs," Mardawi began. "But in our community, the majority will stand with the resistance forces." And again, a reiteration of his main theme: "We are forced by the Israelis to use these operations [suicide bombings] because they attack our civilians."

I left the prison troubled by this warped dogma. The prisoners' benign vocabulary and gentle manner seemed merely to place the harshness of their deeds in greater relief. Contrary to their softly expressed contentions, the suicide bombings were not "operations" but acts of homicide.

Resolution of the Israeli-Palestinian conflict will rest in part on whether people like Sayyed, Mardawi, and al-Deen will seek the path of a Bassam Abu Sharif. With the rise of Hamas to governing power in 2006, the chances of this happening became more remote. Still, Sharif stands as a faint symbol of the possible. A dedicated Palestinian nationalist, he moved from terrorism to pragmatism, from morally abhorrent behavior to civilized disagreement.

* * *

In explaining the state of mind of Palestinian terrorists, some Arab mental health workers appear to rationalize their actions. Dr. Eyad Serraj, a well-known Palestinian psychiatrist, contended that suicide bombing was an act of "absolute despair" arising from living "under the Israeli military occupation."[8] But he failed to acknowledge the glorification of martyrdom as key to this behavior. Nor did Serraj acknowledge the effects of the unrelenting hatred for Israel and Jews expressed in Palestinian school textbooks. And while the "military occupation" has disrupted the lives of Palestinians, this had been true largely since Israeli troops reentered occupied areas in 2002. Before then, following the Oslo agreements, the Israeli presence was minimal. It was in *response* to the terrorism of the intifada that Israeli soldiers returned in force to root out the sources.

Dr. Adel Sadeq, chairman of the Arab Psychiatrists Association in Egypt, was unusually direct in his admiration of suicide bombers. Although he later renounced the killing of innocent people, in early 2002 he told an interviewer: "As a professional psychiatrist, I say that the height of bliss comes with the end of the countdown. . . . It is a transition to another, more beautiful world, because he knows very well that within seconds he will see the light of the Creator. He will be at the closest possible point to Allah."[9]

No less troubling were findings in a study by the Palestinian psychologist Dr. Fadel Abu Hein. He claimed that Palestinian teens who did not participate in hurling rocks at Israeli soldiers suffered more anxiety and depression than who those did.[10] Hein provided no information about how his study was conducted, how anxiety and depression were measured, or whether depressed youngsters might have stayed home for reasons unrelated to rock throwing. But even if Hein's cause-and-effect supposition was valid, should he not repudiate such means of emotional release? Similarly, should not psychologists, like others, condemn suicide murder no matter what the purported reasons? In fact, moral condemnation of terrorism is rarely voiced by anyone in the Arab world.

A notable exception occurred in 2004 at a conference of business and government leaders in Davos, Switzerland. Jordan's foreign minister, Marwan Muasher, declared that suicide attacks against Israeli citizens, as against others, were morally wrong. Arab leaders, he said, should have "publicly, clearly, unequivocally taken a stand against suicide bombs."[11] Few, if any, Arab leaders responded to his remarks or took his advice.

Their refusal to condemn the killing of innocent people in Israel invites others to excuse such killings elsewhere. Altering this manner of thought stands as an overarching challenge to the world community. But while changing such attitudes should be considered a global imperative, it is to the more mundane challenges and lessons related to terrorism that we now turn.

12

Challenges and Lessons

Monday, December 5, 2005, was unseasonably warm in northern Israel. When a young man in a sweatshirt, carrying a shoulder bag, approached the Sharon Mall in Netanya, some passersby became suspicious. They alerted a nearby policewoman, Shoshi Attiya, who yelled at him to stop. When he continued toward the mall entrance and slipped his hand in the bag, Attiya drew her gun. "He's a terrorist," she screamed. "Stop him." Joined by other police, she started running after him but was reluctant to fire amid the crowd of people. At the entrance, a security guard pushed the man against the wall. At that point, the man detonated his bagful of explosives, killing the guard and four others and injuring more than sixty. Soon after, Islamic Jihad took credit for the killings and released a video of the 21-year-old suicide bomber, Lufti Abu Salem.[1]

Should the police have fired, despite the possibility of hitting bystanders? What if the man turned out not to have been a terrorist?

As Israelis were debating these questions, Americans found themselves facing a similar conundrum two days later. On December 7, after passengers had boarded an American Airlines plane in Miami International Airport, a man ran down the aisle from his rear seat, claiming he had a bomb in his backpack. When confronted by two air marshals, he bolted onto the walkway that connected the plane to the terminal.

According to the marshals, after he ignored their calls to stop and seemed to be reaching into his bag, they shot and killed him. The man was Rigoberto Alpizar, 44, an American citizen who lived in Maitland, Florida. Although his wife had shouted during the incident that he was mentally ill, only later was it clear that his bag contained no explosives and that he was not a terrorist.[2]

Should the marshals have held their fire and hoped Alpizar would not detonate the bomb he said was in the bag? What if the bag had contained explosives and the man had been a terrorist?

The ensuing public debate about whether the marshals acted properly was no more satisfactorily resolved than was the debate in Israel. In hindsight, it is obvious that shooting the Palestinian terrorist could have saved innocent lives and that restraint by the U.S. air marshals would also have saved a life. But neither the Israeli nor American actions can be condemned fairly after the fact. In both instances, the responses by the security authorities seemed warranted by conditions of the moment.

These events are reminders that tragedy can be an outcome even when a society's protectors are well rehearsed. They exemplify excruciating challenges that can face authorities when trying to protect a population from a terrorist. Still, failure to prepare for such eventualities in the best way possible would be a dereliction of a government's responsibility to protect its citizens.

* * *

Israel is widely viewed as unusually proficient at providing relief for victims of terrorist attacks and disasters. Israeli rescue and medical teams were invited to help in Kenya after the 1998 bombing of the American embassy, to Turkey following an earthquake in 1999, to India after an earthquake in 2001, and to Sri Lanka in the wake of the tsunami in 2004.

Even past critics of Israel, like Greece and Russia, have sought assistance from the Jewish state when it suited their interests. In advance of the 2004 summer Olympics in Athens, the Greek government invited Israeli security experts to help train their forces to deal with possible terrorist attacks. In the fall of that year, following the Chechen assault on the Beslan school, Russia's foreign minister, Sergey Lavrov, expressed appreciation for Israel's readiness to help in a "counterterrorist coalition."[3] At various times other countries, including France, Germany, Singapore, Australia, China, and the United States, have relied on Israeli advice about riot control and anti-terror techniques.[4]

American law enforcement officials openly prize the information they have gained from Israeli counterparts. Major John Hunt of the New Jersey State Police was part of the delegation to Israel on terror medicine and domestic security in 2005. The muscular officer returned home brimming with enthusiasm about the experience. Impressed by the relationship between Israeli police and community volunteers, he began exploring how the Israeli approach could be applied in his state. Another New Jersey police official, Bergen County's Captain Kevin Hartnett, concluded after meeting with Israeli police from Nahariya: "We can learn a lot more from them than they'll learn from us."[5]

After Charles Ramsey, chief of Washington's Metropolitan Police Department, returned from Israel, red and blue lights began to flash from District of Columbia police cars on routine patrol. Ramsey had picked up the idea from Mickey Levy, the police chief in Jerusalem, where swirling blue lights on police cruisers elevate an impression of police activity and presence. "The Israelis opened our eyes to other types of incidents that we may not have seen before or may not have been used to," said Michael Lauer, head of public information for the capitol police.[6] Ted Sexton, a sheriff in Tuscaloosa, Alabama, and president of the National Sheriff's Association, offered similar sentiments. Among the "invaluable" (his word) lessons he learned in Israel were approaches to bomb dismantlement and ways to keep the public informed without revealing intervention techniques to terrorists.

But beyond sharing information about preparedness techniques, Israel can offer lessons to the United States in more general areas. These lessons, explored in earlier chapters, lie in four spheres: crisis management, national standards, coordination, and communications.

In the case of crisis management, Israel's size seems well suited as a solitary administrative unit. Governed by national authority, practices at one or another Israeli location are generally similar and consistent. In contrast, the vast area of the United States militates against a unitary system of crisis management. State and local authorities already govern most day-to-day activities in education, public safety, business regulations, residential zoning, and more. But the quality of these activities varies from state to state and city to city.

An optimal system for preparedness in the United States would include local or regional management, though under an umbrella of national standards. Especially when considering how Americans might cope with more limited terrorist events, the Israeli experience becomes useful. Administrative jurisdictions that are the size of a state, or portion of a state, seem optimal. The governing structures of states and counties are in place, but national incident management protocols, introduced in 2006, have still not been universally implemented.

Unlike in Israel, the absence of national standards in the United States had permitted a hodge-podge of guidelines and mandates. Some states have enacted requirements for disaster planning and some have not. Most hospitals in the United States are associated with the volunteer Joint Commission on Accreditation, which prescribes disaster management protocols, but several are not. Even designating the nature of an emergency according to color codes varies among U.S. hospitals. Almost everywhere, Code Red means there is a fire in the building. But Code Black in some hospitals signifies a bomb threat, in others a storm, and in still others that the hospital's emergency beds are full.[7] Code Green at the Children's Hospital in New Orleans indicates a disaster that is limited to that facility, but the same color at the Children's Hospital in Cincinnati means "all clear"—the end of the emergency.[8] Physicians and other medical personnel are often affiliated with more than one hospital. And government officials might have to deal with multiple hospitals during a crisis. If codes vary from one institution to the next, the chances for error, especially during emergencies, are increased.

In the past, Israeli hospitals had varying codes that also caused confusion. But in 2002 the Israeli government mandated a 4-step alert level system for all hospitals (4 = highest, 1 = lowest). The new policy was prompted by the outbreak of terrorist attacks. Previous code designations had caused confusion to ambulance drivers and others who were involved with several hospitals. Why wait for a similar crisis in the United States before adopting a uniform system for all American hospitals?

The intifada has underscored as well the importance of a centralized coordinated effort. Israeli emergency responders are part of a single service, the Magen David Adom. (The MDA, which translates as the Red Star of David, is Israel's equivalent of the Red Cross and also the country's Emergency Medical Service.) An MDA commander at an attack site will direct ambulances to area hospitals so that none receives a disproportionate patient load. In the United States, most casualties would be taken to the nearest hospital. At a conference on hospital preparedness in 2006, Dr. David Mozingo, a burn specialist at the University of Florida, recalled his experience with victims of the bombing in Oklahoma City in 1995. The closest hospital "got slam dunked with patients," he said, and the second closest hospital received very few. The Israeli model of "dividing up the patients" would be difficult to implement here, he said, because the American system is so decentralized.

Rather than tolerate this deficiency, policymakers should rectify it. A national plan should require coordinated drills among local responders, along with balanced distribution of casualties among area hospitals. (The most seriously injured patients would in any case be sent to level-1 trauma centers.) Community-wide exercises are now conducted in some U.S. locations, but dividing the patient load is not always part of the drill.

The most commonly cited weakness in American disaster preparedness is in communications between key agencies. The need for remediation is widely understood and needs no reminder from the Israelis, whose system connects hospitals, law enforcement, and the military. In the United States, local departments in many communities cannot "talk to each other" because their equipment operates on different radio frequencies. A survey in 2004 of 192 cities found that in 65 of them, radio equipment in the police, fire, and emergency medical services was incompatible. The problem is magnified when considering inter-county or regional communications. By early 2006, only ten states had statewide radio systems that city and county agencies could join.[9]

After 9/11, New Jersey developed a non-interruptible radio system that connects in-state hospitals, fire, and law enforcement authorities. But the radio frequency does not connect to equivalent agencies in neighboring states. In 2006, the New York City police and fire departments were each still using separate systems, though fire commanders carried an extra radio tuned to the police band. Given financial and technological constraints, Department of Homeland Security officials project that free-flowing communication among agencies throughout the country will not be in place until 2023.

Waiting a half-generation for a nationwide communications system should be deemed unacceptable. As with deficiencies concerning management, coordination, and standards, remediation should be a greater priority than now appears to be the case. The need to correct these flaws is so obvious that citing Israeli accomplishments in these areas might seem unnecessary. Still, the Israeli example demonstrates the value of these features and should further encourage Americans to do the same.

* * *

A 2005 paper by psychologist Jan Shubert, an emergency management specialist with the U.S. Environmental Protection Agency, reviewed lessons from the Israeli experience in the perspective of social psychology and risk communication.[10] Drawing from several studies, she found that Israeli resilience was enhanced by the population's patriotism, trust in social and political institutions, and habituation to the ongoing threat. Survey research also showed that providing information and social support during threat periods was key to helping Israelis cope.[11]

Shubert recognized that because of differing attitudes in the two societies not all worthy Israeli practices are transferable to the United States. For example, the Israelis focus on preparing their people, and the United States focuses on preparing agencies. Israelis feel more confident that the government will act appropriately to protect the population than do Americans. And Israelis are accustomed to the military playing many roles in their lives, but Americans are not. This last fact is especially salient.

Israeli appreciation of the military comes not only from its role in protecting the population but also from broad participation by the citizenry. (Service is compulsory for the Jewish population, though not for Arab citizens of Israel.) Men serve for three years, women for two, and then men continue on reserve status until age 40 to 50 depending on their military specialty. Thus, almost all Israelis feel closely connected to the army either directly or through family members on duty. In contrast, Shubert observes, few Americans "consider protection of the country to be their responsibility."

In the weeks after 9/11, many Americans felt a surge of patriotism. American flags appeared in apartment windows, on automobile antennas, on jacket lapels. Army enlistments rose. But in time, Americans reverted to their private interests and a diminished sense of shared national purpose. Hurricane Katrina provided a telling example.

At a forum in 2006 on Cities at Risk, Baltimore Mayor Martin O'Malley spoke of dismaying television images in the wake of the hurricane. People were stranded on rooftops amid rising floodwater with no relief in sight. Many of the 26,000 evacuees in the New Orleans Superdome exhibited unruly behavior. "We saw a crowd, not a community," O'Malley said.[12] After contacting local Louisiana authorities, five days after the hurricane, Mayor O'Malley dispatched his homeland security adviser, Andrew Lauland, and a team of Baltimore rescue workers to help. When the group reached St. Bernard Parish, a county bordering New Orleans, they were surprised to see the Canadian flag hanging at the local command center.

"Why the maple leaf flag?" Lauland asked the parish fire chief, Jack Stone.

"Because the Canadians were the only outside people to come there," Stone said. A 45-member rescue team from British Columbia had arrived on the third day, a week before the U.S. Federal Emergency Management Agency showed up.[13] The Canadian presence underscored the mismanagement of the U.S. response. The events also recalled the reaction by Dr. Yuri Millo, the Israeli physician at the Washington Hospital Center, who could not imagine Israelis waiting as long as the Americans to help fellow citizens. He attributed the laggard U.S. response in part to an absence of social connectedness.

Not that Americans failed to show concern for the hurricane victims. Belatedly, help came from several out-of-state agencies. Individuals throughout the country sent money for relief programs, and some arrived to help clear debris and repair salvageable homes. But for most Americans, the devastation seemed distant and was not internalized as though a tragedy in their own community.

Jan Shubert's prescription for terrorism preparedness includes having the U.S. government coordinate public education to deal with attacks. Her model is the Israeli Home Front Command. But this model is unlikely to be effective where a citizenry is more self-absorbed and skeptical. Americans would do well to consider activity that enhances a sense of community and national purpose.

If the Israeli experience teaches anything in this regard, it is that military service for young Israelis deepens their attachment to the nation and to each other. Conscription there is necessary for national defense. But the requirement is also a leveling experience for every participant, rich or poor, secular or religious. The shared experience becomes a reference point for a lifetime.

For young American men, who from the 1940s through the 1960s were subject to military draft, service to the country provided similar socialization. Disillusionment with the Vietnam War prompted the end of the draft, diminished patriotism, and weakened our sense of common purpose. Of course the end of the draft is not the only reason for the lessened attachment to community. Political sociologist Robert Putnam postulated several reasons that since the 1970s fewer Americans have joined volunteer organizations and participated in community activities. They include the rise in television viewing, marital instability, two-parent workers, suburban sprawl, generational attitudes, and more.[14] As a result, individuals feel less connected to each other and to the larger society. Because large-scale use of the Internet is so recent, it is too early to know whether blogs and listserves might facilitate social connectedness. But at best, without nonverbal cues, the Internet will still lack the power of face-to-face engagement. No matter how many computers are in use, we remain a nation of people, not laptops.

Meanwhile, adversarial conduct has also been enhanced by the dramatic growth of the American legal profession. For example, in 1995 there were 34 percent more lawyers than doctors in the United States compared to three percent *fewer* lawyers than doctors in 1970.[15] Doubtless, this surge contributed to America's becoming seen as the most litigious society in the world.[16] Not surprisingly, after 9/11 and the anthrax attacks many affected parties filed suit against numerous agencies and individuals including insurance companies, the New York and New Jersey Port Authority, the New York City Fire Department, the U.S. Postal Service, the Federal Bureau of Investigation, and former Attorney General John Ashcroft.

When I asked Israelis whether lawsuits had been instituted against Israeli companies or agencies for damages suffered during terrorist attacks, they were surprised by the question. Suing a bus company whose driver was killed in a suicide attack or owners of a restaurant that was blown up seemed bizarre. The common theme was "We don't sue. We're all in this together."

In 2003, Congressman Charles Rangel of New York introduced a bill to reinstate the draft. Although an opponent of the war in Iraq, he believed that mandatory military service for young men and women would assure that more Americans shared the burden of sacrifice. The proposed legislation also allowed for civilian service as an alternative "in furtherance of the national defense and homeland security, and for other purposes."[17] Fourteen members of Congress co-sponsored the bill, but it failed to receive additional support.

Many countries maintain conscription, including several European states, among them Austria, Denmark, Finland, Germany, Norway, Spain, Sweden, and Switzerland. Most require one or two years of military service for men and permit women to volunteer. German policy allows a draftee to choose nonmilitary service, and about 30 percent of the country's 400,000 conscripts undertake social work in hospitals or senior citizen homes.

Strongly encouraging, if not requiring, young Americans to serve this nation, whether through the military or otherwise, would not suddenly re-ignite national connectedness. But it would be a start. The military is one option, but so are programs that help the needy or enhance the environment. Those opportunities already exist on a limited basis. In 2006, nearly eight thousand Peace Corps volunteers were teaching and working with people in countries around the world. The National Civilian Community Corps (NCCP) enlisted several thousand 18- to 24-year-olds, to work in 10-month programs in inner cities, rural communities, and Indian reservations. Participants in the NCCP receive a modest stipend of $4,000 above room and board. Treating such service as a national responsibility would mean more help for worthy purposes and more Americans with a greater sense of connectedness to their country and to each other.

Service as a rite of passage involves far more than strengthening the population's ability to cope with terrorism or disasters. Yet, as numerous Israelis have found, the spirit of community has been a key element of their resiliency.

*　*　*

On September 11, 2001, Sarri Singer, 28, overslept. The director of a Jewish youth program, she was ordinarily at work by early morning. Her office in the Orthodox Union headquarters at 11 Broadway in lower Manhattan was 20 minutes by subway from her Upper West Side apartment. When she phoned to say she'd be late, a voice responded: "Don't come down. We're being evacuated." Two blocks from her office, the North Tower was burning. Sarri turned on her television. She called her parents in Lakewood, New Jersey, where she grew up, to tell them she was safe. Her father, Robert Singer, a New Jersey state senator, suggested that she not travel until more was learned about the attack and whether there were other assaults to come. Sarri was so frightened that she did not leave her apartment for three days.

In 2005 we met in downtown Newark, New Jersey, where she was directing the regional offices of the OneFamily Fund. Her current work involved fundraising and coordinating overseas programs to help Israelis affected by terrorism. Words flowed easily as she recounted vacations in Israel with her parents and her younger brother, and of other times she spent there on her own. Her face brightened when she mentioned that while confined in her New York apartment on 9/11 she thought a lot about Israel. "I decided at that point to move there," she said.

I was surprised. Just after the attack on the World Trade Center? Wasn't she worried about terrorism in Israel? I asked.

"Fear never entered my mind in all the times I had been in Israel," she answered. "I felt safer in Jerusalem than in New York," she continued. "I feel like Israel is prepared for certain situations, but not New York."

In January 2002, Sarri left for Israel on money she had saved from her New York job. Within weeks she was doing volunteer work for several groups. One counseled youngsters who had been affected by terrorism. Another was Gift of Life, an international society that promotes organ and tissue transplantation. Her assignment was to visit schools where students volunteered to have their cheeks swabbed to establish a registry of blood types. Months later, she found a paying job as program administrator at a girls school in Jerusalem, but she still continued her volunteer activities.

"There's something different about volunteering in Israel," she said. Neither she nor her friends did as much unpaid work in the United States. "But in Israel, somehow it seems to be part of life. The day is very busy, but people there volunteer on a regular basis, whether visiting a family that needs company or going to a nursing home." She twirled the gold ring on her left middle finger as she offered a speculation. "In the U.S., I think we're just more self-involved." Echoes of Robert Putnam.

By June 11, 2003, Sarri's days in Israel were full and pleasant. During the coming summer break she planned to visit the United States and spend time with her family before returning to Israel. Meanwhile, she was looking forward to dinner that evening with a friend. They planned to meet at the Café Hillel, which three months later would be the site of the terrorist attack that killed Dr. David Applebaum and his daughter, Nava.

Sarri, of course, was aware of the numerous terrorist attacks in Israel, but she rode Jerusalem buses regularly and never felt endangered. At 4:30 PM, she boarded No. 14 near the Central Bus Station on Jaffa Road in Jerusalem. The bus was packed, and at first she had to stand. After two stops, a seat became available in the fourth row next to the window. Seconds after sitting down, she felt a huge shockwave against her face. When the wave passed, her left eye was sealed shut and her right eye was nearly so. "I could barely open the eye, but I could see that the roof had fallen in." Her ears were ringing, and she began to scream. Two men appeared outside and yelled at her to leave the bus.

"I can't move," she said.

"You have to. Put your feet against the bar."

"I can't," she repeated. She dimly noticed the back of a passenger's head in front of her. He had white hair and was motionless, as if asleep. She realized he was dead. "I just closed my eye again. I didn't want to see."

She felt tugging on her legs. The men outside were pulling her through a hole. Some time afterward, she saw a picture of the bus and realized the bar they were talking about was part of the frame beneath the floor. It was visible because the floor had been blown open, providing the hole for her rescue.

Sarri was taken to Hadassah Hospital, where doctors found that her eardrums were punctured and that pieces of shrapnel were lodged in her legs. A large fragment had torn through her left shoulder and broken her collarbone. Her left eye was the size of a lemon, and her face was purple from the flying debris. She later learned that an 18-year-old Palestinian dressed as an ultra-Orthodox Jew had detonated a bomb a few rows behind her. Seventeen people were killed and more than a hundred injured.

When Robert Singer received word that his daughter had been hurt, he and his son Eric immediately booked a plane to Israel. The next day they were at her bedside. At Sarri's insistence, her mother, Judie, remained in the United States. "She's very emotional," Sarri said, "and I didn't want her to see what I looked like."

After ten days, Sarri was released from the hospital, and Robert urged her to return to the United States with him. She refused. "I stayed an extra week because I didn't want to be afraid to come back in September," she said. "You know, like if you fall off a horse, you should get right back on." During that week she was allowed outdoors one hour a day. With the help of friends who would accompany her, she carefully planned her daily hour: one at the Jerusalem Mall; a second, lunch at the Ticho House restaurant; a third, a slow painful stroll on Ben Yehuda Street. All places she had been to many times before.

Did she try going on a bus? I asked.

Her voice was subdued, "No."

How about now, nearly two years later?

"No, no, I can't get on a bus yet. It's hard."

When Sarri came back to the United States, she stayed at her parents' home in Lakewood, dividing time between physical and psychological therapy. But in September she returned to her job at the Israeli girls school, while continuing her therapy. Early in 2004, she decided to take the offer from OneFamily to run the office in Newark.

When we spoke again in 2006, she was still going for counseling. "I'm trying to get over the feeling that I have to sit in the back of a restaurant. I won't sit by the door. When I'm next to a bus, I feel heavy anxiety and stress in my chest."

In Israel she met with many of the families affected by terrorism. For some, even years after an incident, the wounds remained raw. She would not guess how long it might take for anyone else to recover. "But I know for myself," she said firmly. "Will I get past this and eventually get on a bus? Absolutely."

Sarri is one of the few people who were personally affected by both 9/11 *and* the intifada. Her story ties into several themes in this book about coping and recovery. Although an American, she displayed an attitude that is common among Israelis, a mix of stoicism and connection to the community. The numerous plans and techniques that Israel has developed to confront terrorism are immensely important. Many can be of value to the United States. But no less important to explain Israelis' resilience is their pervasive civic engagement, their sense of connectedness. Transferring techniques to deal with terrorism and disaster from one country to another is relatively uncomplicated. Transferring attitudes is a far greater challenge. Still, the Israeli attitude is important to understanding how that society has coped and what Americans can learn—if we have the will.

13

Beyond Terror

When interviewed by BBC in 2004, an Egyptian cleric, Sheik Yusef al-Qaradawi, was asked if Islam justifies suicide bombings in Israel. "It is not suicide, it is martyrdom in the name of God," he answered. "It is allowed to jeopardize your soul and cross the path of the enemy and be killed, if this act of jeopardy affects the enemy, even if it only generates fear in their hearts, shaking their morale, making them fear Muslims."[1]

To dismiss al-Qaradawi as a lone religious fanatic would be to ignore the broad support for these sentiments in some quarters. Yasser Arafat, head of the Palestinian Authority until his death in November 2004, regularly referred to suicide bombers as martyrs. Around the time of al-Qaradawi's remarks, the Palestinian Center for Policy and Survey Research reported the results of a poll on the subject: 59 percent of Palestinians in the West Bank and Gaza supported the continuation of suicide bombing inside Israel.[2]

In elections in January 2006, Palestinian voters gave a large majority of legislative seats to Hamas, a group that took credit for numerous suicide terrorist attacks. After the elections, as before, Hamas called for the destruction of Israel. Some analysts contended that Israel's destruction was not an issue for many voters. They just wanted to oust Fatah, the previously dominant group, for its corrupt practices.

Whatever the reasons, the election results and the survey highlighted a continuing question about the purported effect of the attacks. Had the assaults generated fear in the hearts of Israelis, shaken their morale, and inspired fear of Muslims as Sheik al-Qaradawi hoped?

The wave of terrorism induced anxiety in much of the population, but even in the worst years of the intifada, Israelis remained steadfast. Bombed restaurants and shops were quickly repaired and reopened. At first, fewer people rode buses and patronized shopping malls, but in time, the numbers reverted to previous levels. Surveys revealed that patriotism rose during the intifada. Remarkably, the percentage of the population that said they wanted to live in the country climbed to a high in 2002 when the attacks were most frequent. A 2006 study of Israeli resilience concluded that throughout the previous five years, the public responded with flexibility and remained optimistic about the future.[3]

Perhaps these attitudes were a reflexive Jewish response born of millennia of experience. Much of Jewish history is the story of survival in the face of hostility. For two thousand years, after being exiled by the Romans from their homeland in Israel, the Jews tried to make do wherever they lived. Whether in Christian or Muslim lands, they were commonly forced to dwell separately from the rest of the population. For stretches of time they might live in relative tranquility even while non-Jewish neighbors viewed them with suspicion or disdain. Periodically, anti-Semitic dispositions would erupt into violence. Jewish communities might face expulsion, forced conversion, pogroms, murder. But eventually each wave of acute oppression subsided. If not forced to leave, the community would endure the transitory eruption and return to their lives and traditions.

The large exception was the partial fulfillment of the Nazi plan to exterminate every Jew on earth. Still, apart from that twentieth-century nightmare, Jewish communities in new lands or old tended to preserve their patterns of living. Jewish history is a recitation of coping by remaining resolute. In today's context that means Israeli Jews living their lives, to the extent possible, much as they had before the Palestinian surge of terror.

Or perhaps the resilience of Israeli citizens is not particular to the Jewish people, but speaks to a universal impulse. One way of responding to a stressful situation is to ignore it as much as possible. Denial. Unable otherwise to mitigate a terrible condition, a community may react with a collective shrug and carry on as usual. The September 11 attack on the World Trade Center left psychological scars, especially on people close by. But many who lived and worked near ground zero soon returned to their activities there, determined that they, and not fear of terrorism, would control their lives.

September 11 was a terrible tragedy for Americans and was different in degree from Israel's experience. Rather than a single cataclysmic incident, Israelis have suffered lower-decibel tragedies with regularity. Still, in both societies sufferance of unspeakable pain has been coupled with determination to carry on. A signal Israeli response after an attack is to restore the status quo ante as quickly as possible. Within days, a café's shattered glass is replaced, blown-out walls are restored, and patrons are again dining into the evening.

This book has been less an inquiry into the causes of terrorism than the manner of coping with it. While the roots of the Israeli-Palestinian conflict were noted, the central issues here are more straightforward: how Israel has withstood terrorism and what its experience can teach others, especially the United States. We examined the effects of the flood of attacks on different segments of the society—victims and their families, emergency responders, security guards, doctors and nurses, and ultimately the general population.

To focus on the Israeli experience is not to minimize the suffering of the Palestinians. In the course of the conflict, more Palestinians than Israelis have been killed. Israelis have killed terrorists who were preparing to launch attacks. They have assassinated others who recruited and dispatched suicide bombers. They have sought to eliminate members of groups behind terrorism, including Hamas, Islamic Jihad, and the Al-Aqsa Martyrs Brigades. During Israeli actions innocent Palestinians have also become victims. Although it is the policy of the Israeli military to avoid injuring noncombatants, innocents have suffered in crossfire and otherwise become unintended victims. But unlike the deliberate killing of innocent Israelis by Palestinian bombers, these deaths have been inadvertent.

Israeli military doctrine forbids firing at innocent civilians, and Israeli military and security actions are not by any legitimate order directed randomly. Even so, critics have accused Israel of using excessive force. Some have condemned Israel for engaging in "political violence" and deem Israeli reprisals and targeted killings as morally equivalent to Palestinian suicide attacks. This view is disingenuous. It is a warped offshoot of the larger political question that pits the rights of one people against those of another.

On issues of land and resources, Israelis and Palestinians each claim that their competing positions are just. The contention here is that whatever one's position on the claims, it is never appropriate to deliberately target innocent civilians. Suicide bombing is merely a further degradation of this immoral activity. The failure of the international community to condemn terrorism forcefully, wherever it takes place, only makes its repetition more likely.

Exploring these matters has moved the discussion beyond coping, to an understanding that terrorism anywhere is a threat to societies everywhere. Suicide killing of innocents did not begin with the targeting of Israelis, although in the Jewish state it achieved epidemic proportions and extraordinary notoriety. The model has been picked up in post-Saddam Iraq, where suicide bombing and other deliberate violence against civilians has become routine. These widely publicized incidents are likely to prompt similar acts elsewhere.

Security officials in the United States are bracing for suicide bombings on American soil. "I don't want to say it's inevitable," observed Steven Pomerantz, former assistant director of the Federal Bureau of Investigation, "but it's a real threat."[4] The 9/11 Commission offered similar warnings. Established as a national body to assess the attacks of September 11, 2001, the commission issued a report in July 2004, which included an observation that has become familiar to Americans, that they should "expect the worst: An attack is coming; it may be terrible."[5]

During nineteen months of investigation, the 9/11 Commission interviewed more than 1,200 individuals and heard public testimony from 160 witnesses. At a press conference when the report was released, the panel's chairman, former New Jersey Governor Thomas Kean, said: "Every expert with whom we spoke told us an attack of even greater magnitude is now possible, even probable."[6]

The report and the chairman's observation came in the midst of the presidential contest between President George Bush and the Democratic nominee, John Kerry. Partisanship at that time, not surprisingly, was rife. But on the question of the terror threat, there was no daylight between the conclusions of the commission and the presidential candidates or any other reputable analysts.

Anticipating the worst means seeking methods of prevention and, in case of an assault, preparation to respond and provide care for victims. But there is more that needs attention than the response to a particular attack and its aftermath. No less important is to understand and address the long-term effects on the larger population. It is in these areas that the Israeli experience has much to offer.

* * *

One society's practices may not apply to another's because of differences in demographics, cultural norms, or size. Israelis have experienced far more terrorism than Americans, and national attitudes may differ on particular issues. But fundamental social and cultural values are much the same in both societies. Human dignity and individual rights are regarded as self-evident ideals, though fulfillment has been more available to some segments in each society. Still, the will of the citizenry in both countries is expressed, if imperfectly, through democratic institutions. Contested elections, a free press, and an independent judiciary flourish in each. And in the age of terrorism, both societies are struggling to fulfill the state's responsibility to protect its citizens while preserving basic liberties.

The most obvious difference between the two countries is size. Israel's area and population are only a fraction of those of the United States. In fact, Israel's area of 8.5 thousand square miles more closely resembles New Jersey's 8.7 thousand square miles. Similarly, its population of seven million approximates New Jersey's eight million plus. To the extent that Israel's success in addressing terrorism is related to its size, a small American state like New Jersey would seem an appropriately comparable unit.

Thus, if Israel is considered a guide, one lesson for the United States should be to emphasize management of some types of terror attacks through state or sub-state units. This nation's response to Hurricane Katrina in August 2005 proved to be inadequate at all levels—local, regional, and national. The incident offered little optimism that a terror attack causing widespread destruction would have been better handled. Moreover, it is not clear that Israeli experience has much to offer in cases of such widespread destruction. But in managing more limited disruptions or attacks, the Israeli model can be very helpful.

Indeed, when considering a variety of terror weapons, Israeli readiness has been burnished by direct threats. In the 1991 Gulf War, Iraq launched thirty-nine scud missiles into Israel. Fearing that the missiles might be carrying chemical and biological agents, Israeli authorities instructed the population to don gas masks and seek shelter in sealed areas during each attack. The masks had been given to every citizen as part of a kit that included chemical antidotes and protective information. In the end, the worst fears went unrealized, and no poison agents were found. Still, the repeated exercises produced experience-based protocols that could inform others who are similarly threatened.

In dealing with the more frequent type of attacks, those with explosives, Israeli practices should be especially respected. Future terrorist assaults on American soil may well involve explosives. This logic is framed by worldwide experience. Almost all recent terror attacks have involved bombs detonated in confined locations—a bus or subway in London, a train in Madrid, a nightclub in Bali, a school in Baghdad, a café in Jerusalem. Why has there not been a spate of such low-level terror attacks in America? Explanations range from heightened security since September 11 to lack of interest by terrorist groups, at least for now. But few doubt that a dedicated individual or group could concoct a bomb, walk into a crowded shopping mall, and set off a blast. This reality demands that the United States be prepared for such events.

After a terror attack, the speed with which victims are appropriately treated could determine whether they will live or die. It is from the initial moments after an attack, through subsequent months and years of care for victims and families, that Israel's experience is also instructive.

Israeli experience has even given rise to the new field of terror medicine. Dealing with injury and trauma has always been integral to a physician's responsibilities. But the manner, frequency, and severity of the attacks against Israelis, and their effects on the general population, reached a new dimension. The close proximity of the victims to an exploding bomber created traumatic consequences that are rarely seen in large numbers in other societies. Nor have many other societies experienced such a prolonged drumbeat of deliberate attacks against innocent civilians.

Thus, the effects of the terrorism, both physical and psychological, have generated an unusual base of information. That wealth of data has prompted the consideration of terror medicine as a distinctive discipline. The notion became more salient in 2005 with an agreement between two private medical institutions, Hadassah Hospital in Jerusalem and the Robert Wood Johnson University Hospital in New Brunswick, New Jersey, to establish an International Center for Terror Medicine. The Center would include a repository of information based on Israel's cumulative experience that could be shared with security and health officials in the United States and elsewhere.

* * *

Israel has responded on many levels to the years of terrorist attacks. Security forces developed measures that sharply reduced the number of assaults. Rescue and medical workers enhanced their procedures to increase the chances for victims' survival. The general population, even at the height of the suicide bombings, remained resolute.

In mid-2006, Israelis faced yet another form of terrorism from a Lebanon-based group that does not recognize Israel's right to exist. During a month of fighting, Hezbollah launched 4,000 missiles into northern Israel. They were part of a sophisticated arsenal of rockets that Iran provided to the organization after Israel withdrew from southern Lebanon in 2000.

The round of hostilities began after Hezbollah fighters crossed into Israel, killed three soldiers, and kidnapped two others. Israel then bombarded Hezbollah targets in Lebanon, destroying much of the organization's infrastructure and rocket inventory. The parties agreed to a ceasefire in August in accordance with a United Nations Security Council resolution. The resolution's terms included disarmament of Hezbollah and the introduction of the Lebanese army and a sizable UN force into southern Lebanon. Even so, Hezbollah officials said they would not give up their weapons, and the outlook for the agreement appeared uncertain.

Hezbollah's leader, Hassan Nasrallah, had previously made clear that the missile attacks were intended to terrorize and kill Jews. (When a rocket killed some Israeli Arabs, he apologized and said that their deaths were unintentional.) During the attacks many Israelis temporarily moved south beyond the range of the missiles while others made do in underground shelters. Nevertheless, by the time of the ceasefire some fifty Israeli civilians had been killed and Hezbollah was still able to launch more missiles. A national debate in Israel had begun about the country's military performance. But

Israelis in the northern cities were as one with the rest of the country in support of ending the Hezbollah threat—through the ceasefire if possible, but by military action if necessary.

The use of Iranian-supplied rockets was a reminder of the threat posed by Islamic extremists not only to Israel but elsewhere as well. Iranian leaders, like leaders of Hezbollah and Hamas, had previously declared that Israel should be eradicated. By 2006, Iran's reported quest to develop nuclear weapons and intercontinental missiles also alarmed Europeans, whose cities could become vulnerable. The United Kingdom, France, and Germany joined with the United States vigorously to press for an end to Iran's uranium enrichment program. In August, Iran vowed to ignore a UN demand that it halt enrichment efforts and the issue promised to remain contentious.

Although the Shia brand of Islam, predominant in Iran, has long been in conflict with the Sunni tradition, extremists in both camps are dedicated to the establishment of Islamic rule in much of the world. Osama bin-Laden declared that his goal was to attain a "pious Caliphate" when he created "The World Islamic Front for Jihad against the Jews and Crusaders" in 1998.[7] That aspiration helped fuel 9/11 and numerous subsequent attacks, especially against Western targets. In recent years terror assaults, some successful and some thwarted, have been launched in the United Kingdom, France, Germany, Spain, Italy, the Netherlands, and Denmark.

Western leaders in varying degrees have come to realize that the war on terror is not just a battle between countries and some misguided zealots. Rather it is between two value systems. One system esteems human life and freedom of thought and action, while the other demands conformity and sanctifies murder to achieve religious dominance. This bloody contest of values will not end soon.

Terrorism has become the world's problem no less than Israel's, though much can be learned from the long and difficult experience of the Jewish state. Israel has shown how a determined society can withstand sustained terrorist assaults. When Hezbollah's missiles were falling, as when the Palestinians were attacking with suicide bombers, the Israeli population remained steadfast. Their ability to cope was abetted by a profound sense of community, a grassroots network of support, and a determined resilience. Levi Lauer's reaction to his daughter's concern about terrorism during their stroll in 2003 was typical of many Israelis' response to the terror attacks: Recoil at their terrible effects, readjust positions, then keep on walking.

Appendix. *Terrorism Issues in Israel and the United States*

Israel's extensive experience with terrorism offers many lessons for the United States, some best applied at the national level and some at state and local levels. Protocols for drills, communications, and hospital preparedness should be mandated at national levels in the United States, as they are in Israel. This would lead to more uniform capabilities throughout the country. But in dealing with limited-scope events, management is best left to state and local authorities. Thus many states and counties that are comparable in size to Israel can also gain from Israel's management model.

Comparative Examples

	Israel	United States
Preparedness and Response Policies		
Based on:	National mandates; though operations at regional/local levels conducted with flexibility	No national mandates, rather advisories; policies and operations largely determined by state and local authorities
Communications		
Police, fire, medical responders	All use same emergency radio frequency to connect to Emergency Medical Service, Army Home Front	Radio frequencies often incompatible between agencies and between regions; interoperable communications

(Continued)

	Israel	United States
	Command, and police authorities	throughout the country not anticipated until the year 2023
Inter-hospital	All use same emergency radio frequency	Same radio frequencies in hospitals in some states, varies in others
Drills and Exercises		
Range of weapons (conventional and non-conventional)	National mandates to drill for all types of threat	National mandates since 2006, though not fully implemented
Comprehensive and coordinated with police, fire, medical responders, hospitals	Regional, citywide, or local drills 2-3 times per year (every hospital included)	Varies from location to location
Evaluation of hospital drill	Outside observers routinely used	Commonly by in-house (hospital staff) observers
Hospital/Medical Practices		
Code alerts	Four-step alert level same for all hospitals (4=highest, 1=lowest)	Varies among hospitals (e.g., "code black" variously signifies a bomb threat, a storm, or a full emergency department)
Ambulances	Maintained and operated by a single Emergency Medical Service (training and skills are uniform)	Usually maintained and operated by individual hospitals (training and skills vary)
Security		
Security guards	Commonly present at places of public accommodation including restaurants, theaters, trains, etc. (guards check individuals entering public facilities)	Sometimes present at places of public accommodation, often not

(Continued)

	Israel	United States
Airport screening	Careful interviewing of all passengers; singling out some according to profile	Interviewing of passengers rare; search by random designation or for cause, but not by profiling
Explosives (chemical) detectors at airports	Calibrated to be extremely sensitive	Calibrated less sensitively (according to Israeli experts)
Bus drivers	Engage in terrorism/security exercises; security agents often on buses	Engage in terrorism/security exercises rarely if at all
Emotional Trauma		
School teachers	Primed to look for traumatic effects of terrorism on children	After 9/11, some programs to sensitize teachers to traumatic effects on children
Volunteer groups	Hundreds formed to provide emotional and material support	After 9/11, dozens formed to provide support, especially in NYC and Washington DC areas
Social Attitudes		
Unattended packages in public location	Public conditioned to be aware of suspicious objects; children and adults primed to quickly notify authorities	Despite public warnings, no evidence that children or adults notify authorities
Community orientation	Highly community-oriented	More individually oriented
Resilience	Enhanced by strong sense of community	Unclear how lesser sense of community would affect the population under sustained attacks

(Continued)

	Israel	**United States**
Lawsuits in aftermath of terror attack	Virtually none (against bus companies, police, etc.)	After 9/11 and the anthrax attacks, suits filed against the NY and NJ Port Authority, NY City fire Department, US Postal Service, Federal Bureau of Investigation, US Government, and more
Trust in military and law enforcement to provide adequate protection	Positively viewed, in general	More skeptical, mixed views

Acknowledgments

While writing this book I was in contact with scores of Israelis and Americans who were directly affected by terrorism. I am very grateful to them for sharing with me their stories of sorrow, pain, nobility, and resilience. Among the survivors of terrorist attacks and people who lost loved ones I thank especially Debra Applebaum, Natan Applebaum, Kinneret Chaya Boosany, Ora Cohen, Shalom Cohen, Stephen Flatow, Smadar Haran Kaiser, Anna Krakovich, Chava Mor, Yitzak Mor, Ella Nelimov, Sasha Nelimov, Arnold Roth, Frimet Roth, Mary Ellen Salamone, Erik Schechter, Natan Sendeke, Sarri Singer, Nikki Stern, Elad Wasa, and Maytal Wax.

Others helped me understand the extraordinary support system for Israeli families and survivors of terrorism, much of it through volunteer organizations. They include Ruth Bar-on, Chantal Belzberg, Leah Blustein, Micha Feldmann, Yifat Feldmann, Elisheva Flomm-Oren, Shelley Horwitz, Levi Lauer, Talia Levanon, Jessica Losch, Sara Losch, Jonathan Perlman, Yehuda Poch, and Larry Waller.

I had many conversations about terrorism issues with health-care professionals as well as security and law enforcement officials. I am especially grateful to Dr. Shmuel Shapira, the Deputy Director General of the Hadassah Medical Organization in Jerusalem for arranging several interviews and hosting a program in 2005 on terror medicine and domestic security. The American delegation to that program, which I helped coordinate, included Nancy Connell, Robert Eisenstein, Pete Estacio, Jeffrey Hammond, John Hunt, Clifton Lacy, Gerald Ostrov, Leonard Posnock, and William Raisch. Among the Israeli participants were Rita Abramov, Julie Benbenishty, Danny Brom, Yaron Bar Dayon, Esther Galili-Weisstub, Boaz

Ganor, Yehuda Hiss, Zvi Lankofsky, Danny Laor, Shlomo Mor-Yosef, Meir Oren, Avi Rivkind, Estelle Rubinstein, Arik Shalev, and Amitai Ziv.

Additional experts who shared their insights with me concerning the treatment of terror victims (in Israel, the United States, and the United Kingdom) included Alex Kehayan, Nava Braverman, Rony Berger, Paul Carlton, Moshe Daniel, Anat Globerman, Benjamin Davidson, Dvora Hertz, Asher Hirshberg, Yuri Millo, Yoav Mintz, James Ryan, Arik Shalev, Yoram Weiss, Todd Zalut, and Fabio Zweibel.

Several Israeli government officials were also helpful. I especially thank Gideon Meir and Anat Gilead of Israel's foreign ministry, and Orit Stelser of the national prison service, for facilitating my interviews with Hamas prisoners at Ohaley Kedar prison. Mickey Levy, Jerusalem's chief of police, offered valuable descriptions of his city's preparedness for terrorism. I benefited as well from briefings by Avi Dichter, former director of Shabak (Israel's security service) and Lieutenant General Moshe Ya'alon, former chief of staff of the Israel Defense Forces.

Others who helped on various issues related to this book include Zev Alexander, Nava Ben-Zvi, Stephen Donshik, Wallace Greene, Paul Goldenberg, Malcolm Hoenlein, Gillian Laub, Andrew Lauland, Jennifer Mincin, Sheila Raviv, Bassam Abu Sharif, Thomas Vick, and Andrea Yonah.

For reading portions or all of the manuscript and for their valuable suggestions I am indebted to Paul Carlton, Jeffrey Hammond, Richard Karlen, Leonard Saxe, Yuri Millo, Avi Naiman, Anna Olswanger, and David Raab. And for their skillful guidance of this project through publication, I thank my agent, John Thornton, and the staff at Indiana University Press including Robert Sloan, Elisabeth Marsh, Miki Bird, and Elizabeth Yoder. Finally, I thank my wife, Ruth Cole, for her insights and constant support.

Notes

Prologue

1. Ron Marsico, "Israeli Airline Is Bypassing U.S. Screeners," *Star-Ledger* (Newark, N.J.), 11 May 2006, 1.

2. Jessica Stern, *Terror in the Name of God: Why Religious Militants Kill* (New York: Ecco/HarperCollins, 2003); Bruce Hoffman, *Inside Terrorism* (New York: Columbia University Press, 1998).

3. Robert A. Pape, *Dying to Win: The Strategic Logic of Suicide Terrorism* (New York: Random House, 2005).

4. Jewish Virtual Library, www.us-israel.org/jsource/Peace/aksagraph.html. Accessed May 18, 2006.

1. Terror

1. Israel's Law of Return offers safe haven and the right of citizenship to every Jew who wishes to live in the Jewish state. Irrespective of Palestinian claims, this law is consistent with the authority of sovereign states to establish their criteria for immigration and residency. See Israel Ministry of Foreign Affairs, "The Law of Return—1950," http://www.israel-mfa.gov.il/MFA/MFAArchive/2000_2009/2001/8/The%20Law%20of%20Return-%201950. Accessed August 17, 2006; Leonard A. Cole, "A Palestinian Return to Nowhere," *Midstream,* September/October 2001.

2. Joel Greenberg, "Victims' Accounts of a Night of Horror," *New York Times,* 3 June 2001, 4.

3. *60 Minutes,* TCN 9, Australia, aired August 19, 2001.

4. Martin Peretz, "Israel, the United States, and Evil," *New Republic,* 14 September 2001.

5. Diana Lieberman, Shelli Liebman Dorfman, and wire reports, "Tragedy Hits Home," *Jewish News* (Detroit, Mich.), 12 September 2003, 19.

6. Melissa Radler, "Fifteen Doctors Arrive in Israel as Part of Nefesh B'Nefesh," *Jerusalem Post,* 1 August 2004, www.israelnn.com/news.php3?id=67040.

2. ZAKA

1. Mitchell Ginsburg, "Enduring Horror," *Jerusalem Report,* 22 September 2003, 12.

2. Suzanne Goldenberg, "Bomb Shatters Illusions in an Oasis of Civility," *Guardian,* 11 March 2002, www.guardian.co.uk/archive/article/0,4273,4371847,00.html. Accessed April 15, 2003.

3. Buses

1. Egged, www.egged.co.il/Eng/. Accessed December 8, 2004.

2. Etgar Lefkovits, "Ten Killed, 50 Hurt in Suicide Bombing," *Jerusalem Post,* 30 January 2004, 1.

3. Erik Schechter, "Suicide Attacks, A Desperate Strategy," *Jerusalem Post,* 1 April 2003, 1.

4. Robert A. Pape, "The Strategic Logic of Suicide Terrorism," *American Political Science Review,* August 2003, 14.

5. Flavius Josephus, *The Jewish War,* cited by Rabbi Ken Spiro, *Herod the Great,* www.aish.com/literacy/jewishhistory/Crash_Course_in_Jewish_History_Part_31_-_Herod3_the_Great.asp. Accessed December 19, 2004.

4. Survivors

1. www.jewishvirtuallibrary.org/jsource/Terrorism/TerrorAttacks.html. Accessed March 21, 2006.

2. Photographs by Gillian Laub, "The Maimed," *New York Times Magazine,* 18 July 2004, 30–31.

5. Families

1. Meg Laughlin, "Is There Enough to Convict Al-Arian?" *St. Petersburg Times,* 23 October 2005, www.sptimes.com/2005/10/23/Hillsborough/Is_there_enough_to_co.shtml. Accessed October 25, 2005.

2. Israel Ministry of Foreign Affairs, http://www.mfa.gov.il/MFA/Peace+Process/Guide+to+the+Peace+Process/Israels+Disengageme nt+Plan-+Renewing+the+Peace+Process+Apr+2005.htm. Accessed August 24, 2006.

3. Meg Laughlin, "Al-Arian Testimony Gets Dramatic," *St. Petersburg Times,* 17 June 2005, www.sptimes.com/2005/06/17/Tampabay/Al_Arian_testimony_ge.shtml. Accessed October 27, 2005.

4. Berel Wein, "Organ Donation," Rabbi Wein's Weekly Column, 15 March 2002, http://rabbiwein.com/column-393.html. Accessed October 30, 2005.

5. Antiterrorism and Effective Death Penalty Act of 1996, http://usinfo.state.gov/usa/infousa/laws/majorlaw/s735.htm#t2. Accessed November 2, 2005.

6. Matthew A. Levitt, "Sponsoring Terrorism: Syria and Islamic Jihad," *Middle East Intelligence Bulletin,* November-December 2002, www.meib.org/articles/0211_s1.htm. Accessed November 22, 2005.

7. Stephen Flatow, "In This Case, I Can't Be Diplomatic; I Lost a Child to Terrorism," *Washington Post,* 7 November 1999, B-2.

8. U.S. House of Representatives, Hearing Before the Subcommittee on Immigration and Claims of the Committee on the Judiciary, Justice for Victims of Terrorism Act (H.R. 3485), Washington, D.C. 13 April 2000.

9. Naccha Catan, "U.S. Plan To Pay Terror Damages Splits Victims' Kin," *Forward,* 3 November 2000. www.forward.com/issues/2000/00.11.03/news4.html. Accessed June 12, 2005.

10. Jennifer Steinhauer, "19 Months More in Prison for Professor in Terror Case," *New York Times,* 2 May 2006, A-14.

11. Smadar Haran Kaiser, "The World Should Know What He Did to My Family," *Washington Post,* 18 May 2003, B-2; Peter Hellman, "Triumph Over Terrorism," *Jewish Week,* 7 June 2002.

12. Peter Hellman, "Abu Abbas Left a Trail of Victims," *New York Sun,* 21 April 2003, 1.

13. P. David Hornik, "Israel's Deadly Prisoner Deal," *FrontPageMagazine.com,* 12 November 2003. www.frontpagemagazine.com/Articles/ReadArticle.asp?ID=10765. Accessed June 10, 2005.

6. Doctors and Nurses

1. Greg Myre, "Israeli Pathologist Faces Grisly Task After the Bombings," *New York Times,* 24 February 2004, A-1.

2. Daniel Pipes, "Lebanon Turns into Israel's Vietnam," *Wall Street Journal,* 10 March 1999, www.danielpipes.org/article/305. Accessed April 19, 2004.

7. Terror, Medicine, and Security

1. Itzhak Braverman, David Wexler, and Meir Oren, "A Novel Mode of Infection with Hepatitis B: Penetrating Bone Fragments due to the Explosion of a Suicide Bomber," *Israel Medical Association Journal* 4 (July 2002): 528–29.

2. Israel Defense Forces, www1.idf.il/DOVER/site/mainpage.asp?sl=EN&id=22&docid=23457&Pos=1&bScope=False. Accessed August 24, 2005.

3. This description of terror medicine is based in part on Shmuel C. Shapira and Leonard A. Cole, "Terror Medicine: Birth of a Discipline," *Journal of Homeland Security and Emergency Management* 3 (2006): 1–6, www.bepress.com/jhsem/vol3/iss2/9/.

4. Gabriella Aschkenasy-Steuer et al., "The Israel Experience: Conventional Terrorism and Critical Care," *Critical Care* 9 (2005): 490–99.

5. Israel Ministry of Foreign Affairs, "The Palestinian Use of Ambulances and Medical Materials for Terror," 22 December 2003, www.mfa.gov.il/MFA/MFAArchive/2000_2009/2003/12/The+Palestinian+use+of+ambulances+ and+medical+mate.htm. Accessed January 25, 2006.

6. Ralph G. DePalma et al., "Blast Injuries," *New England Journal of Medicine* 352 (2005): 1335–45.

7. "Terrorists Attempted Bio-warfare Attack," *Maariv,* 13 April 2004, http://maarivenglish.com/index.cfm?fuseaction=article&articleID=5889. Accessed June 15, 2005.

8. Laurence Miller, "Psychotherapeutic Interventions for Survivors of Terrorism," *American Journal of Psychotherapy* 59 (2004): 1–16.

9. Panel on Terror Medicine and Domestic Security, Hadassah Hospital, Jerusalem, May 30, 2005.

10. Leonard A. Cole, *The Anthrax Letters: A Medical Detective Story* (Washington, D.C.: Joseph Henry Press, 2003), www.anthraxletters.com.

11. Daphne Berman, "U.S. Doctors Learn How to Deal with Terror from Hadassah," *Haaretz.com,* June 3, 2005. Accessed June 8, 2005.

12. Gil Hoffman, "Hospitals in New Jersey and Israel Establish Center for Terror Medicine," *New Jersey Jewish News,* 2 June 2005, 8.

13. Center for Occupational and Environmental Health, "COEH Alumnus Uses Medical Training to Fight Bio-terrorism," March 2002, http://coeh.berkeley.edu/Alumni/estacio.htm. Accessed November 23, 2005.

8. American Rehearsal

1. "States, Hospitals Learn Emergency-Preparedness Lessons in TOPOFF 3," *ASHP News,* 17 May 2005.

2. David Kocieniewski and Eric Lipton, "New Jersey and Connecticut Get Passing Grades for 5-Day Terror Drill," *New York Times,* 9 April 2005, B-2.

3. Wayne Parry, "Officials Say Terror Drill Lacks a Major Fear Factor," *Record* (Hackensack, N.J.), 8 April 2005, A-4.

4. TOPOFF 3After Action Report of the New Jersey Center for Public Health Preparedness, University of Medicine and Dentistry of New Jersey, Newark, N.J., May 24, 2005.

5. Office of Inspector General, U.S. Department of Homeland Security, "A Review of the Top Officials 3 Exercise," OIG-06-07, Washington, D.C., November 2005.

6. *The 9/11 Commission Report,* Final Report of the National Commission on Terrorist Attacks Upon the United States (New York: W. W. Norton, 2004), 284–85.

7. Michelle O'Donnell, "New Terror Plan Angers Fire Department," *New York Times,* 22 April 2005, A-1.

8. "Chemical Time Bombs: An Insecure Nation" (Editorial), *New York Times,* 10 May 2005, A-16.

9. *Ready or Not? Protecting the Public's Health from Disease, Disasters, and Bioterrorism —2005,* Report by Trust for America's Health, Washington, D.C., December 2005.

10. American College of Emergency Physicians, National Report Card on the State of Emergency Medicine, January 2006, http://my.acep.org/site/PageServer?pagename=wp1_state_map_new_jersey. Accessed March 20, 2006.

11. Testimony of Susan C. Waltman, Senior Vice President, General New York Hospital Association, before the Committee of Health, Education, Labor, and Pensions. U.S. Senate Hearing on "Terror Attacks: Are We Prepared?" Washington, D.C., 22 July 2004.

12. *Ready or Not?*

13. Final Report on 9/11 Commission Recommendations, December 5, 2005, www.9-11pdp.org/press/2005–12–05_report.pd. Accessed April 1, 2006.

14. American College of Emergency Physicians, National Report Card.

15. Meredith Gaskins, Peter D. Rumm, et al., "Terrorism Preparedness Two Years After the Bioterrorism Preparedness Accountability Indicators Project," *Journal of Homeland Security,* December 2005, www.homelandsecurity.org/newjournal/index_articles.asp. Accessed April 29, 2006.

16. Joint Commission on Accreditation of Healthcare Organizations, Disaster Drills, Revised April 13, 2005. www.jointcommission.org/ (search: "disaster drills"). Accessed March 27, 2006.

17. "Hospital Preparedness: Most Urban Hospitals Have Emergency Plans but Lack Certain Capacities for Bioterrorism Response," Report of the Government Accountability Office, GAO-03-924, Washington, D.C., August 2003.

9. Teaching from Experience

1. New Alert Updates, Sheba Medical Center at Tel Hashomer, Israel, February 14, 2005, www.shebamedical.com/shebaclips/05_02_14.html. Accessed January 23, 2006.

2. J. Peral Gutierrez deCeballos, F. Turegano Fuentes, et al., "Casualties Treated at the Closest Hospital in Madrid, March 11, Terrorist Bombings," *Critical Care Medicine* 33 (January 2005): 107–12.

3. Office of the Surgeon General, Resource Site for the Medical Reserve Corp., www.medicalreservecorps.gov/index.cfm?MRCaction=Home.Welcome. Accessed February 12, 2006.

10. Trauma

1. Nikki Stern, "Our Grief Doesn't Make Us Experts," *Newsweek,* 13 March 2006, www.msnbc.msn.com/id/11676434/site/newsweek/. Accessed April 17, 2006.

2. Jennifer Steinhauer, "With a Wrench of the Gut," *New York Times,* 7 September 2005, B-1.

3. Irwin Garfinkle et al., "Vulnerability and Resilience: New Yorkers Respond to 9/11," in *Wounded City: The Social Impact of 9/11,* ed. Nancy Foner, 28–75 (New York: Russell Sage Foundation, 2005).

4. William E. Schlenger, "Psychological Impact of the September 11, 2001, Terrorist Attacks: Summary of Empirical Findings in Adults," in *The Trauma of Terrorism,* ed. Yael Danieli, Danny Brom, and Joe Sills, 100 (Binghamton, N.Y.: Haworth Press, 2005).

5. "Civil War PTSD," *Science,* 17 February 2006, 927.

6. *Diagnostic and Statistical Manual of Mental Disorders (DSM-IV-TR),* 4th ed. (Washington, D.C.: American Psychiatric Association, 2000), 463–68.

7. "The War in Iraq," National Center for PTSD, U.S. Department of Veterans Affairs, www.ncptsd.va.gov/topics/war.html. Accessed March 2, 2006.

8. Scott Shane, "A Deluge of Troubled Soldiers Is in the Offing, Experts Predict," *New York Times,* 16 December 2004, A-1.

9. Project Liberty History, www.projectliberty.state.ny.us/whatwaspl-history.htm. Accessed March 5, 2006.

10. "Survey: 500,000 Israelis Suffer 'Terror Trauma,'" *Jerusalem Post,* 2 December 2004, www.command-post.org/gwot/2_archives/017973.html. Accessed February 3, 2006.

11. Naomi L. Baum, "Building Resilience: A School-Based Intervention for Children Exposed to Ongoing Trauma and Stress," in Danieli et al., *Trauma of Terrorism,* 487–98. Ruth Pat-Horenczyk et al., "Screening PTSD Symptoms, Related Distress and Risk-Taking Behaviors in Adolescents Exposed to Ongoing Terrorism in Israel," Israel Center for the Treatment of Psychotrauma and the UJA-Federation of New York, July 24, 2004 (unpublished).

12. Only 3.6 percent of a U.S. adult population exhibited signs of PTSD at some time during a 12-month period, according to the National Center for PTSD, U.S. Department of Veterans Affairs, www.ncptsd.va.gov/facts/general/fs_what_is_ptsd.html. Accessed March 17, 2006.

13. Jonas Waizer et al., "Community-Based Interventions in New York City after 9/11: A Provider's Perspective," in Danieli et al., *Trauma of Terrorism,* 510.

14. Koby Mandell Foundation, www.kobymandell.org/mission.htm. Accessed March 15, 2006.

15. Malki Foundation, www.kerenmalki.org. Accessed March 15, 2006.

11. Palestinians

1. *Time*, 21 September 1970, cover. The haunting and long-lasting effects on the hostages were recounted more than three decades later by one of the passengers, David Raab, then 17, in "Remembrance of Terror Past," *New York Times Magazine*, 22 August 2004, 56.

2. Bassam Abu-Sharif and Uzi Mahnaimi, *Best of Enemies* (Boston: Little, Brown, 1995), 89.

3. Intelligence and Terrorism Information Center, www.intelligence.org.il/eng/sib/6_04/park_h.htm. Accessed April 16, 2005.

4. Ibid.

5. Palestinian Media Watch, www.pmw.org.il/murder.htm#murder1. Accessed April 18, 2004.

6. Leonard A. Cole, *The Anthrax Letters: A Medical Detective Story.* (Washington, DC: Joseph Henry Press, 2003), www.anthraxletters.com.

7. "Suicide Bombers," Wideangle, Public Broadcasting Service. Aired on Channel 13, New York, July 1, 2004; Nicholas D. Kristof, "Martyrs, Virgins, and Grapes," *New York Times,* 2 August 2004, A-17.

8. Gaza Community Mental Program, www.gcmhp.net/eyad/xyz.htm. Accessed May 18, 2006.

9. Middle East Media Research Institute, www.memri.org/video/segment2_adelsadeq.html. Accessed May 18, 2006.

10. Vivienne Walt, "In Middle East, Conflict Attacks Children's Minds," *USA Today,* 2 October 2001, 8-D.

11. Leonard A. Cole, "A Double Standard on Suicide Terrorism," *Forward,* 20 February 2004, 9.

12. Challenges and Lessons

1. Greg Myre, "Palestinian Bomber Kills Himself and 5 Others Near Israel Mall," *New York Times,* 6 December 2005, A-6; Israel Ministry of Foreign Affairs, www.mfa.gov.il/MFA/MFAArchive/2000 2009/2005/Suicide%20bombing%20at%20Sharon%2 0Mall%20in%20Netanya%205-Dec-2005. Accessed April 16, 2006.

2. Abby Goodnough and Matthew Wald, "Air Marshals Shoot and Kill Passenger in Bomb Threat," *New York Times,* 8 December 2005, A-1.

3. Herb Keinon, "Israel's Experience Can Aid War on Terror—Russian FM," *Jerusalem Post,* 6 September 2004, 14.

4. Margot Dudkevitch, "IDF Teaches US Soldiers Guerilla Response," *Jerusalem Post,* 18 August 2004; "Israeli Security Chiefs Are Advising France on Riot Control," Jewish Telegraphic Agency, December 13, 2005; "Fortune 500 Companies and Foreign Governments Visit Israel for Terror-Fighting Tips," Israel21c, March 5, 2006. www.israel21c.org/bin/en.jsp. Accessed May 26, 2006.

5. Walter Dawkins, "Israel's First Responders Praise Technology in N.J.," *Record* (Hackensack, N.J.), 19 May 2005, L-1.

6. Matthew E. Berger, "A Grim Exercise: Countries Turn to Israel for Advice on Handling Terror," Jewish Telegraphic Agency, July 13, 2005.

7. "Code Black: What Does It Mean?" ABC News, February 6, 2006. http://abclocal.go.com/kgo/story?section=health&id=3895912. Accessed April 6, 2006.

8. Emergency Response, Children's Hospital, New Orleans, www.chnola.org/EmergencyPrepare/EmergencyPrepare.htm. Accessed April 6, 2005; Description of Codes, Cincinnati Children's Hospital Medical Center, http://abclocal.go.com/kgo/story?section=health&id=3895912. Accessed January 23, 2006.

9. Paul Davidson, "Disparate Radios Create Problem," *USA Today,* 29 December 2005, B-1.

10. Jan Shubert, "Social Psychology, Risk Communication, and the Israeli Experience: Tools to help Americans Deal with the Psychological Effects of Terrorism Threats," 2005. (Unpublished manuscript).

11. Avraham Bleich, Marc Gelkopf, and Zahava Solomon, "Exposure to Terrorism, Stress-Related Mental Health Symptoms, and Coping Behaviors Among a Nationally Representative Sample in Israel," *Journal of the American Medical Association* 295 (August 6, 2003): 612–20.

12. Forum on Urban Conversations: Cities at Risk, The New School, New York, N.Y., April 7, 2006.

13. Cecilia M. Vega, "The Parish That Feds Overlooked," *San Francisco Chronicle,* 15 September 2005, http://sfgate.com/cgi-bin/ (initial pathway). Accessed April 16, 2006.

14. Robert D. Putnam, *Bowling Alone: The Collapse and Revival of American Community* (New York: Simon and Schuster, 2000), 367.

15. Ibid., 146.

16. Walter Olson, *The Litigation Explosion: What Happened When America Unleashed the Lawsuit* (New York: Truman Talley Books, 1991).

17. Library of Congress, Thomas. http://thomas.loc.gov/cgi-bin/bdquery/z?d108:h.r.00163. Accessed May 20, 2006.

13. Beyond Terror

1. BBC, July 7, 2004, http://news.bbc.co.uk/2/hi/programmes/newsnight/3875119.stm. Accessed July 8, 2004.

2. Palestinian Center for Policy and Survey Research, Public Opinion Poll #12, www.pcpsr.org/survey/polls/2004/p12b.html. Accessed July 8, 2004.

3. Meir Elran, "Israel's National Resilience: The Influence of the Second Intifada on Israeli Society" (English summary), Jaffee Center for Strategic Studies, Tel Aviv, Israel, January 2006. http://listserv.tau.ac.il/cgi-bin/wa?A2=ind0601&L=tau-jcss-il&D=0&P=384. Accessed May 10, 2006.

4. Tom Bell, "N.J. Cops Get Advice on Suicide Bombers," *Record* (Hackensack, N.J.), 25 June 2004, A-3.

5. *The 9/11 Commission Report,* Final Report of the National Commission on Terrorist Attacks Upon the United States (New York: W. W. Norton, 2004), 364.

6. "Transcript: 9/11 Panel Releases Its Final Report," July 22, 2004. www.washingtonpost.com/wp-dyn/articles/A6014-2004Jul22. Accessed August 23, 2006.

7. Christopher M. Blanchard, "Al-Qaeda: Statements and Evolving Ideology," Congressional Research Service, January 26, 2006, 3. www.fas.org/sgp/crs/terror/RL32759.pdf. Accessed August 30, 2006.

Books for Additional Reading

Abu-Sharif, Bassam, and Uzi Mahnaimi. *Best of Enemies.* Boston: Little, Brown, 1995.

Antosia, Robert, and John Cahill, eds. *Handbook of Bioterrorism and Disaster Medicine.* New York: Springer, 2006.

Bloom, Mia. *Dying to Kill: The Allure of Suicide Terror.* New York: Columbia University Press, 2005.

Braiker, Harriet. *The September 11 Syndrome: Seven Steps to Getting a Grip in Uncertain Times.* New York: McGraw-Hill, 2002.

Byman, Daniel. *Deadly Connections: States That Sponsor Terrorism.* New York: Cambridge University Press, 2005.

Ciottone, Gregory R., ed. *Disaster Medicine.* New York: Mosby Elsevier, 2006.

Coates, Susan W., Jane L. Rosenthal, and Daniel S. Schechter, eds. *September 11: Trauma and Human Bonds.* Mahwah, N.J.: Analytic Press, 2003.

Cole, Leonard A. *The Anthrax Letters: A Medical Detective Story.* Washington, D.C.: Joseph Henry Press/National Academies Press, 2003.

Coopersmith, Nechemia, and Shraga Simmons, eds. *Israel: Life in the Shadow of Terror.* Southfield, Mich.: Targum Press, 2003.

Danieli, Yael, Danny Brom, and Joe Sills, eds. *The Trauma of Terrorism: Sharing Knowledge and Shared Care, An International Handbook.* New York: Haworth Press, 2005.

D'Arcy, Michael, Michael O'Hanlon et al. *Protecting the Homeland 2006/2007.* Washington, D.C.: Brookings Institution Press, 2006.

Davis, Joyce M. *Martyrs: Innocence, Vengeance and Despair in the Middle East.* New York: Palgrave, 2003.

Diagnostic and Statistical Manual of Mental Disorders (DSM-IV-TR), 4th ed. Washington, D.C.: American Psychiatric Association, 2000.

Dorn, Michael, and Chris Dorn. *Innocent Targets: When Terrorism Comes to School.* Macon, Ga.: Safe Havens International, 2005.

Dowty, Alan. *Israel/Palestine.* Cambridge, England: Polity Press, 2005.

Emerson, Steven. *American Jihad: The Terrorists Living Among Us.* New York: Free Press, 2002.

Everly, George S., Jr., and Cherie Castellano. *Psychological Counterterrorism and World War IV.* Ellicott City, Md.: Chevron, 2005.

Foner, Nancy, ed. *Wounded City: The Social Impact of 9/11.* New York: Russell Sage Foundation, 2005.

Ganor, Boaz. *The Counter-Terrorism Puzzle.* New Brunswick, N.J.: Transaction Press, 2005.

Giduck, John. *Terror at Beslan: A Russian Tragedy with Lessons for America's Schools.* Golden, Colo.: Archangel Group, 2005.

Goldberg, Jeffrey. *Prisoners: A Muslim and a Jew across the Middle East Divide.* New York: Knopf, 2006.

Halevy, Efraim. *Man in the Shadows: Inside the Middle East Crisis with a Man Who Led the Mossad.* New York: St. Martin's Press, 2006.

Hall, Harold V., ed. *Terrorism: Strategies for Intervention.* New York: Haworth Press, 2004.

Hoffman, Bruce. *Inside Terrorism.* New York: Columbia University Press, 1998.

Hogan, David E., and Jonathan L. Burstein, eds. *Disaster Medicine.* Philadelphia: Lippincott, Williams and Wilkins, 2002.

Horovitz, David. *Still Life with Bombers: Israel in the Age of Terrorism.* New York: Knopf, 2004.

Kamien, David, ed. *The McGraw-Hill Handbook of Homeland Security.* New York: McGraw-Hill, 2006.

Kehayan, V. Alex, and Joseph C. Napoli. *Resiliency in the Face of Disaster and Terrorism.* Fawnskin, Calif.: Personhood Press, 2005.

Laqueur, Walter, and Yonah Alexander, eds. *The Terrorism Reader: The Essential Sourcebook on Political Violence Both Past and Present.* New York: Meridian/NAL Penguin, 1987.

Laqueur, Walter, and Barry Rubin, eds. *The Israel-Arab Reader: A Documentary History of the Middle East.* New York: Penguin, 2001.

Levitt, Matthew. *Hamas: Politics, Charity, and Terrorism in the Service of Jihad.* New Haven, Conn.: Yale University Press, 2006.

Levy, Barry S., and Victor W. Sidel, eds. *Terrorism and Public Health: A Balanced Approach to Strengthening Systems and Protecting People.* New York: Oxford University Press, 2003.

Lewis, Bernard. *The Middle East: A Brief History of the Last 2000 Years.* New York: Scribner, 1997.

Makovsky, David. *Engagement Through Disengagement: Gaza and the Potential for Renewed Israeli-Palestinian Peacemaking.* Washington, D.C.: Washington Institute for Near East Policy, 2005.

McGlown, K. Joanne, ed. *Terrorism and Disaster Management: Preparing Healthcare Leaders for the New Reality.* Chicago: Healthcare Administration Press, 2004.

Moreno, Jonathan D., ed. *In the Wake of Terror: Medicine and Morality in a Time of Crisis.* Cambridge, Mass.: MIT Press, 2003.

Netanyahu, Benjamin. *Fighting Terrorism: How Democracies Can Defeat Domestic and International Terrorists.* New York: Farrar, Straus and Giroux, 2001.

Oren, Michael B. *Six Days of War: June 1967 and the Making of the Modern Middle East.* New York: Presidio Press, 2003.

Pandya, Anand A., and Craig L. Katz, eds. *Disaster Psychiatry: Intervening When Nightmares Come True.* Mahwah, N.J.: Analytic Press, 2004.

Pape, Robert A. *Dying to Win: The Strategic Logic of Suicide Terrorism.* New York: Random House, 2005.

Putnam, Robert D. *Bowling Alone: The Collapse and Revival of American Community.* New York: Simon and Schuster, 2000.

Pyszczynski, Tom, Sheldon Solomon, and Jeff Greenberg. *In the Wake of 9/11: The Psychology of Terror.* Washington, D.C.: American Psychological Association, 2003.

Reuter, Christopher. *My Life Is a Weapon: A Modern History of Suicide Bombing.* Princeton, N.J.: Princeton University Press, 2002.

Rosenthal, Donna. *The Israelis: Ordinary People in an Extraordinary Land.* New York: Free Press, 2003.

Ross, Dennis. *The Missing Peace: The Inside Story of the Fight for Middle East Peace.* New York: Farrar, Straus and Giroux, 2005.

Sachar, Howard M. *A History of Israel: From the Rise of Zionism to Our Time.* New York: Knopf, 1996.

Satloff, Robert. *The Battle of Ideas in the War on Terror: Essays on U.S. Public Diplomacy in the Middle East.* Washington, D.C.: Washington Institute for Near East Policy, 2004.

Sharkansky, Ira. *Coping with Terror: An Israeli Perspective.* Lanham, Md.: Lexington Books, 2003.

Silke, Andrew, ed. *Terrorists, Victims and Society: Psychological Perspectives on Terrorism and Its Consequences.* New York: John Wiley and Sons, 2003.

Stern, Jessica. *Terror in the Name of God: Why Religious Militants Kill.* New York: ECCO/HarperCollins, 2003.

Stout, Chris E. *Psychology of Terrorism: Coping with the Continuing Threat.* Westport, Conn.: Praeger Books, 2004.

The 9/11 Commission Report. Final Report of the National Commission on Terrorist Attacks Upon the United States. New York: W. W. Norton, 2004.

Tierney, Kathleen J., Michael K. Lindell, and Ronald W. Perry, eds. *Facing the Unexpected: Disaster Preparedness and Response in the United States.* Washington, D.C.: National Academies Press, 2001.

Ursano, Robert J., Carol S. Fullerton, and Ann E. Norwood, eds. *Terrorism and Disaster: Individual and Community Mental Health Interventions.* New York: Cambridge University Press, 2003.

Wiemer, Liza M., and Benay Katz. *Waiting for Peace: How Israelis Live with Terrorism.* Jerusalem: Gefen, 2005.

Index

Leonard A. Cole is an adjunct professor of political science at Rutgers University in Newark, New Jersey. An expert on bioterrorism and terror medicine, he has testified before Congress, made numerous presentations to government agencies, and appeared frequently on national television and radio. Cole's articles have been published in *The New York Times, The Washington Post, Los Angeles Times,* and *Scientific American.* Cole is the author of seven books, including his most recent, *The Anthrax Letters: A Medical Detective Story.*